Getting the Job You Want After 50

FOR

DUMMIES®

A Wiley Brand

Getting the Job You Want After 50

FOR

DUMMIES®

A Wiley Brand

by Kerry Hannon

Getting the Job You Want After 50 For Dummies®

Published by: **John Wiley & Sons, Inc.,** 111 River Street, Hoboken, NJ 07030-5774, www.wiley.com

For general information on our other products and services, please contact our Customer Care Department within the U.S. at 877-762-2974, outside the U.S. at 317-572-3993, or fax 317-572-4002. For technical support, please visit www.wiley.com/techsupport.

Wiley publishes in a variety of print and electronic formats and by print-on-demand. Some material included with standard print versions of this book may not be included in e-books or in print-on-demand. If this book refers to media such as a CD or DVD that is not included in the version you purchased, you may download this material at http://booksupport.wiley.com. For more information about Wiley products, visit www.wiley.com.

This and other AARP books are available in print and e-formats at AARP's online bookstore, www.aarp.org/bookstore, and through local and online bookstores.

Portions of this material originally appeared in *Forbes, Love Your Job: The New Rules for Career Happiness, What's Next? Finding Your Passion and Your Dream Job in Your Forties, Fifties and Beyond* and *Great Jobs for Everyone 50+* and on NextAvenue.org and AARP.org. Reprinted with permission.

Library of Congress Control Number: 2015945226

ISBN 978-1-119-02284-8 (pbk); ISBN 978-1-119-02286-2 (ebk); ISBN 978-1-119-02285-5 (ebk)

Manufactured in the United States of America

10 9 8 7 6 5 4 3 2 1

Contents at a Glance

Table of Contents

Introduction

Welcome to *Getting the Job You Want After 50 For Dummies,* your guide to finding rewarding employment when you're over 50. This book supplies you with what you need to know to find a job today. From building an online presence to revitalizing your résumé to negotiating a salary, this book has you covered, from cover to cover!

Many reasons may have brought you to this book. Perhaps you are just coming back into the workforce or have been laid off and need to find work. You could be looking to make a career change or want to pursue your passion and find more meaning in your work. You may be relocating, or want a job that gives you more flexibility.

The fact that people are living longer, healthier lives opens the doors to possibilities of a variety of work you may want to pursue. Think of it as a bonus chapter of your life. It's a time when, perhaps, the big-ticket items are behind you — paying for children's educations maybe, or a mortgage — and you're free to seek work that's more meaningful and, if you're lucky, not so focused on the size of the paycheck.

Whatever your reason, you want a job, and you want it now.

About This Book

The job market has changed considerably since your first job-hunt, as has the process for finding and landing a job. In the past, you filled out paper applications, printed and sent résumés and cover letters, and networked over the phone and in person to find the right job. Those things are all still necessary — no matter what type of job you're seeking. But mostly they're now done online, thus requiring some technology know-how. In addition, your ego could feel the sting of having to prove yourself to employers who may be half your age and not nearly as qualified as you.

This book provides information on things you may not have a lot of practice in (such as online applications) or things you may need help updating (like interviewing skills). I'm over 50. I get it. It's tough out there. But, with some guidance, you can attain your goals.

Think of this book as your road map to get to where you want to be. You hold in your hands all the direction and resources to help you find and land the job you want, along with instructions on how to use the latest technologies to your advantage. I explain everything from how to bring your résumé into the 21st century to how to network and market yourself online so you're an attractive target for recruiters and employers nationwide.

Within this book, you may note that I followed certain conventions. I often use **boldface** text to label bullet items and other content, so you can easily skim for the information you need. *Italicized* words and phrases represent unfamiliar terminology I define in context. Some website addresses break across two lines of text. If you're reading this book in print and want to visit one of these web pages, simply key in the address exactly as it's noted in the text, pretending as though the line break doesn't exist. If you're reading this as an e-book, you've got it easy — just click the web address to be taken directly to the web page.

Foolish Assumptions

The fact that you're reading this book tells me that you either don't have a job or don't have the job you want. Perhaps you're struggling to figure out where and how to look for jobs and how to make yourself an attractive candidate. Other assumptions I've made about you include the following:

- You're discouraged or getting discouraged that employers and recruiters aren't beating a path to your door and leaving job offers on your voicemail.

- You think employers are reticent to hire someone your age.

- You haven't updated your résumé since the last time you landed a job. You have skills and experience you don't even realize you have; worse yet, they're not listed on your résumé!

- You could use some help using Facebook, LinkedIn, Twitter, and other social media and networking tools to optimize your job search.

- Your job interview skills are rusty, and you really need a refresher course, especially in how to deal with Skype and other new video interview formats.

Icons Used in This Book

Throughout this book, icons in the margins highlight different types of information that call out for your attention. Here are the icons you'll see and a brief description of each.

I want you to remember everything you read in this book, but if you can't quite do that, then remember the important points flagged with this icon.

Tips provide insider insight. When you're looking for a better, faster way to do something, check out these tips.

"Whoa!" This icon appears when you need to hit the brakes and think twice before moving forward.

Beyond the Book

In addition to the abundance of information and guidance on finding a job, acing your job interviews, and negotiating a salary and benefits that have you whistling on your way to work, which happens to be in your home, because you negotiated a telecommuting arrangement, you also get access to even more help and information at Dummies.com (www.dummies.com). Go to www.dummies.com/cheatsheet/gettingthejobyouwantafter50 for a free cheat sheet that accompanies this book. It brings you up-to-speed on job-search fundamentals, job interview guidelines, negotiating tips, and much more. Think of it as this book in a nutshell.

You can also head to www.dummies.com/extras/gettingthejobyou wantafter50 for a few free additional articles that I think you'll find helpful as you begin your journey to the job you want. Here, you find out how to garner contract work through social media, write a knock-out cover letter, identify interview tricks and traps, and discover ten personal branding best practices.

When you're ready to begin your search, start with www.aarp.org/work, with the information and tools you need to help you stay current, competitive, and connected in today's workplace. Features include these and much more:

- A job board
- A list of 285+ employers who have signed a pledge committing to value and hire experienced workers
- Résumé models and tips
- Webinars with experts on technology skills for the workplace
- 21st-century job search
- Guidance on what to do when you lose your job

To explore all kinds of new possibilities that make the most of your interests and expertise, check out AARP's Life Reimagined (`www.lifereimagined.org`), a personalized, interactive website.

Also look for my books *What's Next? Finding Your Passion and Your Dream Job in Your Forties, Fifties, and Beyond* (Berkley Trade/AARP) and *Great Jobs for Everyone 50+: Finding Work That Keeps You Happy and Healthy . . . And Pays the Bills* (Wiley/AARP) to further help put you on the path to finding your next job.

Where to Go from Here

I structured this book so you could use it in a couple of ways. To get the most out of it, read it from cover to cover, so you don't miss out on any valuable information and insight. You may also use it as a job seeker's desk reference; when you need to know something about a specific job-search topic, simply look it up in the Table of Contents or the Index and flip to the designated page to find the answer.

I do recommend, however, that you read Chapters 1, 2, 3, and 5 from start to finish or at least skim them, so you know what's covered in those chapters for future reference. Chapter 1 opens your mind to the possibilities. Chapter 2 helps you inventory your skills and experience and plug gaps that may be holding you back. And Chapter 3 emphasizes the importance of networking. Chapter 5 introduces you to a gaggle of job-search websites where you can start your search. Of course, the other chapters are useful, too, but these serve as a good springboard for starting your search.

As you embark on your journey to find the right job for you, keep in mind that you're a unique individual with skills, experience, and insight that nobody else on the planet has. There's a place for you in all of this — a job that you're uniquely qualified to perform. You simply need to discover it within yourself and in the workplace.

Part I

Getting Started with Finding a Job After 50

getting started with

finding a job after 50

In this part . . .

✔ Figure out what you really want out of a job, in addition to a paycheck and bennies, set a course to get from point A to point B, and discover proven strategies for finding and landing the job you want.

✔ Recognize the skills that employers value most, take inventory of the skills you have, and discover free and affordable ways to build the skills you're missing.

✔ Network your way to your next job by leveraging the power of your personal and professional networks to find jobs, get the scoop about prospective employers, and perhaps even find an inside track to the job you want.

✔ Deal with the financial issues that commonly accompany unemployment and job searches, write off job-hunt expenses on your taxes, maximize your social security benefits, bankroll your own benefits package, and more.

Chapter 1

Scoping Out Your Prospects

· ·

In This Chapter

▶ Understanding current workplace realities

▶ Figuring out what you want . . . and want to do

▶ Finding your place in the workplace

▶ Retooling your job search strategies for the 21st century

· ·

*W*elcome jobseekers! Finding a job, at any age, takes work and dedication. Some older jobseekers assume that employers would rather outsource jobs to cheaper workers overseas or hire younger, less experienced workers for lower wages. Although these suspicions are confirmed by the hiring practices of some organizations, current studies show that employers are increasingly willing to consider older candidates and that age alone isn't necessarily the reason some employers are unwilling to consider older candidates.

In this chapter, I help you shift your attitude about job hunting from one of apprehension to one of hope and possibility and show you a few simple ways to rev up your job-search mojo to today's new workplace reality for 50-plus jobseekers.

Recognizing the Need for and Value of Experienced Workers

The times really are a-changin' and that's good news for your job-hunting prospects. Whether you want to work in an office job, teach yoga, or head up a company, more employers are starting to realize that hiring workers age 50 and older is good for business. More and more employers are discovering the value of experienced workers. Unfortunately for 50-plus job seekers, the fact that demand for experienced workers is on the rise is a well-kept secret. Realizing that employers need you is an important first step in the process of finding and landing the job you want. It gives you the enthusiasm and confidence to set out on what may be a long and arduous journey. In this section, I reveal the reasons the demand for 50-plus workers is rising to invigorate you for the journey ahead and remind you of just how valuable you are to employers who need your skills, talents, and experience.

The job search can be disheartening for anyone, regardless of age. And if that's what you're feeling, never show it to a prospective employer. Always highlight the value you have to offer in every job search communiqué you send out. If you need a confidence lift, take some time and review all your previous achievements.

Noting a change in the current workforce

Many CEOs are increasingly aware that they need to have 50-plus workers on board. As the population ages, the workforce is aging right along with it. U.S. employees 65 and older now outnumber teenagers in the workforce for the first time since 1948. In 2002, workers 50 and older comprised 24.6 percent of the workforce. By 2012, they represented 32.3 percent. And by 2022, they're projected to be 35.4 percent of the total workforce.

This emerging trend isn't likely to change anytime soon. More than one in three workers age 45 and older expects to retire at age 66 or older, compared to just over one in five ten years ago. Moreover, 72 percent of workers ages 45 to 74 envision working in retirement.

Employers are getting worried about their future workforce. In a recent survey by the Society for Human Resource Management (SHRM), one-third of HR professionals predicted that the loss of talent resulting from retirements or departures of workers age 55 and older would be either a problem or a crisis for their organization in the next six to ten years. The Manpower Group 2014 Talent Shortage Survey found that 40 percent of U.S. employers reported difficulty in filling jobs.

Seeing experienced workers as an affordable option

The old concerns that hiring someone our age would probably be too pricey are being debunked. Contrary to common perception, workers age 50-plus don't cost significantly more than younger workers, according to the report "A Business Case for Workers Age 50+: A Look at the Value of Experience 2015," commissioned by AARP and conducted by Aon Hewitt.

Shifting trends in reward and benefit programs mean that adding more age 50-plus talent to a workforce results in only minimal increases in hard dollar total labor costs. These trends include a broad move by large employers to performance-based versus tenure-based compensation, the decline in traditional benefit pension plans, and the fact that healthcare costs are increasing at a slower rate for older workers compared to younger workers.

Meanwhile, in today's global and fast-paced workplace, firms often don't have the time to squander while a younger worker ramps up skills and knowledge. Companies are slowly realizing that to stay competitive, it's smarter to seek out and hire experienced workers. Trust me, you're on the cutting edge of a sweeping change in the demographics of the workplace. And it's being led by the boomer generation.

You may think I'm just looking through rose-colored glasses. But recent surveys show that companies are realizing that it's strategically smart to pay more attention to recruiting and retaining workers age 50 and older. When organizations need someone to step in and do the job right now and solve an existing problem, it's the experienced worker they're eager to hire.

That's what the AARP report unveiled. Findings from a 2014 SHRM survey of HR professionals also back up that trend. SHRM's *The Aging Workforce* survey also found that two-thirds of HR executives canvassed reported that their organization employed older workers who retired from other organizations or careers before joining their organization. Gold stars all around.

The *Aging Workforce* survey, part of a three-year national Aging Workforce Initiative by SHRM and the SHRM Foundation and funded by the Alfred P. Sloan Foundation, also found that 61 percent of the 1,900 randomly selected SHRM HR professionals indicated their organization had attempted to capitalize on and incorporate the experience of older workers in recruitment and retention strategies. (Kudos to them.) The top advantages of older workers were having more work experience (cited by 77 percent of respondents), being more mature/professional (71 percent), and having a stronger work ethic (70 percent). (But, of course.)

Capitalizing on lower turnover

Employers find that workers age 50 and older are more loyal and aren't as likely as younger workers to job jump. And that lower staff turnover benefits the bottom line. The costs of high turnover are tangible. Finding, hiring, and training a new employee is a costly venture, and it becomes even more costly when that well-trained employee decides to jump ship and work for a competitor.

Retaining older workers pays dividends, too!

Depending on your position and industry, the total cost of replacing you can range from thousands of dollars to as much as one-and-a-half times your annual salary. Retaining older workers reduces the one-time costs of turnover, which range from $7,400 to $31,700 or more per employee, according to AARP's most recent survey. This cost includes the time and money that go hand- in- hand with recruiting and advertising your job, bringing people in for an interview, and training a new hire.

Plus, it's hard to put a price on the institutional knowledge that goes out the door with a departing employee. Now tack on the stress that managers and coworkers must shoulder to make up for the work that falls between the cracks when an employee leaves. And, finally, toss in the toll of lost morale that accompanies the departure of a valued team member. Now the employer has a serious problem. And that's clearly a big incentive for hiring a worker over 50. Older workers often anchor a team.

Harnessing the power of highly engaged workers

Aon Hewitt data show that older workers, in general, *love* their jobs more than younger workers do. Yes, we're more engaged than our younger counterparts. Perhaps we're grateful for the jobs in a way that someone new to the workforce has yet to learn to value and appreciate.

For example, 65 percent of employees ages 55 and up in large companies are "engaged," compared to fewer than 60 percent of employees under age 45. Although this gap may seem small, it represents a statistically significant difference in engagement that can have a noticeable impact on business outcomes, according to the AARP report.

In addition to being the most highly engaged age group in the labor force, workers age 55 and older are also the most motivated. A whopping 81 percent of workers age 55 and up are "motivated" — meaning they say that they exert extra effort and contribute more than is normally required in their job — compared to 76 percent of their age 25 to 34 peers. Talk about selling points for older workers on the job hunt!

Reaping additional benefits

In addition to all those wonderful attributes I've already mentioned, older workers typically have the following:

- An ability to make quick decisions and solve problems
- Greater maturity and professionalism
- Superior communication skills, both written and oral
- The ability to serve as mentors
- The critical qualities of reliability and dependability
- More knowledge, wisdom, and overall life experience

Shoulders back. You're valued. Put all this positive juju in your back pocket and never forget how much you have to offer on the job.

Tallying the Benefits of Staying in the Workforce

To get you even more fired up about your job search, let me remind you of five money-wise reasons to stay in the workforce as long as you can:

- **The more years you contribute to your retirement plans, the better off you'll be down the road.** You'll be able to delay taking Social Security, which will dramatically boost your eventual payout. Start collecting at age 70, and your monthly check will be 32 percent higher than if you begin benefits at 66 and 76 percent more than if you start taking benefits at 62 (when most people do).
- **The longer you work, the longer you delay tapping retirement funds, which can continue to grow.**
- **Working longer provides income to pay for health insurance until you're eligible for Medicare at 65.** Fewer employers are offering their retired workers medical benefits, and those who do are ramping up the amount retirees must contribute to the cost of coverage. Even better, you may find a job that offers you access to a health plan.
- **Money aside, you may want to keep working to maintain a sense of well-being.** For people over 50, being engaged, not just involved, is important, according to a report by The Sloan Center on Aging & Work at Boston College. Similarly, when asked about their life and careers,

75 percent of people in their forties and fifties said they want to make their life more meaningful, while 82 percent said they want to give back more, according to a study commissioned by Life Reimagined, which was created by AARP to help people with midlife transitions. Nearly 30 percent plan to make a career change in the next five years; top reasons include having the opportunity to learn more and giving more back to the community. Work gives you a sense of purpose and of feeling connected and needed. It makes you feel relevant. Pinning a dollar figure to that is difficult, but it's real.

✔ **Work sharpens the mind.** Researchers from the RAND Center for the Study of Aging and the University of Michigan published a study showing that cognitive performance levels decline faster in countries that have younger retirement ages. What? Brain cells dying from lack of use? You bet. It's the old "Use it or lose it" axiom. Many aging experts say that to stay healthy, older adults have to learn new things, stay active socially, and exercise.

Bottom line: We're living longer, healthier lives. As a result, we're staying longer in the workforce because we can and often because we need to, in order to have a financially secure retirement.

Reorienting Yourself to Today's Job-Search Realities

What's new since your last job hunt? If it's been a while, you'll quickly find that technology has made job searching easier in some ways but more complex than ever in others. Although the Internet has improved access to openings, it has also increased competition for those same openings. Typically, an average of more than 250 résumés are submitted for every job posting, and the first résumé appears within 200 seconds (just over 3 minutes) of the posting "going live," according to online job-search expert Susan P. Joyce, publisher of WorkCoachCafe.com.

While job-search sites make finding jobs easier, online applications and automated screening technologies pose additional obstacles to getting past the gatekeepers. According to a study by job-match site TheLadders (www.theladders.com), many companies use talent-management software to screen résumés, weeding out up to 50 percent of applications before anyone ever looks at a résumé or cover letter.

Little wonder then that a recent CareerXroads survey shows that only 15 percent of positions were filled through online job boards. So visiting job boards and applying for jobs is probably not the best use of your time, even though you feel like you have to. Most jobs are either filled internally or through referrals. Yes, the old-fashioned way. In fact, only about half of the roughly 5 million jobs now open in the United States are ever advertised publicly. Employers still prefer to hire people they know either directly or indirectly through a referral. In studies of many different employers going back to 2001, employee referrals are the top source of people hired into a company — not a job posting. In fact, employee referrals provided more than 55 percent of the hires in one of the studies.

In other words, employers want to hire someone who has already been vetted in some way, which can save a lot of hassle and cost of the hiring process and of replacing people who don't work out, even if they looked great on paper and interviewed like pros. Employers love it when someone who already works for the organization can vouch for the person. And the employee making the referral often has some skin in the game, so to speak. Many employers pop a bonus reward of up to $1,000 or more for referring someone who's hired and does a good job in the first few months on the job.

Does this mean that applying for a job on job boards isn't worthwhile? Not at all! Scanning the boards gives you a sense of who's hiring, what types of openings are out there, and salary ranges. But it does mean that other approaches, such as networking and marketing yourself, may ultimately forge a better route to landing a job. For more about networking, see Chapter 3. In Part III, you find out how to market yourself and create your own personal brand.

Deciding What (Else) You Want Out of Work

For my book AARP's *Love Your Job: The New Rules for Career Happiness*, I interviewed hundreds of workers about what made them love their jobs. Interestingly, their paychecks aren't generally what get them juiced about going to work. Most people say they're motivated by the people they work with, the opportunity to keep learning and growing, or the mission or cause of their employer's services or the products it makes. Sometimes they say they love the travel opportunities. So don't get locked into a must-have salary. When searching for jobs and comparing offers, be sure to account for other benefits, including the following:

- **Flexible workday:** Being able to work from home or having flexible hours or a compressed schedule is a biggie. It comes down to being treated as a responsible adult and weaving work more seamlessly into the fabric of your life. And that may be getting easier to achieve. A Bank of America Merrill Lynch survey of 650 human resources executives recently found that half of employers are willing to offer flexible arrangements, such as working part-time or job sharing, to their most skilled and experienced workers.

✓ **A healthy work-life balance:** Three in five people interested in a second career midlife say it's very important that the job leaves free time for things they want to do, such as travel, education, or engagement in other activities they enjoy, according to a report by Encore.org, a non-profit organization that's building a movement to tap the skills and experience of those in midlife and beyond to improve communities. Indeed, many of those interested in encore careers appear eager to mix fewer hours of work per week with more years of work in total. Finding more flexibility may make working a few more years more palatable.

✓ **Meaningful work:** More than 25 million Americans 50 to 70 years old are eager to share their skills, passions, and expertise in encore careers that address social needs, typically in education, healthcare, human services, and the environment, according to a 2014 study by Encore.org and Penn Schoen Berland. Of those 25 million, more than 4.5 million are already working for social impact. Another 21 million are ready to join them within the next five years.

✓ **Opportunities to interact with others and stay productive:** Human beings are hard-wired to create, produce, and collaborate, and rewarding work provides opportunities to remain active and productive. A Pew Research Center survey found that working for non-financial reasons, such as job enjoyment or the desire to be productive, increases with age.

✓ **Competitive benefits:** A 2012 AARP/SHRM survey of workers age 50 and up suggested older workers place significance on having competitive benefits and flexible work arrangements. When these workers consider a job offer, health insurance, retirement savings plans, and paid time off benefits play an important role in their decisions. For example, approximately eight in ten workers age 50 and older consider the availability of benefits such as health insurance (82 percent); a pension, 401(k), or other retirement plan (77 percent); and paid time off (80 percent) to be "very" or "somewhat" important considerations in the decision to accept a job.

✓ **Learning opportunities:** Boomers tend to be curious, eager, and adventuresome. They're not geared to be couch potatoes passively absorbing entertainment. As such, they value learning opportunities both on the job and through employer-sponsored continuing education programs.

Employers are increasingly tuning into these incentives. So while they worry that they may not be able to meet your salary expectations, they're discovering that 50-plus workers are attracted to more than pay. So employers are increasingly offering such non-financial perks as flexible work schedules, telecommuting options, and training and education opportunities.

Pursuing Your Passion and Finding Purpose

When it comes to finding a successful and meaningful second act, most people simply don't know what they're passionate about, even when they know that they want to move in another direction. In this section, I encourage you to explore other careers and check out some of the fastest growing job markets to find the right fit. And I provide some tips and cautions to help guide you as you set out to pursue your passion and add purpose to your life.

Pursuing your passion is fine, but you don't want to end up in the poorhouse doing it. Look for ways to align your passion with what's in demand.

Considering other careers

One way to discover a passion that you can transform into gainful employment is to consider other careers. If you've ever thought to yourself, "I'd like to have her job," you have a head start. Think about those jobs you've always dreamed of having. Maybe you've always wanted to be a writer, a graphic artist, a wedding planner, an interior designer, a private investigator, or a sports announcer. Perhaps you've always dreamed of owning a bed and breakfast, brewing your own beer, making candy, or producing movies.

No, it's not too late to start thinking about pursuing a totally new career, and many our age have done so successfully. Think of it this way: If you live to 100 and look back 50 years or so, will you still think you were too old back then to pursue that dream job?

Start now. Pursuing a new career is likely to require a significant commitment of time, money, and effort. The longer time frame you have to plan, the better. Start working at age 50 on a career you might not get around to until age 60. You can start now to research a career you're interested in, take classes, and perhaps even secure an internship in the field to take the new career for a test drive to gauge your true interest in it before going all in.

Test-driving a career in some form is always a good idea. Career changers may enter a period of mourning after starting their new careers. All of a sudden, they realize how much they miss their old careers and aren't really open to replacing what they once had. Check out Chapter 2 for more on internship opportunities — one way to test-drive different work.

Finding inspiration in success stories

Many people find their passion is something they did when they were younger, often in childhood.

One woman I know moved from working in a management position at an insurance company to launching her own business making pillows out of old wedding dresses and crafting other customized pillows and quilts. When Marilyn Arnold was 9 years old, her mother, a skilled seamstress, patiently taught her to sew on a vintage Singer treadle sewing machine. As her feet pumped away at the machine in her family's farmhouse near Paris, Missouri, she was smitten. "I was in love with sewing, even when I stuck my finger and it bled," Arnold told me. But she never dreamed that now, at the age of 66, she would be running her own small business, Marilyn Arnold Designs, in Lee's Summit, Missouri.

Bill Skees has been a bibliophile for as long as he can remember. His favorite haunt growing up in Midland, Texas, was a bookstore called Miz B's. "I'd look at her behind the counter and think, 'That's got to be the greatest job in the world.'" In the decades that followed, Skees crossed the country for various jobs in IT, most recently heading development for a gaming company. But the work was stressful, and every chance he got, he slipped off to a bookstore. All the while, he dreamed of opening his own shop. And at 56, he did. He now owns and manages Well Read Books in Hawthorne, New Jersey.

Someday, you'll be able to add your success story to this list.

Money is the biggest roadblock for most career changers. When you start over in a new field or move to a nonprofit, chances are you need to take a salary cut at least initially. If you have an emergency fund to buy you time, you can do a more thoughtful job search. If you need to, pare back your discretionary living expenses to reflect a more realistic view of what you'll earn. See the later section "Navigating a career change" for details.

Checking out fast-growing job markets

One way to pursue your passion while ensuring your marketability is to consider employment in fast-growing markets. Certain industries, such as energy and healthcare, are experiencing more profound talent shortages than others. According to the ManpowerGroup's 2014 Talent Shortage Survey, here are the top ten jobs that U.S. employers are having trouble filling:

- Skilled trades (welders, electricians, machinists, and so on, prevalent in construction and manufacturing)
- Restaurant and hotel staff
- Sales representatives

- ✔ Teachers
- ✔ Drivers
- ✔ Accounting and finance staff
- ✔ Laborers
- ✔ IT staff
- ✔ Engineers
- ✔ Nurses

Occupations with the most robust job growth by 2022, according to the Bureau of Labor Statistics (BLS), range from personal care and home health aides to interpreters and translators, brick masons and stonemasons, electricians' helpers, and event planners.

Although most of the job growth is expected to be in fields that don't require postsecondary education, jobs that require a college degree or higher are actually growing faster (14.0 percent versus 9.1 percent). And those higher-skilled jobs will pay, on average, more than double ($57,770 per year versus $27,670).

The following sections describe the sectors that are likely to be the hottest over the next few years.

Look for jobs and opportunities that leverage experience. Check out job websites, including www.aarp.org/work, encore.org, www.Job-Hunt.org, retiredbrains.com, and Workforce50.com to get a flavor for what others are doing and what jobs are out there now.

Healthcare

Look for opportunities in healthcare support, such as nursing assistants, physical and occupational therapists and assistants, skincare specialists, physician assistants, genetic counselors, and social workers. According to projections released by Georgetown University in 2015, the United States faces a shortage of 193,000 nursing professionals by 2020. Additionally, a 2015 report from The Association of American Medical Colleges estimates that, by 2025, the United States will experience a shortfall of anywhere from 46,100 to 90,400 physicians. Here again, recruitment and retention efforts aimed at the 50 and older workforce can help address this shortage.

According to the BLS, occupations related to healthcare, healthcare support, construction, and personal care services, such as physical therapists, skincare specialists, and social workers are expected to add a combined 5.3 million jobs in the United States, an increase representing approximately one-third of all employment gains over the coming decade.

The dietitians and nutritionists and nursing assistants occupations are each projected to grow 21.1 percent between 2012 and 2022, according to BLS data. Given the comparatively small size of the dietitians and nutritionists profession, projected growth is expected to result in the addition of 14,200 new jobs. The nursing assistants occupation, however, is far larger. The upshot: The same anticipated growth rate in that occupation is expected to add 312,200 new jobs to the economy by 2022.

Leisure and hospitality

The leisure and hospitality sector is growing. People will be spending money to eat out and go on vacation. Chefs, cooks, waiters, bartenders, and restaurant and hotel managers will be in demand.

Software development

The software developer and programmer sector is expected to add 279,500 jobs by 2022, accounting for about four out of ten new jobs in the computer and math occupations group, according to BLS.

Cybersecurity

Although projected growth in jobs for information security analysts, at 27,400 new positions, is tiny compared to jobs for software developers and programmers, the rate of growth for information security analysts is expected to be 37 percent, making this the fastest growing job in this sector.

Engineering

According to 2013 Current Population Survey data, 22 percent (or 447,000) of engineers in the United States are age 55 and up. As these workers approach retirement age, there may not be enough new workforce entrants to replace their loss in key roles. Focused efforts to retain and recruit older workers can mitigate these gaps.

Skilled labor

BLS projections show that considerable job growth is expected in skilled labor professions, including brick masons, block masons, stonemasons, and tile and marble setters (and their helpers), and electricians' helpers. As mentioned earlier, employers are currently having the most trouble filling openings in these and other skilled trades.

Translators

For those who speak foreign languages, labor experts also project that there will be a rising need for interpreters and translators in courtrooms and other settings.

AARP Employer Pledge: Experience Valued

The AARP Employer Pledge: Experience Valued program (aarp.org/work) is a national initiative to direct job seekers to employers that value and are hiring experienced workers *and* help employers solve their current and future staffing challenges. Employers who sign the pledge agree that they will do the following:

- Recognize the value of experienced workers

- Believe in equal opportunity for all workers, regardless of age

- Recruit across diverse age groups

- Consider all applicants on an equal basis

- Have immediate hiring needs

More than 285 employers have signed the pledge, including AlliedBarton, American Red Cross, AT&T, Charles Schwab, CVS Caremark, General Mills, Google, Kimberly Clark, Manpower, National Institutes of Health (NIH), New York Life, Scripps Health, S&T Bancorp, Toys "R" Us, United Health Care, Walgreens, and WellStar Health Systems.

Taking the first steps in pursuing your passion

"Pursue your passion" is the kind of advice you receive from a friend or relative who either never pursued her passion or knew from the day she was born what she wanted to do. It sounds like great advice until you pause to think about it and realize that you have no idea what your passion is or how to take that first step from point A to point B. Here are some suggestions to ease you into those first steps with a tip of the hat to career coach Beverly Jones:

- **Find a place to start.** You don't need a precise definition before you get going. Start by making a list of what you want in the next phase of your career. Don't look for a perfect path or ideal starting point.

- **Get things moving by taking small steps.** Get moving in the general direction of where you want to go. One small step may be calling someone who works in a field that appeals to you to discuss possibilities.

- **Silence your inner enemy.** If you have a negative refrain that goes through your head and sabotages your efforts to make a change, such as, "I'm too old to do that," make note of it. Write that thought down in a notebook and reframe it with a positive thought, such as, "I have these specific skills, and I'm going to use them in a new career." You need to get rid of that old blocking message to move forward with your dreams.

✔ **Ask the basic questions.** Does your second act fit your lifestyle? Can you afford it? What does your partner think? Ask yourself how a certain career will work with your social life, your spending habits, and your family situation. It will help you to dig deeper and get a clearer picture of what you truly want in your life and your options to get there.

✔ **Keep a journal.** Journaling is a great way to map your new career direction. Make lists: the best times in your life, the things you really like, the experiences you've enjoyed, what you've excelled at, the best moments in your current career. These lists will help you hone in on your passion and visualize yourself harnessing it to pursue something new and exciting.

✔ **Get a business card.** Want to be an artist but still working as a lawyer? Get an artist's business card. As soon as you have a card, it makes the career real. You can get your second-act card long before you finish your first act. Printing your new information on a card can be transformative.

✔ **Have a mental picture of where you want to go.** Tape a photograph to your office wall of what your new career might look like. Or create a collage. Journal about your goals.

✔ **Be practical.** You may need to upgrade your skills and education, but take one class at a time. You can add more classes as your direction and motivation become clear.

✔ **Get your life in order.** Get physically and financially fit. Change is stressful. When you're physically fit, you have more energy. Less debt gives you more choices. Debt is a dream killer. With your finances in order, you have more options. You can be more nimble. See Chapter 4 for more about getting your finances in order.

Need a jump start to get you moving through those steps? Try Life Reimagined. org's LifeMap™, which helps you create your own personal mission statement, implement an action plan, and get advice and encouragement from a certified, online coach.

Don't ruin your hobby. I have a colleague who loves to garden. When she started thinking about what to do next, she considered being a landscape designer. But she quickly realized that she'd get lonely in the garden all day; she prefers working with people. Gardening is a great hobby and escape from work, but it wouldn't be the right career move for her. Make sure you think hard about how your passion will look and feel as a career.

For additional tips on changing careers, check out Chapter 17, visit `aarp. org/work` and `LifeReimagined.org`, and check out my book *What's Next? Finding Your Passion and Your Dream Job in Your Forties, Fifties, and Beyond* (Berkley Books/AARP) (AARP.org/DreamJob).

Putting Proven Success Strategies into Practice

You're not the first person to be looking for a job later in life, and that's good news for you. Others have led the way from unemployment to rewarding work in their 50s and beyond. And although these trailblazers haven't beaten down a path for you to follow (because there are so many paths to follow), they have revealed some strategies and techniques that have survived the test of time. In the following sections, I introduce you to several of the more effective strategies for securing employment, most of which apply to all job seekers, but a couple of which apply specifically to 50-plus job seekers.

Starting sooner rather than later

The sooner you start looking for a job after losing a job, the more likely you'll find a new job. According to the AARP Public Policy Institute report "The Long Road Back: Struggling to Find Work after Unemployment," by Gary Koenig, Lori Trawinski, and Sara Rix, those who waited three months or longer before beginning their job search were less likely to have become reemployed.

Why wait so long to look for work? The most popular answer was that they needed a break. Other reasons survey respondents cited include that they took time to think about what they wanted to do next (57 percent), had savings or other sources of income (56 percent), and found it hard to get motivated (42 percent). Twenty-five percent of respondents waited to begin their job search because of caregiving responsibilities, about the same number who waited because they didn't know how to get started. Whatever the reason, postponing the search for three months or longer worked against them.

Giving yourself a full-body makeover

Being physically fit, well groomed, and properly dressed is better than Botox. Aim to look and dress with an eye toward a vibrant, youthful appearance:

- ✔ If you aren't physically fit, make that a priority. Eat healthy, avoiding sugary and starchy foods and sugary drinks. Exercise at least 30 minutes every other day. Quit or cut back on caffeine, nicotine, and alcohol, if you're so inclined to use those substances.

- ✔ Maintain a well-groomed appearance. Get a haircut. Try a new 'do to give yourself a fresh look.

✔ Spruce up your wardrobe. Get the right look for the job that you're seeking. Free personal shoppers are available at many department stores to help. Or you can also ask friends for tips on looking your best. If you wear glasses, consider getting contacts, Lasik surgery, or new glasses with more contemporary frames.

People do judge a book by its cover. Showing up for an interview looking vigorous, well groomed, and sharply dressed demonstrates that you're up for the job and have the requisite stamina, which is often a concern for employers when they consider hiring someone over 50. This advice also applies to any headshots you use for your social media and networking profiles. (See Chapter 9 for details.)

Using the most effective means to get a job

When reemployed workers were asked about the most effective steps they took in finding their current jobs, the overwhelming majority attributed their success to networking, according to the AARP's "The Long Road Back: Struggling to Find Work after Unemployment." Here are the most effective steps:

✔ Reaching out to a network of contacts

✔ Asking relatives and friends about jobs

✔ Contacting employers directly

✔ Using a headhunter

✔ Consulting professional associations

Based on these findings, I give the next tip and the report's coauthor, Lori Trawinski, project director of AARP's Future of Work@50+ Initiative, gives the last two points of advice to older unemployed job seekers:

✔ If you're interested in a particular industry, join an association connected with it and seek out volunteer openings. Go to industry and professional meetings and conferences. You never know who will know someone who is hiring. And many college and university career centers are reaching out to alumni to help, too.

✔ Volunteer while you're out of work. By putting your volunteering on your résumé, you won't show a blank period of unemployment. To the extent that you can, be out in the world using your skills.

✔ Be aggressive in your job search. Network as much as you can as well as keep an eye out for openings. The people who are aggressive are more likely to be reemployed.

Networking is not optional! As I like to put it, "networking" is just one letter off from "not working." Simply put, many older folks have better networks than do younger people. Employers want to hire someone who comes with the blessing of an existing employee or colleague. It makes their job easier. That's a card younger workers, who often have smaller networks, can't play as often as older workers. LinkedIn, for instance, is a great way to pull together your professional network. And you have got to pick up that darn phone. Ask for help and advice. Here are some concrete ways to network:

- ✔ **Pick up the phone and call everybody you ever worked with and every employer you ever worked for.** That's the way to get an interview. If you don't establish a personal connection to the company, submitting an application is probably a waste of time.

- ✔ **Call friends of friends, people in your faith community, athletic club, volunteer organizations, and parents of your children's friends.** Heck, call your children's friends, too!

- ✔ **Contact trade and professional associations you belong to.** Many have job boards.

- ✔ **Connect with alumni associations and your fraternity or sorority if you belong to one.** College and university placement offices are there to help no matter how long ago you graduated.

- ✔ **Canvas local lawyers, accountants, and bank officers in town and see if they know of any clients who are hiring.** In short, you really have to "kiss a lot of frogs" to find a prince. Leave no stone unturned.

- ✔ **Join LinkedIn and Facebook, find and reconnect with people you know, and let everyone know you're looking for a job.** (See Chapters 9 and 10 for details.)

For additional details about these and other networking strategies and tactics, check out Chapter 3.

For a treasure trove of job search tips and information, head to www.aarp.org/work.

In the following sections, I introduce additional strategies and techniques that are effective in landing a job.

Broadening your job search

Broadening your job search simply means being open to other possibilities — considering a different profession in a different industry, making trade-offs in terms of salary and flextime, stitching together a full-time position with part-time gigs, and so on. It doesn't mean applying to every job opening you find. As I explain in Chapter 11, you really want to focus your efforts in one area for maximum impact. But you don't want to pass up a golden opportunity just because it doesn't happen to conform to your notion of the ideal job.

One way to broaden your search is to think less in terms of job title and more in terms of skills, knowledge, and experience — all these assets may be transferrable to a different profession, a different line of work. If you're focused on a full-time job, you can broaden your search by considering contract work or a temporary assignment, which may lead to a full-time position or even starting your own business.

Making trade-offs

Broadening your job search often requires making trade-offs. According to the AARP Public Policy Institute report, "The Long Road Back: Struggling to Find Work after Unemployment," those who manage to find a job often accept lower pay and benefits, and many have to change occupations.

While some unemployed people have succeeded in finding work with better pay and benefits and more favorable working conditions, others accepted lower wages and fewer benefits, possibly indicating a desire for more flexible work options for work-life balance. Here are some of the ways participants in the study reported broadening their job search:

✔ Looking for a job in a different field. This was the most common response overall (by 41 percent) for both the currently reemployed and the unemployed (43 percent of each).

✔ Looking for a job with lower pay or benefits (37 percent of the reemployed and 39 percent of the unemployed). Perhaps job seekers became more realistic as time

went on about the possibility of finding the types of jobs and pay they had before becoming unemployed.

Occupational change was a common occurrence among the reemployed; more than half (53 percent) had an occupation different from the one they had before becoming unemployed. Almost two-thirds (63 percent) of the long-term unemployed had a job in a different occupation than the one they had before becoming unemployed. By comparison, 46 percent of the short-term unemployed were in a different occupation.

Among the reemployed working in new occupations, 40 percent were earning "a lot less" and 17 percent were earning "somewhat less" on their current jobs. By comparison, 18 percent and 20 percent, respectively, of the reemployed working in the same occupations said they were earning "a lot less" or "somewhat less." Working in a new occupation often means lower pay because a worker's experience may not be as applicable in the new job.

Considering a patchwork approach to your career

As Henry Ford once, said: "Nothing is particularly hard if you divide it into small jobs." You may be able to apply this maxim to piecing together full- or part-time work. For example, you could take on one or two part-time jobs, do some contract work or consulting on the side, and still have plenty of free time and enough money to enjoy that time. Or you may do full-time seasonal work for part of the year and take on a part-time job the rest of the year. And you may want to gradually scale down your workweek over the years as you make a smooth transition into retirement.

Don't be surprised if you find yourself testing a number of different kinds of jobs to find what you really shine at or want to do in the years ahead. You may even strategically build an income stream from a tapestry of work you enjoy and are skilled at doing.

Consider opening a consulting practice and making yourself available for short-term projects. Alternatively, you might find that creating a patchwork of income streams will give you the flexibility you crave.

Navigating a career change

Fifty-five percent of U.S. workers want to change careers, according to a University of Phoenix survey. To make a switch, you'll probably have to learn new skills, make new professional contacts, sock away cash, and more. Here are the best moves to make your change a successful one:

- ✔ Be adaptable and embrace change.
- ✔ Do your research. Reach out to people doing the work you want to do, and ask them all you can about their jobs. How did they get started? What do you need to succeed? And what can you expect to earn, both at first and later on? Because you aren't asking for a job, the discussion should be relaxed. Be inquisitive.
- ✔ Moonlight or apprentice yourself to someone already in the field.
- ✔ If you want to work for a nonprofit in a cause meaningful to you — a common goal among career changers — then volunteer; you'll not only see what the day-to-day work entails but also meet people in the organization.
- ✔ Identify the skills you need. Be prepared to spend the time and money to get the skills, credentials, and contacts you need to get relaunched, but don't assume that you'll need a costly degree. See the next section, "Getting the training you need," for details.

✔ Get financial aid. Fifty-four percent of employers offer tuition assistance to employees, reports the Society for Human Resource Management. You may have to repay the funds, though, if you don't stay with the company for a certain number of years afterward.

✔ Assess your finances. Following your passion is great, but make sure you can afford your dream job. See Chapter 4 for guidance in managing your finances through the transition.

Getting the training you need

Once you reach a certain age, you may be branded with stereotypes that make you vulnerable: resistant to change, technologically challenged, complacent. In a survey by staffing agency Adecco, 39 percent of employers said the greatest challenge with older workers is their difficulty learning new technologies. Of course, this is a misconception — Pew Institute research shows 87 percent of American adults use the Internet — but you may need to demonstrate your tech aptitude to disprove this perception. To increase your market value, obtain the education, training, and certifications required to do the job you're seeking.

Before taking classes or training for new skills, research the demand for those skills locally. In the AARP Public Policy Institute study of unemployment, of the 31 percent who participated in training or education programs in the past five years, more said doing so "did not help at all" than those who said it "helped a great deal." This could be pointing to a mismatch between the training they received and current job openings. Before enrolling in expensive courses or classes, do your due diligence:

✔ Contact a local community college and ask about skills that local employers are looking for. In certain cases, the American Association of Community Colleges partners with AARP Foundation and local workforce agencies and employers to do this; you can find those community colleges in the Back to Work 50+ section on www.aarp.org/foundation.

✔ Talk to graduates and employers to find out whether the educational and training programs are truly valuable.

✔ Consider what you can afford and the return on your investment. Look at free options as well as paid. You'll find more on this in Chapter 4.

Seeking help

During your job search, don't hesitate to ask others for help. People are generally glad to assist if you ask politely for what you need. After all, wouldn't you be eager to help friends or relatives revamp their résumé or assist in any other way you could if they were looking for a job? Sometimes, the most generous people are the least likely to ask for help, never realizing that others may need the opportunity to help someone else. Sometimes, you have to be a taker. Here are common areas where older job seekers often need help:

- ✔ Writing or updating a résumé
- ✔ Getting emotional support (someone to listen)
- ✔ Searching for jobs online
- ✔ Using a computer
- ✔ Navigating LinkedIn, Facebook, Twitter, and other social media and networking sites

Here are some resources to consider checking out when you need help:

- ✔ Family and friends
- ✔ Workforce centers/one-stop job centers
- ✔ Online job-search sites
- ✔ Career or job coaches
- ✔ Your local library
- ✔ Educational institutions, including placement services

Dealing with Ageism

News from the job front isn't all roses. Ageism is real. If you're over 50 and pounding the pavement these days, you face certain challenges. Once becoming unemployed, it typically takes an older worker longer to find a job than it does a younger person, according to the Bureau of Labor Statistics (www.bls.gov/web/empsit/cpseea36.pdf). If you have felt the disappointment of a floundering job hunt at a gut level, you have plenty of company. Many people I have counseled and met with are frankly furious, discouraged, and dumbfounded by their inability to land a job that suits their experience and desired salary.

The key to overcoming ageism is to understand employers' concerns and address those concerns, as I explain here.

Knowing what employers are so worried about

Some employers figure that your salary demands are out of their ballpark, and that if they hire you for less, you'll resent it and probably jump ship if you get a better offer. They often perceive, true or not, that you're set in your ways or lack the cutting-edge skills or even the energy to do the job.

Then, too, some hiring managers might surmise that you have age-related health problems, or are likely to, and you'll be taking too much sick leave. And, of course, there's the nagging issue that you're not in it for the long haul, even if that's far from the truth. Finally, there's concern about reverse ageism — the employer may think you won't want to take orders from a younger boss who is probably making more than you.

Landing a job is difficult for everybody, and everyone seems to have a different take on what it takes to break through. It's not automatically your age that's holding you back. Employers want to hire people they know or can trust. In addition, employers want to reduce their exposure to risk, and you may present a risk regardless of your age. For example, if you made more money than the employer has budgeted for the position, you've been out of work for six months, you've held a higher position (and may be unable to accept a drop in status), or you've had three jobs in the past three years, you may be perceived as a risk. Some of those risks come with age, but they're not caused by age.

Laying their worries to rest

One way to sell a product is to take away every reason a prospective customer has for saying "No," and that's the strategy for overcoming ageism. If you do everything else right in terms of revamping your résumé, marketing yourself online, networking, and so forth, you've already given employers plenty of reasons to say yes. Now, you just have to take away their reasons for saying no. Here are some suggestions for doing just that:

- ✔ **Look your best.** Be physically fit, well groomed, and properly dressed.

- ✔ **Keep up with the times.** Do everything you can to keep up with technology and changes in your field or research the skills or certifications required for your new venture. Add the essential expertise and degrees before you apply for a new job. If you've recently updated any software certifications, or you are proficient in social media, let the recruiter or hiring manager know, even if that's a side comment in your discussion.

- ✔ **Build and maintain a strong online presence.** Invisibility is a liability, demonstrating that someone is out-of-date and unable to navigate the online world. See Chapters 9 and 10 for guidance on building and maintaining a strong positive online presence.

✔ **Establish your ability to learn and adapt.** Speak up about your flexibility in terms of management style, your openness to report to a younger boss, your technological aptitude, your energy, and your knack for picking up new skills. For many employers, it's not only about the candidate with the best credentials; it's about who's the best fit overall for the team. You have to make the case that you're the person who is going to both play your position masterfully and help the team.

✔ **Downplay the risks.** If you held a higher position or earned more money in the past, or if you've been unemployed for some time or worked several jobs over the course of several years, find ways to downplay yourself as a flight risk. If there's a gap in employment, you may explain, for example, that you were financially solvent and could wait for the job you really wanted, and this is it.

✔ **Market your age as a plus**. Think brand management. You're responsible for your own image. Workers 50 and older tend to be self-starters, know how to get the job done, and don't need as much hand-holding as those with less experience. A great benefit to being older is that you have a good deal of knowledge and leadership ability. And whether you realize it or not, you have a network. You have a lot more resources to draw on than do people in their 20s and 30s. So pitch your age as a plus. You need to be able to articulate your value. Strut your stuff.

✔ **Practice positivity**. In truth, one of the biggest stumbling blocks to landing a job is negativity. You probably don't need a Botox treatment. What works better is a faith lift. You've got to believe in yourself. When you do, it shows from the inside out. People dwell on the bad news. "I've been unemployed for too long. I'm too old." Have faith in yourself. After you've been out of work for a while, you forget your value. You take for granted your accomplishments and contributions.

✔ **Stay present.** Don't chatter on in interviews about successes you had ten years ago. Focus on what you've done lately.

Sometimes it's hard to toot your own horn. Self-promotion is uncomfortable, especially if you've always thought of yourself as a team player. Ask people who know you well, whose opinions you value and trust, to evaluate you in writing: your best skills and talents, your personality, the roles you've been really good at.

Guess what comes back? All the accomplishments, all the positives that you need to be reminded of to prove to yourself that you're a talented individual who has a contribution to make. Then when you're in the interview, networking, or doing informational conversations, you can say, "Well, people have said about me that blah, blah, blah."

All of a sudden, you have all the words to use, and it's easier to talk about your attributes because you're using someone else's tribute, advises career coach Maggie Mistal.

Persistence pays

One of my friends in his late-50s started looking for a full-time job when he was laid off from his job as a digital media strategist and senior vice president. He had worked at the firm for 14 years, and the abrupt wave out the door caught him by surprise.

He stayed busy, working part-time in media relations for an environmental nonprofit, writing a blog for an online magazine, and consulting. But his search for a full-time gig left him feeling that while periodic interviews went well, the person across the desk seemed to be looking at his "expiration date."

His frustration was profound.

But there's a happy ending. It took nearly three years, but he did it. He landed a full-time position as digital editorial director for a regional media company. And he loves it. He was hired by the same person who hired him at his former employer. She really didn't care about age because she knew what he could do.

Chapter 2

Using Skills to Your Advantage

In This Chapter
▶ Discovering the skills and qualities employers value most
▶ Taking inventory of your transferrable skills
▶ Adding knowledge and skills to your package

To fill a specific position, an employer chooses the most trusted candidate who has the best track record of doing the job — the person who comes most highly recommended and has the requisite skills and experience. Skills are an essential component to securing employment, so in this chapter, I focus on knowing which skills are valued, identifying the skills you have, and developing the skills you need.

Recognizing the Skills Employers Value

Employers look for skills in two categories: hard skills and soft skills. *Hard skills* (also referred to as *work skills*) are those required to do the job, such as network security, accounting, programming, marketing, data analysis, and graphic design. These skills are typically learned and are quantifiable; for example, you can earn a degree or certification or at least point to a course on a transcript showing that you received training in a particular area. Or you can point to jobs you held in the past that required those same skills. *Soft skills* are more subjective, harder to quantify, such as an ability to communicate clearly, solve problems, manage your own time, and be a team player.

In this section, you discover the hard and soft skills that employers value most and how to dig deeper to find out which skills are most highly valued in a particular field or required for application to a certain position.

Finding out which hard skills are required

Nearly every position, whether advertised or not, requires certain hard skills. I can't possibly cover them all, because they can be highly specific for certain positions, such as knowing how to program in C++, operate a computer numerical control (CNC) milling machine, or translate Farsi. To find out which hard skills are required, hit the job boards, as explained in Chapter 5, pull up job descriptions you're interested in, and make a list.

Following are a few broad hard skill sets that employers look for in nearly every field:

- **Technology skills:** Nowadays, employers expect employees to be comfortable with a range of technological applications. Even if computer work is not a big part of your job, you will do yourself a favor to be somewhat savvy about how to use a computer, tablet, and smartphone and how to navigate your way around the web. See the later section "Getting tech savvy" for details.

- **(Real) social media skills:** In recent years, "social media" has been a popular item in the "skills" section of many job seekers' résumés. But what does it really mean to be skilled at social media? It's more than simply having a LinkedIn, Twitter, or Facebook account. You need to be able to show an interviewer that you're active on these networks and understand the nuances of each one's distinct community. If you don't know the difference between a price tag and a hashtag, you have some work to do.

- **Data analytics:** Some of the fastest-growing occupations between now and 2022 will be information security analysts (37 percent), operations research analysts (27 percent), and statisticians (27 percent), according to the Bureau of Labor Statistics (BLS). This means that candidates with a strong background in data science and analytics will have a real advantage in the job market. Smart employers are looking for people who understand data and its value to a business.

Recognizing the soft skills employers value

Soft skills may seem basic, so bear with me. In many ways, these *softer* skills, which include your outlook and attitude, are gauges of how well you'll fit in. Employers want to be sure that you'll work easily and efficiently with your coworkers, your supervisor, and perhaps the organization's customers or clients. They also want to be sure that you can think on your feet and are equipped to make smart decisions.

Here are the softer skills I'm talking about, arranged in alphabetical order. Rate yourself and mark areas where you may need improvement. Then make a plan to bump it up in those areas, if possible.

- **Analytical thinking:** Employers want people who think logically, can size up situations, seek additional information when necessary, and make fact-based decisions.

✔ **Communication (oral and written):** Employers value workers who communicate well both orally and via the written word. When you're a good communicator, you generally interact better with coworkers, supervisors, clients, customers, vendors, and others.

✔ **Confidence:** Being confident means you can take initiative without the constant need for permission or approval.

✔ **Cooperation (team player):** Success on the job almost always requires an ability and willingness to cooperate and collaborate with others, including coworkers, supervisors, vendors, clients, and customers.

✔ **Creativity:** Even in non-creative jobs, you're expected to be able to think creatively to adapt to changing conditions and solve problems.

✔ **Decisiveness:** If you're a confident decision maker, you're less apt to waste time mulling over options. This doesn't mean, however, that you make rash decisions. You want to establish a healthy balance between analyzing options and being able to make decisions.

✔ **Flexibility:** Most employers I have canvased never fail to mention that they truly value an employee who can easily shift gears. Everyone is multitasking these days, so you need to be able to seamlessly shift from one project to another without missing a beat. You must be willing to put in the extra hours when necessary and to balance assignments — both independently and as a team member — depending on how quickly a project must be completed and the best method to accomplish it.

✔ **Honesty and integrity:** Honesty and integrity are essential in building trust. As an employee, you're a reflection of the organization and its values. The growing popularity of social media has made employers much more sensitive to the image an organization projects all the way down to its employees.

✔ **Leadership qualities:** Leadership doesn't necessarily mean you're prepared to fill in for the CEO. Employers are just trying to get a bead on whether you believe in your own abilities and have an inner confidence that centers you and enables you to focus on the company's needs and not solely your own. They're looking for candidates who are ready and motivated, who want to achieve great things for the firm that reflect back on *all* the team members.

✔ **Learner:** One of my personal favorite soft skills is awkwardly phrased as "learner." Employers know that to beat the competition, they need a team of people eager to keep pushing the envelope, to learn new ways of doing things, and to be fearless about pushing themselves to constantly acquire knowledge and skills.

✔ **Listening:** Listening is a big part of effective communication, and it may take the form of active or passive listening. Passive listening is an ability to hear, understand, and follow instruction. Active listening involves asking questions that elicit the information and insight needed to perform a task, solve a problem, or clear up a misunderstanding. Both are valuable.

Practice listening with a friend. Have your friend tell you a story, work or personal. When she's done, retell the story to make sure you recalled all the key facts correctly.

- ✔ **Literacy (reading and math):** Nearly all jobs require literacy in reading and math. If you have a high-school diploma or a GED, you're covered. If not, work on developing the requisite knowledge and skills. You can find plenty of books and online videos to help you get started.

- ✔ **Organization:** Well-organized people tend to be more efficient and make fewer mistakes. Keeping some sort of day planner on a portable device or in print shows that you can organize your time.

- ✔ **Patience:** Many jobs are stressful, and employers want to see that you can keep your cool when things heat up.

- ✔ **People skills:** Your ability to connect with others and form solid working relationships is exceedingly important for most jobs. Being charismatic is a big plus for sales, management, customer service, public relations, and other jobs that require close contact with others, particularly customers, clients, and the public. Look around at people you like to work with and note what you admire. Try to emulate those attributes.

- ✔ **Planning prowess:** Success in the workplace often comes down to how well you can prioritize your work demands. You've got this one. Just remind yourself of all the times you have had to sift through the piles of to-do lists and urgent delivery dates and made it all work with a professional attitude and didn't skimp on quality.

- ✔ **Positive attitude:** I harp on this one a lot, but you need oomph. This is not a time to be cool and ultra–laid back. Upbeat and energetic people are a plus for most employers, and the truth is, it makes you more engaged in your work, too. It's a win-win.

- ✔ **Problem solving:** If you're a confident decision maker and adept at problem solving, you save your company time and money and regularly keep customers happy, too. Being a good problem solver generally comes down to breaking a problem down into smaller pieces and addressing each piece in turn.

- ✔ **Punctuality:** In some jobs, nothing gets done until everyone shows up. But even if you have a flexible schedule, certain occasions require punctuality. Showing up a little early for an interview helps to demonstrate that you're punctual.

- ✔ **Reliability:** Reliability simply means keeping your promise, and when you agree to work for someone, that's a promise to do your job 100 percent of the time.

- ✔ **Resilience:** The ability to recover from setbacks or failure is essential for success. Employers don't expect you to succeed all the time, but they do expect you to keep doing your job when adversity strikes.

✔ **Resourcefulness:** Resourcefulness is measured by how much you do with what you're given. Creative problem solvers figure out ways to succeed with the resources available.

✔ **Self-management:** Companies are eager to find employees who are able to keep themselves on track with little or no supervision. Employers value someone who shows up on time, gets the job done professionally, and is easy to work with.

Check out the section "Beefing Up Your Skill Set" later in this chapter for tips on how to make any improvements you may need.

Making the Most of What You Have

Nobody makes it to the age of 50 without developing some marketable skills. If you held a job, raised kids, bought a house, played computer games, surfed the web, balanced your bank accounts, read a few books, or did anything else that required getting off the couch and away from the television screen, you've acquired marketable skills. Now, you just need to identify them and put them to use in finding a job. In this section, I show you how.

Auditing your skills

Job seekers often don't know what they know or what skills they already have until they sit down and write a list. I encourage you to make your own list, which will come in handy when preparing your résumé, filling out job applications, and preparing for interviews. Take an inventory of your skills by following these steps:

1. **Write down any formal education you received in high school, college, or trade school that has given you a work skill, such as welding, programming, business management, or public speaking.**

2. **Include any other coursework, seminars, or workshops you attended.**

3. **List any licenses or certifications you currently hold or held in the past.**

4. **Record any proficiencies you have in any subject areas.**

   Perhaps you picked up a foreign language on your own, you taught yourself how to build websites or blogs, or you developed public speaking skills as a member of a local Toastmasters group.

5. **List all office software you're proficient with.**

   This includes spreadsheet applications, presentation programs, database management software, desktop publishing or graphics programs, blogging platforms, and so on.

6. **Jot down any hobbies that have taught you new skills or helped sharpen existing skills.**

7. **List your soft skills.**

   Maybe you're good at solving problems, planning and overseeing projects, or resolving conflict. See "Recognizing the soft skills employers value" for a longer list.

8. **Ask friends, relatives, and former coworkers and supervisors to list your best qualities.**

   You may not realize skills you possess until others call attention to them.

Don't restrict yourself to skills you developed on the job. If you volunteered as treasurer for your local parent-teacher organization, for example, you have experience with financial management and budgeting. If you raised children, you have experience in child-care, scheduling, and training. How you developed your skills is less important than the fact that you have the skills and that you can present those skills in a way that meet an employer's needs.

For additional ideas, search the web for "job skills list" or "jobs skills checklist." The U.S. Department of Labor's CareerOneStop has a Skills Profiler that generates a list of skills in several categories based on the job type and work activities you specify. Check it out at www.careerinfonet.org/skills.

Taking note of transferrable skills

Although you may need additional training and skills to pick up a new job or navigate a career change, many skills are *transferrable* — the knowledge and skill required are the same, but you're applying it in a new way or to a different situation. The ability to manage projects, for example, is a transferrable skill. In the publishing business, you may use this skill to coordinate efforts with writers, editors, graphic artists, and page layout personnel. In a shipping business, you may use the same skill to coordinate pick-up and delivery schedules. Same skill, different application.

When transferrable skills go to the dogs

After three decades in the retail business, dog lover Linda Waitkus retired from her position as a store manager for Bloomingdale's and opened her own retail pet shop, Great Dogs of Great Falls, in Great Falls, Virginia. Her experience in retail business management, customer service, and product marketing were all brought to bear. "I'm good at retail," Waitkus says. "I just transferred my skills to a different stage where I can work for myself."

Look at your skill set and past experience as transferrable to diverse fields. If you're switching industries, you're "redeploying" skills you already have in place.

Most soft skills are transferrable. Every job requires good written and oral communication skills, confidence, creative thinking, problem solving, decision making, self-management, and so on. Whether a hard skill is transferrable depends on the skill and the position you're pursuing. For example, if you worked as a restaurant manager and were in charge of scheduling and budgeting, you can transfer those skills to project management in industrial settings, managing a healthcare facility, or even subcontracting. Knowing how to operate and troubleshoot an injection molding press, on the other hand, wouldn't transfer over to those other fields.

Whether you realize it or not, over the course of your life, every class you've ever taken, every book you've ever read, every job you've ever had has prepared you for this moment. You'll know you've succeeded in finding the right job for you when your preparation meets the right opportunity.

Reframing your experience and skills

Reframing consists of presenting your experience and skills in a way that makes them relevant to the position. For example, suppose you just finished raising your kids and your job experience over the past 15 years consists of volunteer positions you held over the years. You're applying for a job as a director of a temp agency. Instead of merely listing the volunteer positions you held, the years you served, and your responsibilities, you may reframe your experiences and skills to make them relevant to the director position, like so:

President, Norfolk PTA: 2015–2017

- Organized and presided over monthly meetings.
- Introduced and implemented new-member outreach program that grew membership 7% each year.
- Increased fundraising revenue 20% in my first year.
- Led parent-teacher task force to improve student performance by 10% over the course of two school years.

Keep in mind that many experts advise against listing dates on résumés. More on this in Chapter 8.

From phys ed teacher to fitness trainer

Consider this teacher who became a fitness trainer, still using his teaching skills and experience to help his clients get fit.

Dave Kergaard, a former high-school physical education and health teacher, successfully transitioned to a career as a personal fitness coach. "I've always worked out and been involved in sports," he explained.

The work runs the gamut from nutrition counseling to designing workout regimes with weights, bikes, balls, and resistance bands. He has embraced his newfound career — helping a wide range of clients, including a 90-year-old woman who ditched her walker after regaining her strength via the exercise regime he custom-designed for her. Kergaard works with high-school athletes and the 55-plus crowd alike. "Some days I use my psychology degree more than my [physical education] one," Kergaard said.

"Beyond the moderate physical demands, the real challenge for a trainer is giving undivided attention to a student — er, a trainee. Many people won't push as hard unless you are there with them 100 percent," Kergaard said.

Beefing Up Your Skill Set

If you can show a hiring manager that you're taking classes, participating in a workshop, or working toward a professional certification, it shows that you're not stuck in your ways and are open to learning. Plus, the very activity of learning makes you feel unstuck, more alive. Research shows it reinvigorates your brain and stimulates the growth of new neurons and the development of new communication pathways. Yes, even old dogs can learn new tricks.

Of course, you'll never know all there is to know, especially when information is such a rapidly growing and moving target. But you can keep up with changes in your field, acquire new knowledge and skills to change careers, and improve your mental capacity through continuing education opportunities. In this section, I describe several ways to get the education and training you need.

AARP's Life Reimagined has teamed up with Kaplan to create a new online resource to help people find learning opportunities to enhance their current skills. Visit www.LearningAdvisor.com.

The secret to eternal youth

The most creative and resilient professionals tend to engage regularly in learning or self-development efforts. Look around you at the people you respect. Think about the role models you had when you were younger and starting out in your career. No doubt, they were curious, eager learners.

My role model is my dad who, even at the age of 85, was pushing to learn about robotics and the latest developments in technology by reading articles in *The Wall Street Journal* and trade publications and attending lectures at Carnegie-Mellon University in Pittsburgh. It wasn't even his field, but he was intrigued by it. He was the epitome of the lifelong learner.

Look around. There are all kinds of ways you can learn if you're open to it and willing to make a little effort.

Asking yourself some strategic questions to get started

Although I'm a big fan of learning for learning's sake, this *is* a book about landing the job you want, so before you set out on your quest for knowledge, ask yourself the following questions:

- ✔ What skills can I add that will expand my job opportunities?
- ✔ Which skills can I get from a life experience, and which ones will I need to hit the books for?
- ✔ Am I willing to make a hard-and-fast promise to myself to make learning and self-development part of my daily activities? How committed am I?
- ✔ Am I willing to invest the time (and perhaps money) in myself?

Taking classes and pursuing certifications consumes evenings and weekends, and most people are leery of adding one more thing to their to-do list. One way to find the time and the will to shake things up is to start with baby steps, one class at a time. Starting your career education doesn't have to cut too deeply into your schedule or your wallet.

Before enrolling in any program, determine whether it's worth the time, effort, and money:

- ✔ Track down graduates of programs that interest you to get a sense for how valuable it was to them.
- ✔ If it's related directly to learning new job skills, ask someone you trust who knows the field you're interested in or job you're pursuing for his or her opinion.

> ✔ Get a list of employers who have hired graduates from the program.
>
> ✔ If appropriate, ask your former employer to weigh in.

Keep in mind that the shorter the training, the less value it may have. A certificate that you earn in a long weekend probably won't deliver the knowledge and gravitas you would get from one that requires 100 or more hours of class time at a top university.

Checking out community colleges

Take a class at a community college. Community college courses are usually a few hundred dollars per credit. In recent years, community colleges have reached out to adults interested in practical continuing education. The American Association of Community Colleges' Plus 50 Initiative, for example, creates campus programs for people 50 and older, with an emphasis on training for the workplace. If President Obama's proposal for free tuition at community colleges becomes law, even more older students are likely to participate. To meet the demand for continuing education, colleges are creating retraining and certificate programs aimed squarely at this demographic.

Nearly 60 percent of U.S. colleges and universities let older students take classes either tuition-free or at rock-bottom prices. Inquire about specific residency, age, and other requirements at schools in your area.

Try a certificate program. Compared to full-blown degree programs, certificate programs are generally cheaper and more focused on the professional skills you may want to add now. A certificate program may run the gamut from $3,000 if done entirely online to $15,000 for on-campus credit hours. That can be quite a bit cheaper than a public four-year college degree program, which can cost you upward of $650 per credit, or a single course at a private college, which can top $1,300. A master's degree can easily set you back more than $40,000, depending on the school.

Online webinars and workshops offered by industry associations are other avenues to consider. For example, the National Association of Realtors offers a number of continuing education courses for its members.

Enrolling in a Massively Open Online Course (MOOC)

MOOC is the acronym for the trendy *massively open online courses*, offered by education providers such as Coursera (www.coursera.org), EdX (www.edx.org), Lynda (lynda.com), and Udacity (www.udacity.com).

Search for "free online courses" on The Mind Unleashed website (`themindunleashed.org`) for more.

I recently signed up for a free 12-week course called "Think Again: How to Reason and Argue," via Coursera. The class is taught by two professors at Duke University. All I need for the class is a working computer and an Internet connection. Otherwise, it's free.

Offered by top-tier universities like Stanford and Princeton, MOOCs offer cheap ways to learn from their instructors anytime, anywhere. And yes, if I successfully complete the class, I will receive a "Statement of Accomplishment" signed by the instructor. Of course, I'll add that to my LinkedIn profile and let my bosses know I passed with flying colors. Maybe I'll show them what I learned firsthand.

Check out other free course options. You may be able to audit or take free or low-cost courses at your alma mater, or a noncredit personal enrichment program, such as Odyssey (`advanced.jhu.ed`), offered by Johns Hopkins University. Odyssey has a wide selection of courses, workshops, and lecture series delivered by faculty and community experts. Odyssey doesn't have grades or exams.

Taking an educational vacation

One way I keep learning is by traveling. This is a simple way to push your mind and recharge. Travel changes the traveler. You learn, grow, and open your mind when you leave your comfort zone, particularly if you're fortunate enough to visit a foreign country and immerse yourself in a new culture. Try it. Changing places and routines, even for a short while, is motivating and stimulating. And when you get back to the office, it clings to you.

Your travel adventure can be informal, either on your own or with friends and family. You may even just spend one day a month walking around your own town and looking at it through the eyes of a tourist. Stop by an arboretum, tour a historical building, or visit a museum exhibit and shell out a few bucks for the guided headphone explanations of what's before your eyes.

Then, too, if you can afford it, you may want to go all in and take part in a learning vacation. Search online, or try `www.aarp.org/travel`, to find one that fits your interests and budget. If you can afford it, look at vacations offered by National Geographic Expeditions (`www.nationalgeographicexpeditions.com`), Road Scholar Educational Travel (`www.roadscholar.org`), Smithsonian Journeys (`www.smithsonianjourneys.org`), or your alma mater. The alumni association at Duke University, my alma mater, sponsored recent trips to Vietnam, Cambodia, and Peru, as well as the Oxford Experience, where you study for two weeks at the august University of Oxford in England via one of four noncredit enrichment courses led by Oxford tutors. Check out some of the Earthwatch expeditions at `earthwatch.org`. Learning vacations can fill in gaps in your résumé and help you connect with an interviewer. What you learn may not relate specifically to a job, but it shows hiring managers that you're an avid learner and curious. Moreover, you never know who you might meet and learn of potential job opportunities. Can you say networking? And you can add your travel to your résumé under the education section.

Pursuing a degree or certification online

If spending time on a college campus isn't your thing, you can pursue a degree or certification online. Several online universities offer accredited bachelor's and master's degree programs and certifications in high-demand career fields. Many traditional colleges and universities also offer online courses and degree programs. Search the web for your state followed by "online university."

Negotiate for an accelerated degree. You may be able to get your tuition lowered by having the college waive some required courses because of your "experiential" credit. You may have a strong case that you've learned through work and life what some of the required courses cover. Don't be bashful about advocating for yourself.

Acquiring on-the-job training on-the-cheap

Learning by doing is one of the oldest and best ways to acquire a new skill. Trouble is, you're usually required to have the skill to get the job where you can learn the skill by doing it. Still, there are a few ways to get on-the-job training without the experience required to actually land the job. Perhaps you can even earn a little money by doing it. In the following sections, I offer some guidance in this area.

Seeking apprenticeships and fellowships

You can build experience in an industry or job that appeals to you in all sorts of ways. If you want to become a chocolatier, for instance, you may be able to volunteer to help out at a local gourmet grocery or restaurant that makes its own confections. If you're interested in learning the ropes of the restaurant industry, you can offer to help out on weekends in some fashion, perhaps sautéing for the chef or filling in as a greeter or even keeping the restaurant's books if that's your forte. These are all ways people I know have made transitions to new lines of work.

If you're looking for a career with a social purpose, consider applying for an Encore fellowship at `encore.org/fellowships`. These are one-year, paid fellowships, typically in a professional capacity at a nonprofit, to help mature workers re-enter the job market.

Exploring internship and returnship opportunities

Internships and returnships (see the nearby sidebar) can fill a gap in your résumé, and, from the standpoint of an employer, the programs offer a chance to test prospective employees before committing. If you sense that a hiring manager is interested in hiring you but still waffling because you have been out of work or are making a career shift, consider asking whether he would consider an internship, to appraise you based on your work for several weeks. Think back on the movie *The Internship,* where two 40-somethings, played by Vince Vaughn and Owen Wilson, scored sought-after summer internships at Google and, amazingly, are ultimately hired full-time.

To get some leads on internship programs for 50-plus workers, visit these sites:

- ✔ iRelaunch (`www.irelaunch.com`) is a company that helps connect individuals who want to return to work after career breaks with employers interested in hiring them. The site features a list of Career Reentry Programs Worldwide (`www.irelaunch.com/CareerReentry`). As of this writing, 124 programs are listed.

- ✔ OnRamp Fellowship (`onrampfellowship.com`) is a program that places experienced women attorneys with law firms for a one-year, paid training contract. This experiential learning program gives returning women lawyers — many of whom have opted out of the legal field for a period of time to raise children — an opportunity to demonstrate their value in the marketplace while also increasing their experience, skills, and legal contacts. Nineteen law firms are currently participating in the program.

Older interns are sometimes paid respectable wages. For example, attorneys with OnRamp are paid a one-year stipend of $125,000 ($85,000 in smaller markets, such as New Orleans and Birmingham) and benefits, which are paid by the law firm, the fellow works full-time on complex legal projects and receives ongoing feedback from a designated partner advisor.

A growing number of organizations — the National Institutes of Health, Stanley Consultants, and Michelin North America, among many others — have programs designed to attract and keep workers past 50. Companies with internship programs for older workers include Harvard Business School, McKinsey, MetLife, PwC, and Regeneron.

What's a "returnship"?

Goldman Sachs launched the first "returnship" program in the fall of 2008 to give individuals who had taken a career break, primarily women raising children, an opportunity to restart their careers after an extended absence (two or more years) from the workforce. The returnship is a paid ten-week program designed to help facilitate the on-ramping process in a variety of Goldman Sachs divisions.

Since then, other companies have followed Goldman Sachs' lead. The British bank Barclays recently announced plans to launch an internship program in the U.K. for mature workers in the second half of 2015. (At the moment, Barclays says it has no plans to take this apprenticeship program to the United States.) The goal: to give an as yet undetermined number of older job seekers the same opportunities the bank offers the 2,000 or so 16-to-24-year-olds who enroll in its apprenticeship program each year.

Consider looking for organizations in your area that offer similar programs or even suggesting such an arrangement to an organization you want to work for that doesn't have such a program in place.

Three years ago, Intel introduced the Intel Encore Career Fellowship — a program that pays a one-year, $25,000 stipend to help retiring employees transition into post-retirement careers with a nonprofit organization. So far, 200 retiring Intel employees have become Encore Fellows, said Julie Wirt, Intel's global human resources retirement design manager. "And the momentum for the program is clearly building," she said. "It's not only a retirement benefit for our employees, it's having an impact on communities around the country."

Taking on a part-time job in the field of your dreams

To get a feel for what a new career will really be like, take on a part-time job in the field that interests you. (Try moonlighting if you're currently working to see how you like the different field.) If you're interested in teaching, you may offer to guest lecture at nearby colleges or universities. You may discover that teaching is your calling or that it's not as great as you had dreamt it would be. Even if you have to do the job for free, it's probably still worth your time so you can make sure this is what you really want. If the dream fits, you can go all in to sharpen your skills and pursue the degree or certifications you need. If the dream fizzles, you haven't lost a huge investment.

Some careers, such as teaching and real estate, may require a new degree or certificate. Others may require a new set of skills that you may not even realize you need until you work in the industry. For example, if you open a bakery or any retail business, you'll need to learn about inventory management, bookkeeping, and marketing to be successful.

Getting started as a volunteer

Look for opportunities to volunteer for a nonprofit organization that provides opportunities to build the skills you need. In addition to helping with skill-building, volunteering gets you outside of your own head and that swamp of negativity and helps you gain some perspective on others' needs.

Search for prospects at AARP's Giving Back (www.aarp.org/giving-back) or Create The Good (www.createthegood.org), HandsOnNetwork (www.handsonnetwork.org), and VolunteerMatch.org (www.volunteermatch.org). If you're good with numbers, look into AARP Foundation Tax-Aide program (www.aarp.org/taxaide), where volunteers help lower income seniors do their taxes. It's a great way to get some tech skills (taxes are done on computer). AARP trains all volunteers.

Seek out nonprofits that need your particular professional expertise through the Executive Service Corps (escus.org) and Taproot Foundation (www.taprootfoundation.org). Idealist (www.idealist.org) has a searchable database of both volunteer and paid positions.

Never sit around feeling sorry for yourself. If you're unemployed, try volunteering or doing pro-bono work that keeps your skills current. These activities allow you to network and potentially get your foot in the door with a future employer. They also plug gaps in your résumé. Moreover, you may meet someone who will lead you to a job opening elsewhere.

Gaining experience through contract gigs

Consider taking a contract job that can lead to a full-time post or gives you the ability to weave together a patchwork of jobs in the Me Inc. mode. All jobs are a work in progress. After you get in the door, you can make the job your own and grow the position to fit your talents. For more about contract work, check out Chapter 6.

Getting tech savvy

Employers worry that older workers are behind the times in technology, so if you're not tech savvy, your number-one priority is to get plugged in and up-to-speed on the latest office and consumer technologies. At the very least, learn to communicate through email, to cruise the Internet, and to use Microsoft Office applications, particularly Word, Excel, and PowerPoint. Here are some suggestions on how to hone your computer skills:

- ✓ **Check out AARP TEK.** AARP's Technology Education Center (www.aarp.org/tek) is a one-stop resource for workshops, tools, and tips. You'll find training videos, information about AARP TEK workshops offered in major cities, tutorials for online banking and online safety, a link to AARP's Social Media Education Center, buyer's guides, how-to books, and more.

✔ **Take classes at your local library or community center.** Many local libraries and community centers offer a range of classes, including computer and technology courses that suit skill levels from beginner to advanced. You can often find introductory classes to Microsoft Excel, Quickbooks, and more. Some courses may be offered online as well.

✔ **Watch videos.** Although videos don't provide the tactile learning required to become comfortable with technology, videos show you how it's done, so you can try it yourself. You find helpful videos on YouTube (www.youtube.com) and on educational sites such as the Khan Academy (khanacademy.org) and TED (ted.com).

✔ **Read books.** You can find plenty of books on a variety of technology topics, including computer basics, Microsoft Office applications, blogging, building websites, computer graphics, and more. I recommend reading such books when you're sitting at the computer and that you practice the skills being taught.

✔ **Get help.** Ask a tech-savvy friend or relative to help or contact a local high school or college to see whether a high-school or college student may be interested and available to tutor you.

Chapter 3

Harnessing the Power of Other People

*O*ne of the most powerful resources when looking for a job is other people. Look to your friends, past colleagues, or relatives as a valuable job-seeking asset. They can assist with many job-searching tasks from retooling your résumé to building an online presence.

In this chapter, I encourage you to let go of any reservations you may have that are keeping you from reaching out for help in your job search, and I show you ways to get the help you need.

Think about it. If your friend needed a job and you could help her, wouldn't you feel bad if she didn't ask for your help? Well, you're the one needing the job, so do your friends a favor and let them know you need their help.

Networking Your Way to Your Next Job

No matter where you live or what position you're after, whether you're a top-level executive, a graphic designer, or a plumber, most people in your field find and get the jobs they want as a result of networking. Only a tiny percentage of job postings ever make it to the job boards. Employers want to hire people they know or those recommended by someone they know and trust.

This reassures them that you are who you say you are and will show up and do the job.

As a 50-plus worker, you probably have an edge in the networking department over younger workers. All your years have brought you into contact with more people. Make the most of this key advantage you have over your younger competitors. In this section, I show you how.

Starting with the people you know

Networking sounds harder than it is. You already know the people in your network. All you need to do is reach out to them and let them know you're looking for work. Here are some ways to do just that:

- **Brainstorm.** Meet with your significant other and/or friends and brainstorm a list of people to contact. Write down the names of previous employers and colleagues who may be in a position to help you find openings or introduce you to others who may know about openings. Here's a short list to get you started:

  - People in your faith community or other social circles you belong to who could offer support and encouragement.

  - People you volunteer with or have volunteered with

  - Neighbors

  - Trade and professional organizations

  - Local businesspeople, including lawyers, accountants, and bank officers

---

Networking works

The AARP study "The Long Road Back: Struggling to Find Work after Unemployment" asked people who had been unemployed in the last five years and are now back at work which steps were the most effective in landing a job. The results speak to the clout of networking over sending out résumés and cover letters and submitting applications. Reaching out to professional contacts was the most helpful, followed by asking relatives and friends — both ways to network.

A recent survey by Jobvite reinforces the fact that networking is the best way to land a job, showing that four out of ten workers found their best jobs through personal connections. So don't be bashful. Now's the time to tap your professional and personal network for a helping hand to get in the door for a job interview.

✔ **Pick up the phone and start dialing.** Make at least one call a day to someone who may be in a position to help. When you run out of names and numbers, call everyone else you know, even if you think the person can't help you; you never know where that next job lead will come from. Connecting in person and over the phone are the best ways to get an interview with a potential employer. If you don't establish a personal connection to the company, filling out an application is probably a waste of time.

A phone call is much more effective than an email or text message. A face-to-face meeting over coffee or lunch is even better. Send an email message only if you can't find the person's phone number.

✔ **Tap your family ties.** Don't be embarrassed to call immediate and extended family members when you're out of work. No need to keep up a pretense that everything is fine. Push past any worries about look-ing needy or vulnerable. Being out of work is a blow to your ego and may make you feel less than 100 percent, but realize that it's okay. Most people understand, have been in your shoes before, and are happy to make a connection for you if they can.

✔ **Reconnect with former classmates.** School alumni organizations are a great source of contacts for your job search. Alumni directories help you find old friends, classmates, and even teachers/instructors/ professors. They can also connect you with people you didn't know who are currently working for your target employers or in your target industry/profession.

✔ **Touch base with former coworkers.** Many employers have "alumni" groups, on LinkedIn, Facebook, and elsewhere on the Internet. Search "[employer name] alumni group" to find former colleagues, bosses, and even those you knew only slightly who also worked for the same employer. Having worked for the same organization is common ground that warrants an invitation to get connected. If the company doesn't have an alumni group, start one or help organize a reunion.

Don't stop there. If you know vendors, clients, or even competitors from your former days with a company, reach out to them. Using these connections and others, you can build a highway to a new job. Just comply with any non-compete clause you may have signed with a former employer.

Networking online

Online networking doesn't hold a candle to pressing-the-flesh schmoozing, but it enables you to track down people you'd probably never be able to find otherwise and keep in contact with hundreds of people with very little effort.

If you need further convincing, here are some of the top benefits of online networking for experienced workers:

- ✔ It's free.

- ✔ You can learn what someone from your past has been up to since you last talked and do your reconnaissance via online profiles before you reach out. That can go a long way in smoothing the initial contact. You may comment on something they're doing, a trip they took, a child's college graduation, or a recent award or recognition for their work.

- ✔ It's a fast way to connect with new and old contacts without even leaving your house or mustering up the courage to make that phone call.

- ✔ You can have targeted discussions with more folks online than you can at an in-person networking event where meeting three new people is considered success.

In this section, I offer suggestions for networking online via the big three sites: Facebook, LinkedIn, and Twitter. For additional guidance on getting started with Facebook and Twitter, see Chapter 9. For more about LinkedIn, turn to Chapter 10.

Use online networking as one of several networking tools at your disposal. It's not the be all and end all. A face-to-face meeting generally has more lasting impact and builds a stronger bond. Even if you're meeting new contacts online, look for opportunities to meet in person or set up a phone call or Facetime or video chat via Skype, for instance.

LinkedIn

When you join LinkedIn Groups, you can share your expertise, possibly catch a recruiter's eye, and, perhaps most importantly, contact other group members without being formally introduced. Best practices for networking on LinkedIn include the following:

- ✔ **Invite people you meet in person to connect with you on LinkedIn.** Whenever you meet someone with the potential to form a mutually beneficial relationship, look the person up on LinkedIn and send an invitation to connect. It's a crafty way to combine a "great to meet you" with a "let's connect on LinkedIn" message, and most people will agree to connect after an in-person meeting.

- ✔ **Post daily status updates.** On your LinkedIn home page, post something relevant to your profession daily; for example, an inspirational quote, a link to a compelling and informative article or blog post, or something you read in an industry newsletter. Also, tap into LifeReimagined.org's discussion group on LinkedIn, "A new you, within reach." The group has more than 20,000 engaged users.

Follow Influencers to get a steady stream of relevant content delivered to your feed so you have content to share with others in your network. LinkedIn Influencer is a designation given to approximately 500 professionals who've been invited to publish on LinkedIn. As leaders in their industries, geographies, and seniority, they discuss topics of interest, such as leadership, management, hiring and firing, disruption, and how to succeed.

✔ **Share an article you find on another website.** Many websites and blogs include buttons you can click to share content on LinkedIn, Facebook, Twitter, and other sites. Simply click the button to post a status update or tweet that link out to the article or post. Before posting the update, add a comment of your own to indicate what you think about the content you're sharing or to explain why you think people should read it.

✔ **Comment on and share other people's status updates.** Show you care by engaging with the people in your network.

Facebook

A survey from the Society for Human Resource Management found that while a whopping 94 percent of employers who responded said they trolled LinkedIn to find job candidates, and 54 percent tapped Facebook, which has 1.39 billion monthly users — four times the size of LinkedIn. Although Facebook is more social than professional, it provides a smooth, subtle way to get back on someone's radar and possibly even pick up contract work or job leads. Here are a few tips for networking on Facebook:

✔ **Engage with the community.** Share and comment on status updates that your Facebook friends post. Don't merely post your own status updates.

✔ **Check out Facebook groups.** You can find a wide range of special interest and local job-search and industry groups. Many of these groups list hourly jobs that run the gamut from employers looking for carpenters, electricians, or plumbers to local auto dealers who need a part-time salesperson or a child-care center that needs a teaching assistant.

✔ **Be professional.** Although Facebook isn't designed for professional networking, assume that any future employer can read what you share, and post accordingly — no off-color jokes, no texting shorthand (using 4 instead of "for," for example), no inappropriate photos, and no emoticons (such as the smiley face). And be careful with your spelling and grammar, too.

Don't adopt a laissez-faire attitude toward your online social life. A recent CareerBuilder nationwide survey found that more than two in five hiring managers who use social media to research potential employees said they found information online that caused them not to hire a candidate. Here are some of the biggest turnoffs for potential employers:

- Candidate posted provocative or inappropriate photos or information: 50 percent.

- Sites had information about candidate drinking or using drugs: 48 percent.

- Candidate bad-mouthed previous employer: 33 percent.

- Candidate had poor communication skills: 30 percent.

- Candidate made discriminatory comments related to race, gender, or religion: 28 percent.

- Candidate lied about qualifications: 24 percent.

Twitter

Twitter is a great place to network, because that's about all you do on Twitter. To maximize the return on your Twitter time investment, follow these suggestions:

- Follow the thought leaders and companies in the industry or line of work you're interested in doing.

- Retweet and favorite tweets that resonate with you and are relevant to your line of work.

- Post regularly about the line of work you're interested in so you become a recognized thought leader in this area.

- Include a person's @handle when you post something you think may be of particular interest to him.

- When attending a trade show, meetup, or other event connected with your field, tweet out a few pithy quotes from a speaker or panelist that hit home with you.

- Look for interesting people to follow and connect with on Twitter accounts, such as @CareerSherpa and @TheLadders, which are devoted to sharing job-search advice and career tips with their followers.

- Join in Twitter chats, parties, meetups, or Tweetups. These are a few of the names assigned to live business networking events on the Twittersphere. During a tweet chat that may last around an hour, a cadre of people meet at a set time to discuss a specific topic, using a prearranged hashtag for each tweet. A host or moderator poses questions to get the conversation rolling. This is a great way to meet new connections and learn about your industry.

✔ Consider cold tweeting. If you've found a person in your field who's active on Twitter, consider contacting him via a direct tweet and letting him know you're looking for new job opportunities. Ease into it first by interacting through a string of retweets, comments to tweets he's posted, or after a Twitter chat you both participated in. In other words, build a Twitter rapport before you make that cold tweet asking for advice on your job search.

Many firms today have their own Twitter handles devoted to their employment efforts, such as @StarbucksJobs and @TargetCareers. Run a quick search for Twitter accounts with the words "jobs" or "careers" and you'll find a roster of prospective employers who tweet job postings. You can also search for hashtags to discover new opportunities shared by employers and recruiters. Here are a few to check out:

#Careers	#JobListing	#JobSearch
#JobFairy	#JobOpening	#JobTips
#JobHuntChat	#Hiring	#TweetMyJobs

Joining meetup groups

Look for a local networking group for people in your profession, or start your own if you can't find one. Joining a group, a job club, or meetup group for job seekers can help you stay on top of trends and hear about job opportunities.

Try finding locals with similar interests on Meetup.com (www.meetup.com). Some groups focus on boomers and may organize hikes in local parks, group dog walks, volunteer outings, or trips to area museums. Although these are non-work activities, you never know where you might meet someone who can help you connect with a job opening. Meantime, it's a relaxed setting where you bond over common interests, which is a great way to grow a new friendship and, in turn, your network.

Importantly, some meetup groups are specifically for job seekers. You can search your city on Meetup.com, for example, to find one near you. Studies have shown that these kinds of support groups are helpful because you feel accountable to group members and you can help each other out with leads. Even better, from a psychological standpoint, these can be a great way to get out of your house if you're not working.

Another way to network is through LifeReimagined live local events (www.lifereimagined.aarp.org/events), where you'll meet members of the Life Reimagined community who will offer support and encourage you to explore new possibilities.

Overcoming introversion

If you happen to be too shy or have trouble meeting new people, I recommend immersion therapy — join a networking group. Available groups vary depending on where you live, but you usually have several to choose from, including Business Networking International, MasterMind Groups, LeTip, Women in Business Networking, your local Chamber of Commerce or Convention and Visitor's Bureau, local merchant associations, Rotary, Kiwanis, and Optimists.

I'm a member of The Transition Network, (`www.thetransitionnetwork.org`) a nonprofit networking group for women over 50. It's based in New York, but lucky for me, the group has a great chapter in Washington, D.C., where I live. Peer groups like this are a great way to fight the shyness barrier that stands in the way of making new contacts and friends. It's a safe, friendly environment, and the events tend to be fairly intimate.

When you're ready to mingle, here are my top five networking tips for those of you who are on the quiet side:

- **Show up early.** If you hear of a local event that sounds intriguing, push yourself to make room in your schedule. Get there early. The best time to schmooze is before things get rolling.

- **Build relationships.** Networking isn't about finding someone to help you get a job today. It's a process of developing contacts gradually over time through people who connect with and trust each other.

- **Be curious.** Networking is not work. It's about being interested in what other people are doing and being open to learning from them. Ask questions and try to get people to talk about themselves. Spend twice as much time listening as you do talking.

- **Set goals.** Before heading to a new event, tell yourself that you'll try to meet three or four new people and get their contact information. Afterward, jot down a note on the back of their business cards reminding yourself where you met and what you discussed.

- **Follow up.** The day after the networking session, send a note to your new connections, telling them how much you enjoyed meeting them and proposing a future date to get together informally. Email works fine, but, hey, if you've got a personal notecard, send it! These days, people rarely receive mail other than bills, junk, and magazines, so your recipient will likely be delighted to get your card and, perhaps even more likely, to become a devoted member of your personal network.

Make it personal

My networking often has nothing to do with work. I always write a quick note of congratulations when I find out someone in my group has had a child or send condolences if they've had a loss. I try to introduce people to one another if I think they might make a connection, either personal or professional.

I keep folks up-to-date on my life, too — within reason. Sometimes I seek advice or ask whether they know someone who may be willing to be interviewed for a story or to help me solve a problem.

That goodwill comes back to me in spades. Some of the early members of my group send work my way or pop me a note that makes me feel good about something I've achieved.

Revisiting Your College Career Center

If you attended college for any amount of time, you may qualify for help from your school's placement office or career center. Many colleges have special relationships with businesses that recruit through the college. Career center staff can help you revamp your résumé and cover letter. They may also provide you with an online account where you can post your profile and résumé, access online podcast seminars, view job and internship listings with contact information, sign up for career center appointments, and get the latest news on job fairs and recruiter visits.

Alums and would-be grad students are tapping into online web refresher courses on résumé writing, interviewing, and even navigating social networking sites. Many schools offer free career coaching and welcome alums back at job fairs and for company informational meetings. Some schools assist alumni in setting up interviews. You can bone up on job-hunting skills (free of charge in most cases) and link to a vast network of people predisposed to lend a hand. Consider it added value — a degree that keeps giving back.

Search for your school on LinkedIn and tap into your alma mater's LinkedIn network for additional connections.

At Duke Fuqua School of Business, MBA alums have not been bashful about asking the career management center for help. The seekers are generally unemployed, recently laid off, or sensing that job stability may be a little shaky with their current employer. The guidance ranges from strategic assistance, for those who want to move in a different direction and are looking for support and counsel on how to get there, to a very tactile need to dust off résumés and get started again.

Working with a Mentor

If you've decided to change careers, fly solo as a freelancer, or start your own business, you should seriously consider finding a mentor to guide you, someone who's been there and done that. Almost universally, the workers I know who have made a successful transition to new work after age 50 had at least one person they could turn to when the ground got shaky. The person inevitably was someone experienced with the ins and outs of the new line of work. A mentor or sponsor can play several roles, from teaching you the ropes to encouraging you and even recommending you to potential employers or customers.

In this section, I offer guidance on tracking down the right person to mentor you.

Be prepared to nurture your mentoring relationship over an extended period of time. A good mentoring relationship grows organically and gradually.

Finding a mentor

Finding an able and willing unpaid advisor takes time and patience. First, make a list of the people in your network who you deem able to provide you with the guidance you need, individuals who have knowledge and experience in the line of work you're interested in doing and are likely to be wise and patient guides. Think Obi-Wan Kenobi, Luke Skywalker's wise and patient mentor.

After settling on the person you want to serve as your mentor, ask the person for some specific advice about an issue or problem you're facing. Ease into the relationship with baby steps. You don't even need to mention the word "mentor," but if you're looking for a more formal mentor-mentee relationship, you can eventually broach that subject with an invitation. At some point, you'll want to schedule regular meetings, even if only to have a cup of coffee and touch base on how things are going. Mentorships and sponsorships frequently turn into mutually beneficial friendships. The main reason most mentors and sponsors say they take the time to counsel and help is the elusive gratification they get in paying it forward.

If you decide to look for a mentor or sponsor, be clear about your goals for the relationship. Write them down to help you focus on what you hope to achieve. You may have a certain business task at hand, something as simple as wanting someone to give you advice on how to spruce up your image in the workplace, such as proper attire. Or it could be someone who can tell you which business courses are most worthwhile or which people at a certain organization to approach about getting a job there. Or perhaps you're looking for someone who can help you learn the ropes of a new business area or skill.

Considering reverse mentoring

Mentoring is the buzzy concept in the work world these days. And for people over 50, at least, the latest twist is *reverse mentoring,* partnering with someone younger (typically of the same sex) to learn from each other. Reverse mentoring is especially effective when the mentor and mentee complement one another, for example, when the younger person is more tech savvy and the older person knows the business.

For the last five years, I've been in a few reverse-mentoring relationships. One is with a friend who's two decades younger, far hipper and more attuned to navigating social media. Because I'm not that tech savvy, it's nice to have someone I can call or email with a quick question who doesn't think I'm a bonehead. On the flipside, as an author and longtime journalist, I've helped market her book, introduced her to people who can further her career, and written recommendations.

Many millennials have a contagious energy and entrepreneurial attitude. Their drive and that passion to achieve success can be a great motivator.

Navigating the high tech world or social media apps and more can be frustrating. AARP sponsors a free program called Mentor Up (`www.mentorup.org`) in communities around the country, which connects people 50 and older with someone younger who can help them learn the ropes.

Hiring a virtual mentor

If you can't seem to find someone in your professional and social circles who's willing and able to mentor you in person, consider hiring a virtual mentor, who can offer guidance from a remote location. Virtual mentoring is less personal, but it can still provide the guidance and connections you need to find the job you want.

To get connected with a virtual mentor, contact a mentor matchmaking firm, such as PivotPlanet (`www.pivotplanet.com`), which offers video-conference, phone, and in-person mentoring for individuals for a fee. (It also offers Pivot Enterprise, a platform that universities, large nonprofits, and companies use to connect employees and alumni with subject-matter experts. Check with your HR department or alumni association to see whether it's offered to you free as a benefit; if not, ask whether your organization or alma mater might consider it.)

The mission of PivotPlanet is to offer easy access to expert advisors in hundreds of fields, from acupuncture to financial planning to landscape design, and serve people looking to "pivot" from an existing career to another. It's networking and counseling for job seekers of all stripes — from aspiring entrepreneurs to people burned out in the corporate cubicle and baby boomers planning encore careers at a fraction of the cost of hiring a career coach. Most one-hour sessions range from $40 to $125.

To get started on PivotPlanet, here's what you do:

1. **Use the key word search on the PivotPlanet home page to describe the type of work you want to explore, and choose from the list of advisors resulting from your search.**

   You can also click Find an Advisor, at the top of the page, to browse advisors by career type, job title, or any key word. Compare advisors by reading their biographies, watching their videos, scanning their photo galleries, and reading client reviews.

2. **Set up a PivotPlanet account or log in if you already have an account.**

3. **Send a message to an advisor requesting a one-hour live video or phone conference and provide up to ten times and dates that work for you.**

   In-person mentorship sessions are also available. Work directly with PivotPlanet staff to schedule a full-day or half-day in-person session. Your advisor will suggest three one-hour time slots for the conference, based on your preferences.

4. **Accept and book one of the slots.**

5. **Have a list of questions ready to go and a pad and pen for note-taking.**

6. **Connect with your advisor for your video or phone conference.**

I've used the individual services of one of PivotPlanet's mentors, who lives in Florida, hundreds of miles from my home in Washington, D.C., to hone my public speaking goals and business plan. I found my one-on-one sessions incredibly useful and empowering, and the $180 fee well worth it.

The mentor-mentee relationship can evolve over a series of sessions at regular intervals and on an as-needed basis.

Connecting with a Career Coach

If you know you need a change but are unsure of what to do, a career coach can help you set goals, clearly outline the steps to take you there, and motivate you to make it happen. I personally used a coach to give me the kind of unbiased help a friend or family member couldn't. I found her through my dog. She and I met when training our puppies a few years ago. While serendipity allowed me to meet my career coach, asking friends for recommendations is a good place to start. You can also research online, where you'll find a slew of directories.

Countless career coaches representing a dizzying array of styles and philosophies tout their services online, and winnowing down the field requires due diligence. The Life Planning Network (www.lifeplanningnetwork.org) and 2 Young 2 Retire (www.2young2retire.com) offer coach directories geared to midlife workers.

To find the right coach for you, follow these suggestions:

✔ **Look for qualifications.** Career coaching is a self-regulated industry and emerging profession. Many coaches have been doing it for years without adding professional designations. But designations are a sign of formal training and of adherence to general standards of professionalism.

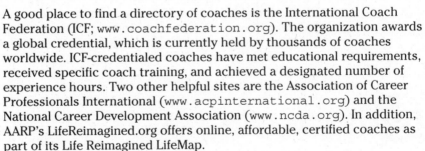

A good place to find a directory of coaches is the International Coach Federation (ICF; www.coachfederation.org). The organization awards a global credential, which is currently held by thousands of coaches worldwide. ICF-credentialed coaches have met educational requirements, received specific coach training, and achieved a designated number of experience hours. Two other helpful sites are the Association of Career Professionals International (www.acpinternational.org) and the National Career Development Association (www.ncda.org). In addition, AARP's LifeReimagined.org offers online, affordable, certified coaches as part of its Life Reimagined LifeMap.

✔ **Explore the past career path of potential coaches.** Find out as much as you can about their career path, both in the coaching field and in the regular work world. Don't be too timid to question potential coaches about their level of expertise for your particular needs.

✔ **Ask for at least three references.** Of course, no one is going to hand over the names of clients who didn't love them, but asking for references is an important step in your process. You never know what you might learn when you get someone on the phone. Plus, it's imperative to know a potential coach's work style and how she succeeded with other clients starting a new career. Ask references how they worked with the coach, for example, by phone or in person and specifically how the coach helped in his or her job search.

✔ **Find a coach who conducts one-on-one sessions.** These can be in person, by phone, Skype, Google+ Hangout, or email, but you want his or her full attention. Phone sessions are commonplace these days, which in many ways is to your advantage. You aren't restricted to signing on with a coach in your town, and you don't waste time getting to and from meetings and making small talk.

✔ **Expect a free initial consultation.** After you've narrowed your search, you'll want to interview a few candidates. Never agree to work with a coach without a trial run. This initial session should be gratis.

✔ **Ask about fees.** Rates vary significantly, anywhere from $50 to more than $200 per hour. Some coaches require a minimum number of hours. On average, coach-client relationships last from six months to a year. You may sign on for one or two meetings to jump-start your job search. Some coaches provide resources, such as books, and give homework assignments to prepare for future sessions.

✔ **Check out the coach's website or blog.** This should give you insight into the coach's areas of expertise and what she has published. Search the coach's name on the web and see if you find uncensored comments written by other clients.

✔ You can find coaches who have blogs via directories such as Alltop.com (visit www.alltop.com and search under "career") or who are on Twitter by searching "WeFollow" under #coach.

✔ **Get a written agreement.** This is a business relationship, so treat it like one with a formal agreement that defines the duties of each party. Verbal agreements can be risky and leave both the client and the coach susceptible to unexpected misunderstandings.

If you're unemployed, your local unemployment office may be able to set you up with free career counseling. Look for library, community colleges, and the alumni offices of your alma mater for coaching sessions and workshops. CareerOneStop (www.careeronestop.org), sponsored by the Department of Labor, offers coaching for job hunters and also special programs for military members moving into the private sector at various locations around the country. These could be small groups but are helpful nonetheless to get you moving forward.

Getting Discovered: Busting Recruiter Myths

Although getting a call from a recruiter is flattering, arrangements can get complicated. A good recruiter gives you the inside track on great jobs — ones that may never have hit your radar. If you get the gig, the recruiter earns a fee, paid by the employer, for playing matchmaker. Yet this seemingly symbiotic relationship can be confusing for a job seeker, especially if you've never worked with recruiters before and aren't sure what their role is in getting you hired.

In this section, I bust seven myths about recruiters and, in the process, explain how to find and team up with a recruiter most effectively.

Myth #1: Recruiters find you from industry colleagues

Although recruiters may discover you through their networking efforts, it's not so much the norm anymore. Recruiters increasingly are using the web to seek out experienced candidates. That's one of the reasons you should have a strong online presence, as explained in Chapter 9.

Recruiters also search job boards such as CareerBuilder, Indeed, and Monster. Still others look at Instagram and Pinterest, where folks with visually oriented jobs (such as graphic design) post résumés.

Myth #2: Recruiters find you, not vice versa

That may be true, but not necessarily. If you have what employers want, recruiters don't care whether you find them or they find you. If you want to work with a recruiter as part of your job-hunting strategy, go for it. You can track them down by using the methods they employ to find their candidates: via networking, referrals from colleagues, and social media. Here are some online resources on where you can find recruiters:

✔ Bullhorn Reach (www.bullhornreach.com)

✔ LinkedIn (www.linkedin.com)

✔ Riley Guide Directory of Recruiters (www.rileyguide.com/recruiters.html)

You can have your résumé distributed to recruiters on these sites:

✔ EmailMyResume.com (www.emailmyresume.com)

✔ ResumeArrow (dist.resumearrow.com)

✔ Resume Rabbit (www.resumerabbit.com)

You can also search the web for recruiters in your area that serve specific industries. For example, if you enter "Food Manufacturing Recruiter Plano, Texas" into the Google search engine, you'll find links to several recruitment websites. In most urban areas, you can find trade associations of executive recruiters that provide a website with their members' names and expertise listed. LinkedIn groups and Twitter chats, such as #OMCChat and #InternPro, also provide the means to connect with recruiters.

Look for a recruiter who has expertise in the industry in which you're interested, and choose one or two who specialize in your field or the field you're pursuing.

Don't submit your résumé to more than a couple of recruiters, because it can cause conflict at the hiring company if several recruiters are pitching you to the same employer.

Keep in mind that a recruiter you contact may not have time to meet with you or talk to you at length until a job opening that's right up your alley crosses her desk. Recruiters typically prescreen over the phone and then file your résumé in their database for future jobs.

Myth #3: The recruiter works for you

The voice on the other end of the phone is super friendly. Your calls are returned in a nanosecond. The recruiter assures you that you're perfect for the job, and, naturally, you get your hopes up. Despite the pursuit, chances are you're only one of four or five great candidates the recruiter is presenting to the client. Recruiters generally work for a finder's fee paid by the employer. The recruiter works for the employer, not for you.

Be careful not to fall under the spell of the courtship, or you'll be upset when the recruiter suddenly goes into "radio silence mode" and stops returning your calls. Don't take it personally. It's business. If you don't get a call, the company probably filled the position in-house or changed the criteria of what it was looking for. As soon as the job is off the table, so are you.

The bottom line: Recruiters are salespeople. It's about closing the deal. Time is of the essence.

Myth #4: Recruiters know what the best job fit is for you

Many times, recruiters who call you are simply fishing to round up a batch of potential candidates. They may actually know very little about your work experience and current situation beyond what they've seen via your social media profile and online résumé.

It's up to you to take charge so that you don't waste your time getting calls for jobs that don't interest you. Ask upfront if the recruiter has a specific job in mind for you, and be clear about the salary you require. Prepare to answer detailed questions about your résumé, job experience, and any gaps in employment.

Many recruiters look at how often candidates have switched jobs, and they're likely to dismiss job hoppers. They also want a list of references. And the recruiter may need to know if you are willing to relocate. If you have to travel to get to an interview, be clear on who's paying the travel expenses.

Depending on the job opening and employer, the recruiter will probably ask if you're willing to agree to a drug test, criminal background check, reference checks, educational background checks, and credit checks.

Stick to business. A recruiter is not your career coach. Don't mention money concerns or insecurities about your chances of landing the job. And unless it's part of the job description, this is not the time to ask about telecommuting policies or other flextime options. Save that for after you get an offer.

Myth #5: If you don't get the job, they'll stay in touch

It's a recruiter's job to find people for jobs, not jobs for people. That said, many of the best recruiters network with other recruiters. So even if they don't have an open requisition that's perfect for you right now, if you have built a good rapport with them, they may know of another opportunity and make an introduction.

Myth #6: Recruiters are résumé wizards

Résumé writing is not a recruiter's job, but it's generally in his or her wheelhouse. Although good recruiters will take the time to fine-tune your résumé for the specific job at hand, this isn't a revamp for you to use universally. The onus is on you to bring a job-winning résumé.

Recruiters may ask that you revise your résumé, however, and they may offer some guidance. For example, a recruiter may request that you remove any objectives and replace them with a bulleted list of quantifiable accomplishments that reflect your skills and talents.

Myth #7: The recruiter negotiates your salary with the employer

Recruiters aren't paid to negotiate your salary. That's your job. Recruiters are paid by the employer, so technically it's in the best interest of the recruiter to help the employer keep your salary within the set parameters. If you've established good rapport with your recruiter, however, she may give off-the-record advice such as, "I wouldn't take their first offer" or "If it were me . . . ," or she may send you to sites such as Glassdoor.com (www.glassdoor.com) and Salary.com (www.salary.com) to get salary ranges for the position.

Checking Out Job Fairs

One way to meet with potential employers is at a job fair. These aren't just for recent college graduates. Employers also use job fairs to recruit experienced workers. Job fairs are a great way to connect with employers and recruiters and expand your network.

In this section, I explain how to make the most of job fairs, whether they're brick-and-mortar (in-person) or virtual (online) events.

Brick-and-mortar career fairs

To gain entrance to a brick-and-mortar job fair, you're typically required to pay a small entrance fee. The payoff, though, is you get direct entrée to lots of employers and are able to pass along your résumé, plus you can listen in to presentations by company reps and local career experts. To reap the full value of these in-person events, do the following:

- ✔ Dress in proper business attire and be well groomed. First impressions count. Although you probably won't have an interview per se, prepare as if you will.

- ✔ In addition to connecting with company reps, introduce yourself to other job seekers, tell them what you do, and ask what they do.

- ✔ Share contact information.

- ✔ If you make a good connection, you may agree to share leads with a fellow job seeker.

✔ Bring along a simple business card that includes your name, your target job title, your expertise, and your contact information. Use a plain type font, such as Times Roman or Arial. Make sure the size is big enough to read without squinting.

✔ Carry twice as many copies of your résumé as there are exhibitors. You generally leave one at a company's booth and hand one to anyone you speak to directly. If you have a few versions of your résumé geared to specific jobs, bring along copies of each.

✔ Visit as many booths as you can. Smaller companies may be a better bet than the bigger names.

✔ Always show your interest in a company by first asking about specific vacancies the company is looking to fill and asking any specific questions about the firm that show you've done your research. Then you can deliver your pitch if it makes sense to do so.

✔ If they mention a position that appeals to you, but the résumé you have tucked in your bag isn't geared to that specific job, hold off handing over your résumé. You can send a résumé in a day or two after you've had a chance to tweak it.

✔ Ask for business cards from every company representative you speak to, so you can follow up with an email and a call within a week.

Virtual career fairs

Digital career events are on the rise and are a win-win for job seekers and companies. While these events are an inexpensive way for employers to meet potential employees, you can share your résumé with companies that are hiring. Furthermore, for the 50-plus job seeker, your participation in a virtual career fair sends a strong signal that you are tech savvy — an important factor for many hiring managers. You may be able to nab an initial, albeit brief, interview with a recruiter or hiring manager — without having to leave the comfort of home. But this is not a casual browsing event. Take it as seriously as you would an in-person interview.

To find an online career event that's geared to your job search, canvas job board websites, including Brazen Careerist (www.brazencareerist.com) and Monster (www.monster.com) for upcoming fairs. LinkedIn, industry groups, and membership associations such as AARP (www.aarp.org/virtualcareerfair) can also direct you to upcoming job fairs they're sponsoring or are connected to in some fashion. (Some companies offer their own virtual fairs. Check their websites or social media accounts.) See which businesses have a "booth" with job openings and a recruiter or hiring manager available during the fair hours.

To make the most of a virtual job fair, follow these suggestions before, during, and after:

- **Do your research.** Review ahead of time the roster of the employers participating and what kinds of jobs are available. Go to company websites and their social media pages, and search Google News (news.google.com) to find out any recent news. This will help you have a savvier and more energized conversation about why you're a good fit for the job and the organization.

- **Update your résumé and social media accounts.** When you register, you'll probably have to create a profile and upload a photo and a basic résumé. Tweak your résumé, or, better yet, create several versions of it to match jobs you want. Don't forget to proofread them for grammar and spelling errors. Save each résumé on your desktop so you can quickly refer to it and have it ready to email to a recruiter. Be sure to scrub your online profiles of any "unprofessional" posts on Facebook, LinkedIn, and Twitter. (See Chapter 8 for more about fine-tuning your résumé and Chapters 9 and 10 for more about Facebook, LinkedIn, and Twitter.)

- **Get your computer ready.** Generally speaking, a Mac or PC desktop or laptop is fine. After registering, you'll likely receive a confirmation email with instructions to see whether your computer meets system requirements. If your Internet connection is spotty at times, find a cubicle at a local library with free Wi-Fi or ask a friend if you can set up at her place.

- **Keep your conversations professional and focused.** Your goal is to connect with all the companies you have on your list. These can be instantaneous conversations, so be careful to keep it formal. Use "Mr." and "Ms." Avoid emoticons and watch for typos. Post sticky notes on your desk to remind you of your three main selling points. These will help you stay focused when a conversation gets rolling. Be patient for a response. With lots of questions coming in from other job seekers, the recruiter may take some time to answer.

- **Be prepared for an impromptu video interview.** Recruiters may ask if you can launch into a video interview, usually Skype, on the spot. This means that you need to understand in advance how these virtual interviews work. Check out my tips for a video interview in Chapter 13.

- **Surf the chat rooms.** Stop by not just the firm's "booth" but also its chat room. Recruiters and hiring managers are often accessible in the chat rooms. In chat rooms, you're able to read what other participants post and hear more from the hiring managers staffing the booth about the company culture and more.

✔ **Send thank-you notes.** Always send thank-you emails to anyone you talked to online, and be sure to attach your résumé. Reference something from your conversation with them as a reminder of who you are. Handwritten notes are great, but you may not have access to that mailing information. Doing both doesn't hurt, particularly if you want to share more with the interviewer or ask additional questions.

✔ **Be realistic.** Not many people actually get hired via the job fair itself. Employers mine these events to gather résumés that potentially lead to future phone and in-person interviews. The networking and educational opportunities these fairs present are far-reaching. You never know where these contacts can lead you in your job search.

Chapter 4

Tackling Common Financial Issues

In This Chapter

▶ Running a tight financial ship

▶ Paying for any additional education and training you can't get for free

▶ Taking tax deductions to offset the costs of job hunting or running a business

▶ Putting together your own benefits package

*W*hether you're unemployed, underemployed, or planning to change careers or start your own business, a solid financial platform gives you the time and options needed to successfully navigate your transition. You'll want to make sure you can afford the basics: food, shelter, healthcare, and so on. If you're out of work, you may need to slash expenses and take advantage of government-sponsored safety-net programs to support yourself and your family through a period of unemployment. If you're planning a career change, you may need to take a job for significantly less money than you had been making to get started in the new field. And if you're planning to start a business or become a contract worker, you can expect to work for several months before you see any income or profit.

Being unemployed is a double whammy; you have no income plus some added expenses. If you need additional training to enter the workforce, for instance, you may have to pay for it, along with transportation to and from the training center or school. Creating, printing, and mailing applications, résumés, and cover letters also cost money, especially if you need to hire someone to help you. And if your employer supplied health insurance, even if you choose to continue that coverage through COBRA, you're faced with paying the entire premium or dropping coverage.

In this chapter, I offer guidance on how to tighten your belt and take advantage of tax breaks and other government programs. This two-pronged attack — spending less while tapping available resources — puts you in a better position to support yourself and your family as you work toward achieving your career goals.

Filing for Unemployment Benefits

When you lose a job, you may be able to apply for unemployment benefits. To qualify, you must meet the following conditions:

✔ You're unemployed through no fault of your own, meaning you didn't quit or get fired for *gross misconduct* — committing a dangerous or illegal act, such as stealing from your employer.

✔ You received enough wages to establish a claim. Requirements on wages earned vary among states. Contact your local unemployment office or visit your state's unemployment website for details.

✔ In most states, you also need to be physically able to work, actively looking for work, and ready and willing to accept work.

If you qualify, don't let pride get in the way of filing for unemployment insurance benefits. These programs are in place to alleviate some of the financial pain and pressure of being unemployed.

Getting Your Financial House in Order

When money gets tight, your options are limited. You can earn more money, spend less, or do both. You may need to make some painful choices, such as downsizing or even moving to a more affordable city or town. In dire circumstances, you may even consider asking friends or family members for help or taking advantage of government-sponsored assistance programs.

In this section, I help you get motivated to make the changes that are often necessary to firm up your finances, and I suggest ways to cut expenses and tap your own financial resources for temporary relief.

Motivating yourself to get started

Spending money is much more fun than cutting expenses, but debt is a dream killer. It drives people to make choices out of desperation that often limit their opportunities to achieve future wealth. If you need additional motivation to get started, consider the following reasons to strive toward financial fitness:

✔ **When you're nimble financially, you have more choices.** You can accept a job that may not pay as much as your last one because you *want* the job instead of *need* the job. You can turn down a job that's not right for you, because you can afford to wait for the right opportunity. You can choose to become a contract worker or start your own business knowing that you can survive for months without pay as you establish yourself.

✔ **You're more confident and less apt to appear desperate or needy.** As you search for a job, engage in interviews, and negotiate the terms of your employment, you can operate from a position of power, and your confidence shows.

✔ **You can focus on finding your ideal job.** Having to worry less about paying bills, you can focus more time, energy, and effort on finding the job you want or launching your own business.

✔ **You can afford to pay for the additional training and services you need to pursue your career goals.** By having savings socked away, you have the resources available to ramp up your skill set.

Focusing on the fundamentals

If you never had to concern yourself with finances in the past, focus first on these fundamentals:

✔ **Chart a budget.** Write down your income, what you owe, and what you have socked away. Look at what you're spending every day, every month, and every year. This will help you find ways to pare back your spending. Begin by keeping track of how much you spend each day and on what. (Pay in cash or put everything on a credit or debit card, as long as that doesn't lead to increased spending.) Then, on a monthly basis, study your credit card, bank statements, and log of cash payments to see where your money is going and what can be trimmed back or eliminated. Do you dine out too often? Are you traveling too much? Do you spend a lot on groceries or clothes?

✔ Track your finances on a website, such as Mint (www.mint.com) or You Need a Budget (www.youneedabudget.com). These free sites are designed to help you streamline your bill paying and dissect your monthly spending.

✔ **Increase your savings.** If you're unemployed, increasing your savings obviously is not an option, but if you're still working and planning ahead for a career change or business startup, grow your nest egg. A savings cushion of six months to a year of living expenses will stave off dipping into your retirement savings or taking on debt. (Aim for a year's worth of expenses, if you can swing it.)

✔ **Stay liquid.** Emergency funds typically belong in bank accounts or money market funds that don't fluctuate in value and are easily accessible by check, ATM, or teller window. I also suggest putting some of your emergency cash in bank CDs with maturity dates of six months or less so you can eke out a little more interest than from a savings account. You generally find the highest rates at online banks and credit unions. A great place to comparison shop is Bankrate (www.bankrate.com).

✔ **Review your credit report and score.** Get a free annual report at www.annualcreditreport.com, and check for errors. Pay a little extra to get your credit score. Your credit score is important for two reasons:

  • With a higher score, you can borrow more money at lower interest rates, which gives you more choices. Good credit can provide the funds you need to start a business or pay bills as you transition to contract work.

  • Many employers are now checking credit scores prior to hiring. (They must ask your permission to do so.)

✔ **If your credit score is lower than 700, work toward improving it.** Pay all bills on time, and don't open new accounts, transfer balances, close accounts, or cancel credit cards, all of which show up on your credit report and negatively affect your credit score.

✔ **Consolidate debt.** If you have several sources of debt, you may be able to consolidate loans and credit card balances into a single loan with a lower overall interest rate.

✔ **Reduce or eliminate debt.** Pay down credit card balances and refinance your mortgage at a lower rate, if possible. Consider downsizing your home, depending on where you live and the real estate market. If you have enough equity built up in your current home, you may be able to sell it and pay cash for a more affordable home, eliminating your mortgage.

If you've experienced a financial setback, such as unemployment, contact your creditors and try to negotiate payment options. Banks are often willing to work out arrangements with people who are responsible enough to call them and make a sincere effort to work out a solution.

✔ **Consult with a fee-only financial planner.** Look for experienced, credentialed advisers. As a rule, an adviser should have the Certified Financial Planner designation, awarded by the nonprofit Certified Financial Planner Board of Standards. These national groups of financial planners offer searchable databases with contact information: the Certified Financial Planner Board of Standards (www.cfp.net), Financial Planning Association (www.plannersearch.org), Garrett Planning Network (www.garrettplanningnetwork.com), and National Association of Personal Financial Advisors (www.napfa.org).

✔ **Take a personal finance course or read a book.** Many community colleges offer personal finance courses. Check out *Personal Finance For Seniors For Dummies,* by Eric Tyson and Robert C. Carlson (Wiley).

Tapping your financial resources

If you're over 50, you may have built up quite a nest egg in the form of equity in a home, savings and retirement accounts, and other valuable possessions. Although you don't want to deplete these resources, you may be able to borrow against some of them and cash out portions of others to make it through a rough patch or fund a career change or business startup. Think creatively — and then consult with your financial adviser. Here are a few suggestions to kick your imagination into gear:

- ✔ **Take out a home equity line of credit.** If you have equity built up in your home, a home equity line of credit enables you to cash out that equity on an as-needed basis.

  Use a home equity line of credit only as an emergency fund, perhaps to cover mortgage payments to avoid foreclosure while you try selling the property. It's a great safety net to have in an emergency.

- ✔ **Downsize.** Look for a more affordable housing option. Many people who downsize enjoy the resulting increase in financial freedom and wish they had made the move sooner.

- ✔ **Use your assets to earn money.** For example, you may be able to lease one or more rooms in your home (or your entire home, if you move to more affordable accommodations). You can use your car or van to provide delivery services or to work as a taxi driver for a service such as UBER (visit www.uber.com for details).

- ✔ **Sell your assets.** You can always sell your assets, for example on eBay or craigslist, to turn them into cash. (For guidance on listing and selling items on eBay, check out *eBay For Dummies,* by Marsha Collier, published by Wiley.)

Financing Any Additional Education and Training

If you need additional education or training to return to the workforce or to change careers and you can't find it for free, you need to come up with the cash to cover the costs of the training and any books and other materials required for the courses you take. Fortunately, student financing is available even for older students, some of which is available exclusively for older students. In this section, I help you explore your options.

Paying for your education

Although certain educational offerings are entirely free, many programs, especially those that offer a degree or certification, cost money. If you're currently employed, you may be able to take advantage of employer-reimbursed education and training opportunities, or you may have enough money and time to work on your degree or certification one course at a time. If you're unemployed and strapped for cash, the financial aid department at the school you're interested in can help you explore available options, including scholarships, grants, fellowships, and student loans. In this section, I reveal several options to help pay for your education.

Taking advantage of employer education/training opportunities

Roughly half of employers offer tuition assistance to employees, according to the Society for Human Resource Management. Many employers offer tax-free tuition-assistance programs (up to $5,250, not counted as taxable income), and the contribution doesn't have to be attached to a full degree program.

You may have to repay the funds, though, if you don't stay with the company for a certain number of years afterward. And you may need to earn a minimum grade or get your manager's approval for the curriculum to be eligible for this workplace perk.

Admittedly, if you choose a field that doesn't directly relate to your current employment, you may need to convince your boss that your course of study will resonate, even tangentially, with your job. But nothing ventured, nothing gained. In essence, you'll need to explain how continuing education will make you a more productive and creative worker. In other words, what's in it for the company?

IBM's Transition to Teaching program

IBM's Transition to Teaching program, begun in 2006, is one of a growing number of corporate-sponsored programs that help current workers make a smooth transition to their next chapter. The program reimburses $15,000 of educational expenses to become certified as a math or science teacher. The program also allows employees to continue working while going to school and to work with their managers to adapt class work to day-to-day job responsibilities. The program even provides networking assistance when the time comes to help employees get a foot in the door for initial job interviews with the school district.

Getting a break from Uncle Sam

The federal government has a vested interest in keeping you in the workforce. The longer you continue to work, the more tax revenue you generate. So don't hesitate to seek out government assistance to fund your continuing education. Government assistance typically comes in the form of tax breaks and low-interest loans. Here are a few resources to check out:

- ✔ Visit the Tax Benefits for Education Information Center on the IRS website (`www.irs.gov/uac/Tax-Benefits-for-Education:-Information-Center`). The Lifetime Learning Credit, for example, can give you a tax credit of up to $2,000 to cover up to 20 percent of annual tuition; you don't have to be enrolled in a degree program. (The benefit phases out completely for married couples earning $124,000 and singles earning $62,000.)

- ✔ Consider a low-interest federal Stafford loan. There's no age limit, and you're eligible as a part-time student, too.

- ✔ Search the web for your state followed by "college financial aid" to find links to sites that contain information about state financial aid programs for higher education.

Certain forms of financial aid are often available only to students working toward their first bachelor's degree, but some schools will waive this requirement for older students returning to college to pursue a career change.

Go to FinAid.org (`www.finaid.org/otheraid/nontraditional.phtml`) and Edvisors.com (`www.edvisors.com`) for information on scholarships and grants for older students.

Considering Pell grants

For an undergraduate degree, check out federal Pell grants. They're interest-free and don't need to be repaid; the most recent maximum award is $5,730. The amount you'll qualify for depends on factors such as your financial need, tuition costs, and whether you'll be a full- or part-time student. For more on this type of aid, go to the Pell grant area of the U.S. Department of Education's website at `www2.ed.gov/programs/fpg/index.html`.

Paying with tax-free money: 529 plans

To make the most of the money you have available to pay for classes, consider socking away money in a 529 plan. This tax-favored program, run by the states, isn't just for your child's or grandchild's college tuition. People of any age can invest money in a 529 plan and use the cash for their future education costs. A 529's earnings are tax-free when you withdraw the money to pay higher education expenses. Some states even let residents deduct 529 contributions from their state income taxes. And if you wind up not using some or all of the money, you can transfer the funds to another beneficiary, such as your child or grandchild. You can research 529 plans at the College Savings Plans Network (`www.collegesavings.org`).

Scoring scholarships, grants, and fellowships

Try to score an older-student grant, scholarship, or fellowship. Some groups and foundations offer them, though it may take some investigating to track down this interest-free financing. The American Association of University Women, for example, offers fellowships and grants for women going back to school to advance their careers, change careers, or reenter the workforce. For more on grants, scholarships, and fellowships, check out the sites www.fastweb.com and www.finaid.org.

Choosing the right loan for you

If you must borrow, be conservative. The Consumer Financial Protection Bureau (www.consumerfinance.gov) has excellent college financing advice to help you choose the right loan and pay the least amount of interest. Try to get a Federal Direct Loan. Rates on these loans are fixed and low.

You may be able to get your monthly student loan payments reduced if you work in public safety, public health, education, social work, or the non-profit sector. Learn more at the Public Service Loan Forgiveness Program area of the Department of Education site (www.studentaid.ed.gov/repay-loans/forgiveness-cancellation/public-service).

Avoiding additional debt

Consider your future finances before taking on any significant student debt. Look at it as a short-term investment and weigh the potential return on that investment and the risk. Ask yourself how likely each educational opportunity will produce a return on your investment. Consider your future financial condition if everything goes as planned and if the outcome doesn't live up to your expectations. Is it worth the risk?

If you're already strapped for cash, do your best to avoid taking on more debt. Spending $5,000 for training to become a truck driver, for example, may make sense if you're certain to land a job soon after graduation that pays enough to cover your expenses and the loan in your first year on the job. If you can find a trucking company to cover the cost, even that expense can be avoided.

Applying for student financial aid

The first step to take to pay for additional education and training is to contact the financial aid department at the school or training center you plan to attend to find out whether the program you plan to enroll in is eligible for student financial aid. If it is, you'll probably be required to submit a Free Application for Federal Student Aid (FAFSA). Nearly all educational institutions require that students submit their FAFSA to become eligible for any form of student financial aid, regardless of whether the aid is based on financial need. Students of any age can submit the FAFSA and are eligible for federal student financial assistance. Soon after submitting your FAFSA, schedule an appointment to meet with someone in the financial aid department of the school or training center you plan to attend.

If you're quitting a job to return to school, request a "professional judgment" review to adjust your income, so your financial aid package is based more on projected income than on your past year's income.

The school's financial aid rep will put together a financial aid package for you that shows the various forms of financial aid and the amounts you qualify for and how much cash you're expected to contribute. For example, a financial aid package may show the amounts you qualify for in the form of scholarships, grants, fellowships, work-study programs, and subsidized student loans. You may be able to secure additional student loans not included as part of your financial aid package if you can't come up with the cash to meet your projected obligation.

Be sure to submit your FAFSA by your state's or school's deadline — typically early to mid-February for the school year starting in the fall. You'll need information from your tax return to complete the FAFSA, which is kind of tricky; if you don't have all your W-2s and other documents to complete your tax return, you'll have to estimate your income for the year and then file an amended FAFSA later if your estimates are off.

If you're currently employed, ask your employer's human resources office about the availability of employer tuition assistance. Many large employers provide some form of tuition assistance. Up to $5,250 (in some cases more) in such assistance is excluded from gross income for income tax purposes. They may require you to maintain a minimum GPA to get the assistance and commit to working for the organization for a certain number of years after receiving the assistance (or you have to pay it back). Often the assistance is provided as a reimbursement after the fact, so you'll need to budget for your cash flow needs.

Visit FinAid (www.finaid.org), click Other Types of Aid, scroll down to the Student Profile-Based Aid section, and click Older and Nontraditional Students for more information. FinAid is a free comprehensive source of student financial aid information, advice and tools — on or off the web.

Applying for grants and scholarships

Although your financial aid package may contain one or more grants or scholarships, you can find and apply for additional grants and scholarships on your own. Research scholarships at Fastweb (www.fastweb.com), where you can find more than 50 awards that have a minimum age restriction of 30 years or older, more than 230 awards with a minimum age restriction of 25 years or older, and more than 1,800 awards with no age restrictions.

Ask the financial aid rep at the school you plan to attend about Silver Scholarships. The Serve America Act authorizes the Corporation for National and Community Service (CNCS) to award fixed-amount grants to community-based nonprofit entities to carry out a Silver Scholarship Grant Program, which provides $1,000 higher education scholarships to individuals age 55 or older who complete at least 350 hours of service in a year in an area of national need. The grant may be transferred to a child, grandchild, or foster child.

Leveraging tax breaks to lower costs

The federal government provides tax deductions and credits to offset educational costs. (A *deduction* lowers the income on which taxes are calculated, while a *credit* lowers the taxes owed by a certain amount.) Here are a few of the more substantial federal tax deductions and credits available:

- ✔ You can deduct the interest you paid on student loans. This benefit applies to all loans (not just federal student loans) used to pay for higher education expenses. The maximum deduction is $2,500 a year.

- ✔ The Lifetime Learning Credit allows you to claim up to $2,000 per student per year for any college or career school tuition and fees as well as for books, supplies, and equipment required for the course.

- ✔ You may be able to withdraw from an IRA to pay for qualified higher education expenses for yourself, your spouse, your child, or your grandchild without having to pay an early withdrawal penalty. You will still owe federal and state income tax on the amount withdrawn.

Consult a tax specialist to find out more about federal, state, and local tax breaks to help cover education expenses.

For more information, read IRS Publication 970, "Tax Benefits for Education" (www.irs.gov/publications/p970) to see which federal income tax benefits may apply to your situation.

Writing Off Your Job-Hunt Expenses

When you're looking for a job, you need all the breaks you can get, and depending on your situation, you may qualify for federal and state income tax deductions to help offset your job-hunting costs. Be obsessive about saving receipts.

Job-hunting deductions apply only to searching for a job in your current field. If you're switching careers, they're verboten.

Depending on your situation, you may be able to itemize your expenses for a tax deduction, using Form 1040 and Schedule A. You can claim a federal tax deduction only for job-hunt costs exceeding 2 percent of your adjusted gross income. That being said, I highly recommend you seek professional tax help for your situation. Here are a few deductions that may apply:

- **Outplacement and employment agency fees:** These costs are acceptable whether or not you land a new job, assuming, of course, that you're looking for a job in the same line of work. Career-coaching fees may also be deductible.

- **Résumé preparation and postage:** Paper, ink-jet cartridges, fees paid to a résumé writer, printing costs, and postage are all probable write-offs.

- **Dues, subscriptions, and association fees:** Membership dues to professional organizations and subscriptions to certain industry publications may be deductible if you use the services provided in your job search. If challenged, you will need to show documentation that a job board at your professional association, for example, was a direct source of leads for you.

- **Business travel:** You can deduct the IRS standard mileage rate if you use your personal vehicle for business, but be sure to keep travel mileage logs in case you're asked for documentation. Airfare, train tickets, and taxi fare are deductible, provided they're specifically related to your job hunt. You can't, for instance, take a five-day trip to Washington, D.C., to visit the museums, spend a single day interviewing, and then count the entire trip as a write-off.

- **Business meals:** If you're job searching and meeting with sources or other business contacts, keep track of whether you pick up lunch or coffee, as 50 percent of the total cost of those meals can be deducted.

- **Moving costs:** If you accept a job that requires you to relocate, you may be able to write off all expenses associated with your move if your new employer doesn't offer to reimburse you. Your new workplace must be at least 50 miles farther from your old home than your old job location was from your old home. If you use your vehicle to move, you can deduct mileage. For more information, see IRS Publication 521 "Moving Expenses" (www.irs.gov/publications/p521).

✔ **Internet access:** You should be able to deduct work-related Wi-Fi expenses and fees for online job sites and networking services such as LinkedIn (if you upgrade to a paid, professional account). Again, you must be able to show evidence that these were tools used in your job search.

✔ **Home office deduction:** If you're working as a freelancer, contract worker, or consultant while you pound the pavement for a new full-time gig, you can write off some of your home office costs if you have set aside a specific place solely for work. You must file Form 8829 "Expenses for Business Use of Your Home." The IRS now allows a "Simplified Option for Home Office Deduction," which permits you to deduct $5 per square foot of your home office on your tax return, with a maximum write-off of $1,500 (based on a maximum of 300 square feet). It is usually a better option to take the traditional home office deduction. You should run the numbers. You can read all the home office rules in IRS Publication 587, "Business Use of Your Home" (www.irs.gov/publications/p587).

✔ **Skill building:** The cost of job-search seminars and networking events is generally deductible, but again, you must be certain you can prove that they're connected to your job search. Tuition money to acquire or improve job skills may qualify for the Lifetime Learning Credit, which has limitations and income restrictions that are explained in IRS Publication 970, "Tax Benefits for Education" (www.irs.gov/publications/p970).

Accounting for Social Security Benefits Reductions When You Work

If you start receiving Social Security retirement benefits before reaching your full retirement age, your benefits are reduced if you earn more than a certain amount. For example, in 2015, if you're younger than full retirement age during all of 2015, $1 is deducted from your benefits for each $2 you earn above $15,720. If you reach full retirement age during 2015, $1 is deducted from your benefits for each $3 you earn above $41,880 until the month you reach full retirement age. For people younger than full retirement age during 2015, here's the breakdown:

If your monthly Social Security benefit is . . .	And you earn . . .	You'll receive yearly benefits of . . .
$700	$15,720 or less	$8,400
$700	$16,000	$8,260
$700	$20,000	$6,260

If your monthly Social Security benefit is . . .	And you earn . . .	You'll receive yearly benefits of . . .
$900	$15,720 or less	$10,800
$900	$16,000	$10,660
$900	$20,000	$8,660
$1,100	$15,720 or less	$13,200
$1,100	$16,000	$13,060
$1,100	$20,000	$11,060

If you work for someone else, only your wages count toward Social Security's earnings limits. If you're self-employed, only your net earnings from self-employment count. Other income, such as other government benefits, investment earnings, interest, pensions, annuities, and capital gains, don't count toward your earnings limit. For details, read the pamphlet "How Work Affects Your Benefits" at www.ssa.gov/pubs/EN-05-10069.pdf.

For more about Social Security, read *AARP Social Security For Dummies,* by Jonathan Peterson (Wiley).

The amount your benefits are reduced, however, isn't truly lost. Your benefit will be increased at your full retirement age to account over time for benefits withheld due to earlier earnings.

Taking Advantage of Additional Public Benefits

If you're unemployed or experience a significant reduction in income, you may qualify for benefits from federal, state, and local governments that you hadn't previously qualified for, including the following:

- Unemployment insurance benefits (see the earlier section "Filing for Unemployment Benefits")
- Subsidized health insurance
- Food assistance
- Gas or electricity subsidies
- Free or low-cost phone service
- Low-cost auto insurance

When you work, a portion of your taxes goes toward funding these benefits for others. When you're unemployed or underemployed, take advantage of these benefits to get back on your feet, so you can start paying taxes again to help other unfortunate souls.

To find out which federal benefits you may be eligible to receive, visit www.benefits.gov. To find out about benefit programs in your state, mouse over Benefits in the menu bar near the top, click By State, and click the state you reside in. To find out about local benefit programs, contact a family services organization, community center, or church.

Providing Benefits for Yourself

If you're self-employed, unemployed, or underemployed, you don't have access to employer-sponsored benefits, such as health insurance and pension programs, so you need to provide them for yourself or make do without them. The good news is that if you're not earning enough to fund these benefits yourself, the government may help by subsidizing your health insurance premiums and expanding your tax breaks for any surplus you may be able to squirrel away in a retirement account. In this section, I help you explore your options.

Planning for retirement

If you're starting a business, working on contract, moving to a nonprofit, or joining a small firm without an employee retirement plan, open your own. Your three key options are solo 401(k), SEP-IRA, and a Simple IRA.

- ✔ **Solo 401(k):** This plan is best if you're self-employed with no employees and have income of $100,000 or more. The maximum amount you can contribute is 20 percent of net self-employment income plus $18,000, up to $53,000 in 2015; if you're 50 or older, you can contribute up to $6,000 more. The deadline to open an account to be eligible for a deduction is December 31. You can make contributions until your business's tax-filing deadline.

- ✔ **SEP IRA (Simplified Employee Pension):** An SEP is a good choice if you're running your own business with no employees. The maximum contribution is 25 percent of self-employment income, up to $53,000 for 2015. The SEP has no "catch-up" provision allowing people age 50 or older to invest more than younger people. The deadline to open is April 15 to be eligible for a deduction for the previous tax year or October 15, if you file for an extension.

✔ **Simple IRA:** You may opt for a Simple IRA if you have fewer than 100 employees. You can also have a SIMPLE IRA if you don't have employees. If you do have employees, you typically must match up to 3 percent of their compensation. The maximum contribution is $12,500 up to $15,500 if you're 50 or older. The deadline to open an account is October 1 to be eligible for a deduction in the current tax year.

Don't worry about having to max out your contribution; save as much as you can. Opt for an auto-deposit program if your bank and financial firm permit so that you can have a set amount automatically shifted from your business's bank account into a retirement plan every month.

Low-income individuals or couples can qualify for a special Savers Credit of up to $1,000 for an individual or $2,000 for a couple for retirement plan con-tributions. To be eligible in 2014, single taxpayers couldn't earn more than $30,000 (or $60,000 for married couples).

Getting health insurance

If you're not eligible for an employer-sponsored health insurance plan, shop for insurance on the new healthcare exchanges via Healthcare.gov (www. healthcare.gov). Don't drop your current job insurance (you can continue it for a time under a law known as COBRA) until you have a new policy in place. Note that with COBRA, you're likely to lose your employer's contribu-tion, so be prepared for your health insurance premium to double or worse.

Check your state insurance department website, too, because it may list health insurance choices for residents. Also be sure to ask your doctors which insurance carriers they accept.

Crunch the numbers when comparing health insurance plans. You may save money by choosing a high-deductible plan and using a health savings account (HSA) to pay for medical, dental, and medication costs with untaxed money from your HSA. But you may not. To compare plans, take the following steps:

1. **Multiply your monthly health insurance premium by 12 months under one of the plans you're considering.**

2. **Calculate or estimate your total annual out-of-pocket costs under this particular plan.**

   This is the tricky part. If the plan covers everything except a small deduct-ible, simply use the deductible as your total. Likewise, if the deductible is high and you expect your out-of-pocket costs will meet the deductible, use the deductible as your total. But if you're healthy and rarely meet your deductible, you may want to estimate your annual out-of-pocket costs based on previous years' amounts.

3. Perform Steps 1 and 2 for each plan you're considering.

4. Compare the plans.

For example, suppose that you're comparing a gold plan that covers everything except for a $200 deductible and costs $680 per month to a bronze plan with a $3,000 deductible that costs $180 per month, and you think you'd probably meet that $3,000 deductible under the bronze plan:

- ✔ Annual cost of gold plan = ($680 × 12) + $200 = $8,360
- ✔ Annual cost of bronze plan = ($180 × 12) + $3,000 = $5,160

In addition, you could have an HSA under the bronze plan and use it to pay your out-of-pocket expenses with non-taxed dollars, saving you additional money, so the bronze plan would be best, all other things being equal (such as whether the doctors you want to see accept that particular plan).

You may be charged a small annual fee of about $40 for a health savings account from a no-load mutual fund company, such as Vanguard or Fidelity. You can contribute up to $3,350 to a health savings account for individual coverage (a maximum of $4,350 if you're 55 or older). For families, the limit on contributions is $6,650; $7,650 if you're 55 or older. Most banks also have HSAs.

If you're shopping for an individual health policy, you can also compare premiums, deductibles, and out-of-pocket costs at such websites as eHealth (www.ehealthinsurance.com), GoHealth (www.gohealthinsurance.com), Insure.com (www.insure.com), and NetQuote (www.netquote.com). Always check to see whether your preferred doctors are in-network before you select a plan. Or have a local health insurance agent to shop around on your behalf. Look for one at the National Association of Health Underwriters website (www.nahu.org).

Part II
Launching Your Job Search

Using Lesser-Known Online Job Boards

Website	Description
Coolworks.com	Database of seasonal jobs, amusement park jobs, and more
Job-hunt.org	Comprehensive list of job-search resources and links to employer recruiting pages
Ratracerebellion.com	Geared for work-at-home opportunities
Retiredbrains.com	Online job board that connects to thousands of jobs for those over 50; includes lots of part-time job opportunities
Retirementjobs.com	Geared toward 50-plus job seekers
Seniorjobbank.org	A career site for boomers and seniors with an active job board
Seniors4hire.org	Submit a résumé, post a description of your model job, or apply for posted jobs
Workforce50.com	Employment and career change resources

Visit www.dummies.com/extras/gettingthejobyouwantafter50 for a bonus article on finding contract work through social media.

In this part . . .

- ✔ Check out the hottest job markets to discover your options, and tap into popular and lesser-known job boards, leaving no stone unturned in your search for the job you want and were made to do!

- ✔ Consider the option of flying solo and creating your own job through contract work, launching your own business, becoming a "social entrepreneur," or buying a franchise.

- ✔ Make the most of special circumstances, such as veteran status, disabilities, relaunching a career after an extended absence from the job market, and working abroad in retirement.

Chapter 5

Scoping Out Promising Job Markets

*W*hen job hunting, you're faced with two challenges: figuring out what you want to do for a living and then finding someone who's willing to pay you to do it. In this chapter, I help you meet both of those challenges by steering you to the hottest job markets and listings. By knowing what's out there, you can find a job with more of what you want and employers need. In the process, you narrow your focus so that your subsequent job-seeking efforts have greater impact.

As you get rolling with your job hunt, I urge you to consider a wide range of options and broaden your search to different fields. In the AARP report "The Long Road Back: Struggling to Find Work after Unemployment," many older workers who had been unemployed were able to find work by considering new occupations. In fact, of those who succeeded in finding jobs, more than half had an occupation different from the one they had prior to becoming unemployed.

Exploring the Possibilities and Gathering Ideas via Job Boards

At the age of 50, it's a little late to start thinking about what you want to do when you grow up, but more and more people who are looking at 50 in their rearview mirrors are thinking about what *else* they want to do now that they've grown up. Times have changed, and maybe the employers of today no longer need what you used to do. And maybe you really don't want to do what you used to do anyway. The time has come to explore exciting new opportunities and perhaps consider opportunities you passed up along the way.

One of the best ways to start thinking about work opportunities you're interested in and qualified for is to browse online job boards — websites where employers post job openings or the site itself gathers postings from around the web. Job postings via online jobs boards can be a first-rate source of intelligence about who's hiring for what jobs and where. In this section, I lead you on a tour of well-known and lesser-known job boards.

If you're looking for a new job right now and still holding down a current one, tread carefully. With so much recruitment or job hunting done online these days, getting "found out" by a current employer is a growing risk. See the later section "Harnessing the power of apps/websites," for details about apps designed to keep your job search confidential.

Checking out the big boards

Start with the big job boards, where you'll find the greatest number and diversity of listings:

- ✔ **CareerBuilder** (`www.careerbuilder.com`) is among the leading job boards, providing job listings, career advice, and other employment resources along with a place to post your résumé. CareerBuilder pulls from career sites of more than 1,000 partners, including 140 newspapers and leading portals, such as MSN and AOL.

- ✔ **Craigslist** (`www.craigslist.org`) is a mostly free online classifieds site. It's organized by location — city or state or country. The cost of posting a job is typically free or very low ($25 to $75), in comparison with the majority of job sites, so you'll find job postings from a wide range of employers. However, watch out for scams. The site organizers police postings for scams, and you can "flag" postings that may be considered inappropriate. To help its visitors, craigslist has a section called "Avoiding Scams and Fraud." Protect your privacy if you post your résumé. Those postings are visible to anyone who visits the site, so limit the contact information and details that you include.

Be especially careful on craigslist, because anyone can post a job opening. Research the employer carefully before sending any sensitive information, and don't go to your initial interview alone. (See the later section, "Taking extra precautions with online job postings.")

- ✔ **Glassdoor** (www.glassdoor.com) allows you to sign in via Facebook to find Inside Connections at a company through your Facebook network, so you can see whether any of your Facebook friends work there or did so in the past. You can browse the latest job listings as well as view company-specific salary reports, recent interview questions, employee ratings and reviews, CEO approval ratings, interview questions and reviews, office videos, and more.

- ✔ **Indeed** (www.indeed.com; see the later section "Exploring job boards for older workers") lets you search for jobs by job title, key words, or company name and by location. After conducting a search, you can filter results by salary, title, company, location, job type, and employer/recruiter. Sign up and log in for additional features such as saved jobs, job history, email alerts, and résumé upload.

- ✔ **Jobaware** (www.jobaware.com/jobs) lets you search for jobs by key words and company and by location. Sign up and log in for additional features, such as job tracking and search history.

- ✔ **Job-Hunt** (www.job-hunt.org) is a free online guide with links to thousands of employers and associations and their job boards. Click Job Search Help, near the top of the page, and click Boomers to access the Guide to Boomer Job Search, with links to articles specifically for job seekers over 50.

- ✔ **LinkUp** (www.linkup.com) is a job-search engine that uncovers unadvertised jobs listed on company websites.

- ✔ **Monster** (www.monster.com), one of the original job boards, has expanded to include other resources. You can search for and apply for jobs online, post a résumé, review company profiles, and get salary information and career advice. BeKnown is a networking feature that puts you in touch with possible connections via Facebook.

- ✔ **SimplyHired** (www.simplyhired.com) is another leading job board with a smorgasbord of listings. You can search for jobs by job title, skills, or company and location or browse by category.

Also, check out Mynextmove.org (www.mynextmove.org), O*Net Center (www.onetcenter.org), and O*Net OnLine (www.onetonline.org) for more job-finding information.

Check out Payscale (www.payscale.com) or Salary.com (www.salary.com) to research salary ranges based on position and location. Payscale has a feature called Get Your Personal Salary Report and a new tool to help find your dream job. PayScale's database filters search results based on salary, location, education, and flexibility.

Job boards are great for conducting research, but you should be aware of the following potential drawbacks:

- ✔ Online job postings aren't always removed in a timely fashion, so the job opening may no longer exist by the time you discover it.

- ✔ Recruiters sometimes post jobs to determine whether the description is alluring for job seekers. If too few people respond, they change it and the true posting goes live a few days or even weeks later.

- ✔ Sometimes recruiters put up faux posts to gather résumés for future headhunting searches.

- ✔ Employers may post jobs to satisfy the public posting requirement before hiring the in-house applicant who already has been chosen.

- ✔ Scammers collect résumés and other information from job seekers.

Combing niche job boards

Large job boards, such as CareerBuilder, Indeed.com, Monster.com, and SimplyHired, are popular for employers and employees alike. They give job seekers access to plenty of openings, but the competition for those openings is stiff. You may find more success by becoming a bigger fish in a smaller pond — by combing through smaller job boards that are more focused on workers with your talents and interests. Here's a short list of niche job boards to help narrow your search:

- ✔ **CrunchBoard** (www.crunchboard.com) is one of the more popular job boards for Internet and technology jobs.

- ✔ **Dice** (www.dice.com) is the site for tech job seekers. You can search by company, job title, key word, and location. The site also features career advice and tech news for job seekers.

- ✔ **Engineering Daily** (www.engineeringdaily.net) is "a web-only magazine dedicated to providing engineers with access to relevant and useful content on a variety of topics." The site features a large engineering-exclusive job board.

- ✔ **HealthJobs Nationwide.com** (www.healthjobsnationwide.com) bills itself as the largest healthcare talent acquisition job-board network in the United States.

- ✔ **Mediabistro** (www.mediabistro.com) provides access to job postings in the media, including newspapers, magazines, book publishing, television, radio, and the web. You can browse the job board or register to have postings that may interest you delivered to you via email. The site also posts jobs for freelancers.

✔ **SalesGravy** (www.salesgravy.com) features an area for sales talent sourcing and recruiting. Click the Job Seekers link, in the upper-right corner of the home page, to log in and search for jobs in sales.

✔ **Snagajob** (www.snagajob.com). If you're looking for an hourly gig, this online marketplace has more than 300,000 job postings available at any one time. You can search for specific jobs by title, industry, or company and filter results by location.

✔ ***Work At Home Vintage Employees LLC (WAHVE)** (www.wahve.com) is a site for professionals "phasing" into retirement who work from home for insurance firms. Most positions are long-term, but some are short-term for projects that are a minimum of three months. Positions range from bookkeeper to claims support to customer service.

✔ **The Write Jobs** (www.writejobs.com) is a great place for exploring job listings exclusively for writers, especially technical writers, and editors.

These and other smaller, more targeted sites, including those operated by industry and professional associations, usually include openings that don't show up elsewhere. They also sometimes offer contact information for the hiring manager instead of routing you to a generic application, which means your résumé is less likely to disappear into a black hole. And although applicants from niche sites tend to be more qualified — because their skill set more often matches what the employer is looking for — you'll compete with fewer candidates there than you would on well-known sites.

Small businesses in particular tend to opt for niche boards to find candidates because they tend to get applications from higher-quality applicants, which means they have to filter through fewer applications to find the spot-on hire. If a hiring manager is seeking a dynamo sales representative, for instance, she may post that opening on Sales Gravy.

Digging up more niche job boards

Each industry has its own niche job board(s) and sometimes job boards for sub-specialties within the industry. They're not as front and center as the gigantic job websites, so you have to do a little sleuthing to find one that's relevant:

✔ Visit the websites of professional organizations in your field, such as the Society for Technical Communication, to see whether the site has a job board or links to other sites that post relevant jobs.

✔ Ask people who work in your industry about where they look or have looked for jobs, or ask hiring managers at businesses in your field where they post openings.

✔ Search the web for <your city> or <your state> or <your county> followed by "jobs" to find any local job boards. For example, DCJobs.com (www.dcjobs.com) caters to job seekers in Washington, D.C. You may have to scroll down through several pages of results to find more specialized job boards, because the top search results are likely to steer you toward the big job boards.

✔ Search the web for <your industry> followed by "jobs." Again, you may need to scroll through several pages of search results to find more specialized job boards.

Exploring job boards for people 50 and older

Now that you're included in the category of workers 50 and older, you can take advantage of the job boards that eliminate some of your competition:

✔ **AARP job board (www.aarp.org/work):** You can search for jobs by job title, key words, or company name and by location.

✔ **Encore.org (www.encore.org):** This is the place to go for boomers attracted to second careers in the nonprofit sector. Mouse over Resources, near the top of the page, click Resources for Encore Seekers, and scroll down to the "Explore social sector jobs" section for links to organizations that may be able to help you track down meaningful employment for your encore career.

✔ **National Older Worker Career Center (NOWCC; www.nowcc.org):** The NOWCC is "a national nonprofit organization dedicated to promoting experienced workers as a valuable and critical component of the nation's workforce." Mouse over Applicants, near the top of the page, and click Current Openings to browse job openings listed by state and find a link to submit your application.

✔ **RetiredBrains (www.retiredbrains.com):** This online job board, specializing in part-time gigs, connects to thousands of jobs for those over 50.

✔ **RetirementJobs (www.retirementjobs.com):** This site is geared toward full-time positions for 50-plus job seekers.

✔ **SeniorJobBank.org (www.seniorjobbank.org):** This is a career site with an active jobs board for boomers and seniors.

✔ **Seniors4hire.org (www.seniors4hire.org):** Job seekers can submit a résumé, post a description of their model job, or apply for posted jobs.

> ✔ **Workforce50.com (www.workforce50.com):** Workforce50.com's core
> mission is "to find and provide job listings from employers truly inter-
> ested in hiring from the over-50 community." Here, you can also find
> information and articles related to job searching.

Check out AARP Employer Pledge: Experience Valued program (www.aarp.
org/work), directing job seekers to more than 285 employers that value and
are hiring experienced workers.

Looking into government jobs

Government jobs are often available at the federal, state, county, and
municipal levels. The largest employer in the United States is the federal
government, which employs more than 2,723,000 employees. In 2015, for
example, the federal government is expected to hire around 95,000 new workers, up from 80,000 in 2014, and more openings are expected. Roughly a quarter of the 2.1 million federal civilian workers are now eligible for retirement,
and as the economy improves, more workers may be headed for the exits.

Employment in the state and local government sector is projected to increase
by 929,000, to reach just over 20.0 million in 2022. This increase is more than
two-and-a-half times the increase seen in the 2002 to 2012 period. The projected job growth in the sector is driven by increases in both state and local
educational services, with almost half of the growth coming from the local
government educational services industry.

To find out what's available, do the following:

✔ Visit USAJobs.gov (www.usajobs.gov) to search for jobs by key word,
   job title, government agency, and location, or start at www.usa.gov,
   track down the government agency you want to look for, and check its
   list of openings. Most agencies have their own job boards, and you may
   see additional positions on those sites that you don't see on the broader
   site. In most cases, you still have to go through USAJobs to apply, but
   some positions are exempt from the competitive system and allow for
   more direct hiring.

✔ Visit GovernmentJobs.com (www.governmentjobs.com) to search
   specifically for jobs posted by employers in the public sector. You can
   search by job title or key word and by location or browse jobs by category or location.

✔ Search for your state's website, access it, and then poke around to find
   job-related links. You may find links for jobs in education or a more general Jobs or Human Resources link that leads to an area where state job
   opportunities are posted.

✔ Search for your county's or city's website, access it, and look for job links. Less populated counties and municipalities are less likely to have their own websites or to post jobs on those sites, but it's worth a try.

Landing a federal job can be quite a challenge. Talk to practically anyone who has tried to secure a job with the federal government, and she'll tell you the hiring process can be painfully slow and bureaucratic. Follow these steps to expedite the process and improve your chances of success:

1. **Find the right fit.**

   Find the job you want and are qualified to do in the agency you want to do it. If you're passionate about the environment, for example, use that as a starting place to figure out which agency will be the most compatible for you. Look for openings at the Environmental Protection Agency (EPA), the U.S. Department of Agriculture (USDA), and other agencies dealing with environmental issues.

   Find out more about the various agencies by attending events sponsored by government-related associations, such as the American Council for Technology (ACT) and the International City/County Management Association (ICMA) to name two. You can also tap into government-related websites, such as Go Government (www.gogovernment.org), which can help you research federal agencies and government careers, and Best Places to Work in the Federal Government (www.bestplacestowork.org).

2. **Go directly to the agency's website.**

   After pinpointing the agency you're aiming for, check out its job board directly, which may contain additional job openings that aren't posted on USAJobs.gov. You still need to apply on USAJobs.gov, but these positions may be exempt from requirements for posting jobs there.

3. **Apply.**

   Even if you find and eventually secure the job through your networking efforts, you need to jump through this hoop. Regardless of where the job is posted and how you find out about it, you must apply for openings on USAJobs.gov (www.usajobs.gov). See Chapter 11 for details on submitting your application on USAJobs.gov.

4. **Network.**

   Although the application process is rigid, it helps to reach out to anyone you know who works for the federal government. You want to get a sense of what it's like from an insider. It's not just about the job but the culture and environment as well. In addition, federal employers are no different from those in the private sector; they want to hire people that they know or that someone they know knows.

Consider starting with a short-term appointment, which involves working on a specific assignment or project for one year or longer. You can find term appointments on USAJobs.com. Check out special programs. For example, the Peace Corps actively recruits retired leaders to be volunteers for short-term shifts. Some positions are paid. The Presidential Innovation Fellows program recruits the best and brightest in the technology field to do a yearlong stint in federal service. Government-sponsored fellowship programs, such as Code for America and Fuse Corps, place leaders from the private sector into government positions for one-year assignments.

When looking for a government position, expect the usual bureaucratic delays and be persistent. Although timing varies from one agency to the next, 80 to 90 days between application and hiring is the norm. You can easily wait four months or longer to get an offer. I always encourage prospective job applicants to apply to numerous jobs over a series of months and give it time. A friend of mine applied to 40 jobs over three months. He got four interviews and two offers. The time from first application to starting the position was approximately three months.

Going to college . . . to find a job

College towns and colleges, which tend to be recession-resistant, are often great places to live and work in the 50-plus years. In addition to supplying ample jobs for people not yet ready to clock out, colleges offer affordable entertainment, sports, and lifelong learning opportunities.

Explore the websites of colleges and universities that interest you and click the link for Jobs or Human Resources to see what's available. Nearly every higher education facility in the nation posts its openings on its website for all to see. Or check the site HigherEdJobs (www.higheredjobs.com). You can screen by location, institution, job title, category and full- or part-time positions.

Many colleges and universities welcome older workers. AARP's Best Employers for Workers Over 50 program, which ran from 2001 to 2013, often included colleges and universities along with healthcare providers in college towns. Past winners include Cornell University in Ithaca, New York; West Virginia University in Morgantown; the University of Pittsburgh; and Virginia Commonwealth University in Richmond.

Some schools make a special effort to appeal to older workers. Penn State University, for instance, has a retirement community on campus that offers residents free college classes and priority tickets to games. For culture buffs, the Penn State Center for the Performing Arts presents music, dance, and theater.

Harnessing the power of apps and websites

Many of the job sites mentioned in this chapter, including CareerBuilder, craigslist, Indeed, Jobaware, Monster, LinkUp, SimplyHired, and SnagaJob, have corresponding smartphone apps. Networking apps and websites for Facebook, LinkedIn, Monster's BeKnown, and Twitter are also very useful for networking and checking out job listings.

Here are a few additional job-search apps to check out. They're geared to those who are employed but open to new prospects. You either transfer your profile from Facebook, which is then edited to keep you incognito, or you fill out a questionnaire with information about your credentials and the kind of jobs and companies that interest you. The service then pairs you with potential employers, while keeping your identity top-secret. If there's a match and both parties indicate an interest, the service introduces you and enables you to communicate with one another and set up an interview. These apps and websites are appealing to recruiters, who almost always prefer employed over unemployed candidates, especially when seeking candidates with specialized skills and experience.

- **Jobr** (www.jobrapp.com): You build a Jobr profile by signing into your LinkedIn account and importing your profile (or you can use a résumé). Your photo, contact info, and other identifying information are removed, so you remain anonymous. Jobr then sends you job openings based on your salary preferences, location, skills, education, and work experience. You browse proposed job listings and then swipe to the right on jobs you want to apply for and left on jobs you don't. Employers and recruiters do the same. If you both select one another, a recruiter may request a full résumé by email or schedule a phone interview.

- **Poachable** (www.poachable.co): Poachable is a website that has listings for an assortment of job functions in a variety of places. The focus right now is technology, and jobs tend to be for engineers, product managers, and designers. Poachable also has a blog with posts on how job seekers can make themselves more attractive to employers.

- **Poacht** (www.poachtapp.com): Like Switch and Jobr, but instead of using a Tinder-like swiping process to match you with potential employers, Poacht asks you a few screening questions, such as the salary you're seeking and whether you're willing to relocate. The app then notifies you when an employer is interested. At that point, you can accept or decline the introduction request.

- **Switch** (www.switchapp.com): Originally for tech jobs in New York City, Switch has plans to expand to other major metro markets. It works like Jobr; you and your prospective employer swipe to show interest, and the app introduces you.

Most of these apps and sites are pretty new, so they may not list as many jobs as do the big job boards. Although most offer a range of jobs in a variety of places, they're currently geared to start-up technology, engineering, and digital media, located in techie locales, including New York and Silicon Valley.

Taking extra precautions with online job postings

Be careful when responding to online job postings, especially on generic classified sites, such as craigslist, because anyone can post a job listing. Look for the following warning signs:

- ✔ Any posting that requests sensitive personal or financial information, such as your Social Security number or a credit card number. Work-from-home postings are notorious for *phishing* expeditions (gathering personal and financial information to steal your identity or worse), charging to get started, and promising payment that never comes.

- ✔ Requests to email your response to a free email address ending in gmail. com or yahoo.com, for example, instead of to a company email address ending in something like wiley.com or ibm.com.

- ✔ A link that redirects you to somewhere other than the place indicated in the link. You can usually mouse over the link and look in the status bar near the bottom of your web browser or email window to see the actual address of where the link will take you; if it differs from the address in the link itself, don't click the link.

- ✔ A job listing that requires any form of payment to gain access to additional information or to qualify for consideration.

When first responding to a job listing via email, share your name and email address and little else. Indicate your interest in the position and request the organization's name, physical address, and phone number, so you can do your own background check to make sure the organization is legitimate. Explain that when responding to online job postings, you take certain precautions to ensure that the posting is legitimate before sending any detailed information. They'll understand and appreciate your concern. You may include a scaled-down version of your résumé, with your work experience, education, and so on, but excluding sensitive information, such as your birth-date and the names of education institutions and the dates you attended. Scammers could use detailed information to contact places you worked or went to school to find out more about you.

Protecting yourself against scammers is another reason networking is such an effective means for finding and landing a job. Networking eases the concerns not only of prospective employers who want some assurance that you are who you say you are but also of job seekers like you who need to know that job postings are legitimate. Before responding to a job posting, use your connections to find out whether anyone you know works for the organization. If someone you know works there, you can be less concerned about submitting your application or résumé.

Investigating Opportunities by Category

Another way to discover what's out there is to search for jobs by category in healthy job sectors or categories, including part-time, seasonal, and holiday jobs; work-at-home opportunities; and jobs for animal lovers. In this section, I reveal the hottest job sectors and explore additional categories to consider as you figure out what you want to do and find someone to pay you to do it.

Compensation varies depending on the employer, your experience, and where you live. Jobs may be full- or part-time or have flexible hours. Some may require you to return to school for specific training, while others enable you to repurpose skills you already have.

Focusing on the hottest industries

One way to conduct your search is to focus on the hottest job markets — industries that have reported rising numbers of vacancies or have projected an increasing need for employees. This section covers five sizzling sectors to consider.

Healthcare

The aging population and longer life expectancies are spurring a wide range of healthcare-related jobs. In fact, for the period 2012 to 2022, the U.S. Bureau of Labor Statistics projects that industries related to healthcare will generate the most new jobs, about 5 million. New jobs are cropping up all the time for people in their 50s, 60s, and 70s that cater to people in their 80s and 90s. The jobs can run the gamut from repairing gurneys and wheelchairs at a hospital to transcribing medical records at a physician's office.

Look for jobs at public and private hospitals, nursing and residential care facilities, and individual and family services. Specific jobs to explore in the sector include dietitian and nutritionist, patient advocate, personal and home healthcare aide, massage therapist, physical therapist (and aide/assistant), registered nurse or licensed/practical nurse, nurse practitioner, school nurse, paramedical examiner (screening individuals applying for life or healthcare insurance), senior fitness trainer, skincare specialist, home modification professional, medical equipment maintenance and repair, and medical records administrator.

Financial

As boomers slide into their retirement years, they're increasingly seeking help with managing their money, whether it's bill paying, estate planning, or choosing the right insurance policy. There's growing awareness that people need to have financial plans in place to help avoid outliving their savings.

Moreover, as traditional employer-provided pensions are being replaced by do-it-yourself IRAs, 401(k)s, and similar plans, demand is on the rise among all age groups for experts who can make sense of retirement investment. Little wonder that the Bureau of Labor Statistics (BLS) predicts job growth in the financial activities arena to rise about 10 percent in the next decade.

Jobs to explore in the sector include accountant, personal financial adviser and planner, insurance broker, retirement coach, bookkeeper, financial manager, and tax preparer.

Leisure and hospitality

Given the snowballing number of retiring workers, demand for travel and leisure activities has surged. A recent Manpower survey found that 23 percent of employers in this field were planning to take on more workers in the first quarter of 2014. The BLS sees long-term growth, too: about 1.3 million new jobs between 2012 and 2022.

Jobs to explore in the sector include barber and hairdresser, cosmetologist, casino worker, caterer, chef, cruise line worker, landscaper, pet sitter/walker, recreation worker, resort worker, tour worker, bartender, waiter, and hotel shuttle van driver.

Retail

It's not exactly shop 'til you drop, but most experts predict that the rising population will translate to a greater demand for workers in the retail trade.

Jobs to explore in the sector include cashier, customer service representative, package preparer, e-commerce analyst, direct salesperson, retail salesperson, sales representative, and product demonstrator.

Professional and business services

Jobs in this sector are forecasted to grow by nearly 20 percent — roughly 3.5 million new jobs between 2012 and 2022. Jobs to explore in this sector include grant/proposal writer; green-business consultant; human resource specialist; information security analyst; database administrator; management consultant; market research specialist; meeting, convention, and event planner; and translator/interpreter. Spanish is the most in-demand language, but other languages are increasingly needed, such as Arabic. Specializing in translating in a particular field, such as the judicial system or healthcare, and knowing its special terminology increase your job opportunities.

Cast a wide net. Seek out openings at small businesses and big corporations.

Narrowing your focus to the hottest occupations

If looking at the hottest industries didn't spark any ideas, try narrowing your focus to these fastest-growing occupations (according to the BLS *Occupational Outlook Handbook*) listed in Table 5-1.

Table 5-1	Fastest-Growing Occupations (2012–2022)	
Occupation	*Growth*	*Annual salary*
Industrial-organizational psychologists	53%	$83,580
Personal care aides	49%	$19,910
Home health aides	48%	$20,820
Insulation workers	47%	$39,170
Interpreters and translators	46%	$45,430
Diagnostic medical sonographers	46%	$65,860
Helpers for brick masons, block masons, stonemasons, and tile and marble setters	43%	$28,220
Occupational therapy assistants	43%	$53,240
Genetic counselors	41%	$56,800
Physical therapist assistants	41%	$52,160
Physical therapist aides	40%	$23,880
Skincare specialists	40%	$28,640
Physician assistants	38%	$90,930

Occupation	Growth	Annual salary
Segmental pavers	38%	$33,720
Helpers for electricians	37%	$27,670
Information security analysts	37%	$86,170
Occupational therapy aides	36%	$26,850
Health specialties teachers, postsecondary	36%	$81,140
Medical secretaries	36%	$31,350
Physical therapists	35%	$79,860

Considering positions you may have overlooked

The Department of Labor's *Occupational Outlook Handbook* includes many new job-related profiles that you may not have considered before. These include the following:

- Compensation, benefits, and job analysis specialists
- Computer network architects
- Emergency management directors
- Fundraisers
- Genetic counselors
- Information security analysts
- Nurse anesthetists, nurse midwives, and nurse practitioners
- Phlebotomists
- Solar photovoltaic installers
- Training and development specialists
- Web developers
- Wind turbine technicians

Finding a job after 50 is different from when you were younger, as I write extensively about in my book *Great Jobs for Everyone 50+: Finding Work That Keeps You Happy and Healthy . . . And Pays the Bills*. I highly recommend you read the book for my jobs workshop and smorgasbord of jobs to consider. More often, the big-ticket items are out of the way — child-care, college tuition, and mortgages — and you have the flexibility to stretch and try new kinds of work that make you happy and give you purpose. Find a job that ramps up your learning curve, maybe even scares you a little. Perhaps you want to aim for one that sweeps you into an entirely new field where you're able to draw on your previous talents and add new skills as you go.

Contemplating part-time jobs

To streamline their operations and avoid having to pay employee benefits, many employers hire part-time workers. As a result, more and more employees have to take on two or more part-time jobs to make ends meet. This isn't necessarily a bad thing, if you can earn enough from your part-time gigs to pay the bills and cobble together your own benefits package. In addition, working a couple of jobs can be an attractive proposition for people who don't want to work full-time or are easily bored. Here are a few sites I recommend to help find part-time work year-round.

- ✔ **FlexJobs.com** (www.flexjobs.com) lists jobs in more than 50 categories, from business consultant and translator to project manager and small nonprofit executive director, with a variety of scheduling arrangements. To get the full listings, the basic fee is $14.95 for a month.

- ✔ **Rat Race Rebellion** (www.ratracerebellion.com) specializes in work-at-home jobs, scrutinizing its postings to ensure legitimacy and delivering them in a free e-newsletter. You'll find a variety of positions, from customer service representatives to freelance writing. Many pay under $20 an hour, but you can find some higher-paying ones.

- ✔ **Elance.com** (www.elance.com) and **Guru.com** (www.guru.com) list freelance opportunities in fields such as web development, graphic design, and business consulting.

Pounding the pavement for seasonal jobs

If the idea of changing jobs every season appeals to you, seasonal jobs may be in your future. Consider the following possibilities:

- ✔ **Limo driver:** Limo services provide work year-round, but their dance cards fill up during prom and wedding season from April to June. Most limo companies provide on-the-job training but require an impeccable driving record. If you're 70 or older, insurance restrictions may be a stumbling block.

- ✔ **Shuttle bus driver:** Colleges, car dealerships, car rental agencies, airport parking facilities, hotels, and motels commonly use shuttle bus drivers. You'll need a commercial driver's license (CDL) for most jobs.

✔ **Tax preparer:** Large tax firms, for instance, H&R Block and Jackson Hewitt, hire thousands of tax preparers each year to come on board from January until May 1. You usually need to take the firm's income tax course in the fall to prepare. To fly solo, become an enrolled agent with the Internal Revenue Service. Under new IRS rules, any individual who, for compensation, prepares or assists in the preparation of a tax return or claim for refund must have his or her own Tax Preparer Identification Number, which costs $64.25 per year. See `www.irs.gov/Tax-Professionals/PTIN-Requirements-for-Tax-Return-Preparers` for details. To gain experience, check out AARP Foundation Tax-Aide (`www.aarp.org/taxaide`), where volunteers help lower income seniors do their taxes. AARP trains all volunteers.

✔ **Substitute teacher:** To work during the school year and have your summers (or a good part of your summers) off, consider registering with local school districts to work as a substitute teacher. If you have any sort of degree, preferably a bachelor's or better, you have a great chance of being included in the pool. You're usually paid per day you work.

✔ **Private tutor:** If you're a certified teacher; have a strong background in finance, medicine, law, editing, or business; or know and can teach a foreign language, you'll find plenty of opportunities as a private tutor throughout the school year. Some test-prep firms hire tutors to help teens and adults with standardized tests and professional certification exams. Certified teachers are preferred, but you can fly solo. You may get your foot in the door by volunteering at a local library and spreading the word at local schools.

✔ **Park service employee:** Each year, the National Park Service as well as state and local parks hire temporary and seasonal employees. The best way to find a job at a National Park is to go to each park's individual website, or USAJobs.com, and click on its jobs or employment opportunities link. For a state park opening, check with your state's division of parks and recreation.

✔ **Nursery worker:** If you're a skilled and knowledgeable gardener, local nurseries could probably use your expertise during their busy seasons with answering customer questions or doing some light to heavy lifting. It helps to know the difference between an annual and a perennial, of course, and which plants do best in the shade versus the sun. Consider taking a master gardener class to boost your résumé.

✔ **Ballpark worker:** In the spring, summer, and fall, ballparks around the country need ushers, ticket takers, box office attendants, cashiers, bartenders, suite attendants, in-seat servers, concession stand workers, and more. If you're a people person, know the game, and are familiar with the home team, you have an edge over the competition.

✔ **Amusement park personnel:** Amusement parks require a lot of personnel in the summer months to keep those roller coasters rolling and Ferris wheels spinning, not to mention manning the game booths and concessions stands. If you live near an amusement park or are willing to temporarily relocate, you may find a summer job that suits your taste. Be aware, however, that the competition from college and high-school students is stiff.

Finding holiday jobs

For many retirees and 50-plus workers looking for short-term gigs, the holiday season is a great time to pull in some extra dough. And you have what employers are looking for: They're keen on hiring people who are responsible and reliable. Plus, a temporary gig can lead to future employment after the holiday rush fades, particularly if the economy continues to be robust. You've got a foot in the door, and hopefully you've demonstrated your competence and built a relationship.

If you're interested in looking for a holiday job, follow these suggestions for getting started and improving your chances:

✔ **Cast a wide net.** Retailers have a seasonal demand not only for sales clerks but also for customer service helpers, cashiers, stockroom clerks, and security guards. You may also find openings at restaurants as greeters, wait staff, bartenders, and baristas. Package delivery firms such as UPS and FedEx are inundated with a surge in demand and hire accordingly. Small boutiques, mall kiosks, catering companies, and florists add staff at this time of year. You may even pick up work as a holiday decorator, party planner, babysitter, or pet-sitter for those taking holiday vacations.

✔ **Tap your network.** Ask friends and family members who work at companies that add seasonal workers for a heads-up if they know of positions that are unfilled or opening up.

✔ **Play the familiarity card.** At slack times, stop by businesses where you're already a customer and talk to the person in charge of hiring seasonal helpers. Knowing you're a loyal fan of the business can make it easier for a manager to add you to the team.

✔ **Make it personal.** Online applications are often standard fare at big national employers. An in-person visit to a specific location, when possible, allows you to meet the store or restaurant manager and is hands down the best way to get noticed. Be enthusiastic and energetic and dress professionally in case a casual encounter leads to an interview.

✔ **Follow up.** It's good business, and good manners, to call or email the person you met or interviewed with to thank him for his time. If the business has no immediate openings, don't be a pest, but try to keep tabs on hiring plans. As customer traffic builds during the remainder of the year, opportunities may pop up. By staying in touch, you position yourself to be top of mind for last-minute hiring decisions.

✔ **Be flexible.** You have a better chance of getting hired if you're willing to work whenever needed. Employers are often in the dark about just how many hours of help they'll require until the shopping season really gets percolating. So be clear that you can come in at the drop of a hat, work weekends and nights (if you can), and are open to tackling many kinds of jobs.

✔ **Highlight your availability.** It never hurts to let a manager know during an interview that you can also be available at other busy times during the year. For some employers, knowing they have to go through the hiring and training process only once can be an incentive to hire you now, knowing that they're filling future needs as well.

Going green with eco-friendly work

If you're eco-conscience, working for an organization involved with climate change awareness, renewable energy, wildlife conservation, or green construction not only provides a paycheck but also a great deal of personal satisfaction. Whatever your specialty, green organizations can use your expertise and your genuine interest in the environment.

If you're looking for a green career or resources to help you find a green job, check out the Environmental Career Center (www.environmentalcareer. com), a job-posting resource for the eco-friendly sector. I also recommend GreenBiz.com and its Green Jobs and Sustainability Careers Center, jobs.greenbiz.com.

Here are three green jobs to consider, depending on your skills and interests:

✔ **Green building consultant:** Older buildings, in particular, are getting serious facelifts. States, counties, and cities are offering incentives targeted at green building projects. Find out about the Leadership in Energy and Environmental Design (LEED) green building certification program at www.usgbc.org/leed.

✔ **Waste consultant or waste reduction coordinator:** If you're a recycling devotee, you'll revel in the chance to help companies and residential communities reduce waste. The National Recycling Coalition (www. nrcrecycles.org) offers webinars on a range of recycling topics and more. Some states now offer recycling certification programs via local colleges.

✔ **Eco-landscaper:** As an eco-landscaper, you'll be designing and building sustainable gardens and landscaping that are cheaper to maintain and environmentally friendly. The Ecological Landscaping Association (www.ecolandscaping.org) is a great place to find out about the training and credentials required. Many community colleges and universities offer certificates and degrees in sustainable landscape design.

Green employers want to hire job candidates who walk the talk. Claiming that you're committed to the environment isn't enough. Employers will know in a heartbeat if you aren't authentic. If you want to pursue a second, green career, get involved in environmental causes in your community, the nation, and the world.

Taking your job search on the road

To combine work with travel, consider work camping — taking on jobs at campgrounds, national and regional parks, marinas, and resorts. Jobs may include office work, grounds keeping, housekeeping, maintenance, handyman work, coordinating social activities, managing rentals, serving as an interpretive guide, or handling retail sales. Past experience in the type of available work helps. Expect on-the-job training if necessary.

To find out about work-camp opportunities, visit CoolWorks.com (www.coolworks.com) and Workcamper News (www.workcamper.com). The most popular gigs are as hosts, housekeepers, and maintenance workers at campgrounds and government-owned parks. Many also work at NASCAR tracks, wildlife sanctuaries, Christmas tree lots, and pumpkin patches.

Feeling at home with home-based jobs

One of the great American dreams is to work at home, having a flexible schedule and working as much or as little as desired or needed to make ends meet. Unless you require a lot of social contact primarily obtained through work, you'll probably like working at home as much or even more than you had imagined. The two big questions you need to answer before you make the leap are: "Is the work safe" and "What sorts of opportunities are available?" In this section, I answer those two questions.

Is it safe?

Con artists often dangle the home-based job as a carrot to get people to hand over their cash or their personal information, which the con artists use to steal. Still, many work-at-home opportunities are legitimate. Organizations often save money by outsourcing work to home-based workers, avoiding the overhead of maintaining office space and equipment and paying benefits.

Although you may not be able to avoid risks entirely, you can minimize your exposure to risk by taking the following precautions:

✔ Work only for brick-and-mortar employers — those that have a physical address, a phone number, and a domain name.

✔ Never give any personal or financial information, such as your Social Security number, birthdate, or bank account or credit card numbers over the phone or online until you've done your research and confirmed that the organization and the person claiming to represent it are legitimate.

✔ Search the web for the organization's name followed by "scam," "rip-off," or "complaints" to tap into any online discussion about the organization that may reveal it's not legitimate. Also, search the organization's name at the Federal Trade Commission's website (www.ftc.gov).

✔ Check for complaints with the Better Business Bureau (BBB) in your area and the area in which the company is headquartered, and verify the organization with its local consumer protection agency and state's attorney general.

✔ Contact one of the organization's reps and ask what specific tasks you'll have to perform, whether you'll be paid by salary or commission, who will pay you, and when and how frequently you'll be paid. Ask what the total cost to you will be, including supplies and equipment. Get answers to your questions in writing.

✔ Be wary of overstated claims of product effectiveness, exaggerated claims of potential earnings, and demands that you pay for something before instructions or products are provided.

✔ Be wary of personal testimonials that never identify the person so you can't investigate further.

What sorts of opportunities are available?

If you've set your sights on a work-from-home job, go straight to a company you'd like to work for and see whether it hires remote workers. A good place to start is the career section of its website. Sites such as FlexJobs.com (www. flexjobs.com) focus on legitimate work-from-home jobs and prescreen each job and employer to be certain they aren't scams. Here are some great work-from-home jobs to consider:

✔ **Translator-interpreter:** Fluency in two languages generally qualifies you for the job, but to work for certain employers, you need to know specialized vocabulary, such as legal or medical terms.

✔ **Mediator:** Arbitration and alternative dispute resolution (ADR) have steadily gained converts from those hoping to bypass lawsuits with onerous fees and often a drawn-out legal process. For guidance on how to make it as a mediator, check out *Success as a Mediator For Dummies,* by Victoria Pynchon and Joe Kraynak (Wiley).

✔ **Graphic designer:** If you have a talented and well-trained eye and know your way around graphics programs, you can find plenty of assignments designing websites, logos, letterhead, business cards, restaurant menus, marketing brochures, and much more. Local colleges and universities and the American Institute of Graphic Arts (www.aiga.org) are great places to go to find out how to get the training and certification required . . . and to find a job when you have what it takes.

✔ **Writer/editor:** If you have a flair for the written word and a clear grasp of spelling, grammar, punctuation, and usage, you can find a wide range of writing and editing jobs. Reach out to local associations and organizations, community newsletters, and other regional publications. Ask if they need an extra hand on an assignment basis for online and print articles, brochures, and press releases. Freelance writers can find postings on Elance (www.elance.com) and Freelancer.com (www.freelancer.com).

✔ **Grant/proposal writer:** If you have a knack for research, are detail-oriented, and have fundamental writing skills, grant/proposal writing could be in your future. To find out how to succeed as a grant/proposal writer, check out *Grant Writing For Dummies,* by Beverly A. Browning (Wiley). Check online job boards such as the Chronicle of Philanthropy (www.philanthropy.com) for job postings.

✔ **Bookkeeper/accountant:** Duties run the gamut from processing payroll checks to handling invoicing, accounts receivable, accounts payable, and other financial reporting. Some firms may ask you to monitor checking and savings accounts and track credit card bills. Although you may find work without being a certified public accountant (CPA), that certification will open a lot of doors. Visit the American Institute of CPAs (www.aicpa.org) to find out how to become a CPA.

✔ **Customer service representative:** You'll need an up-to-date computer (usually a PC), a high-speed Internet connection, a dedicated landline telephone during business hours, a telephone headset, a quiet place to work, and people and communication skills. Potential employers include American Airlines, 1-800-Flowers.com, and Hilton Hotels. Others use third-party companies who then hire home-based workers.

Barking up the right tree: Jobs for animal lovers

Nearly two-thirds of U.S. households have a pet, and last year they spent an estimated $60.59 billion on them, an increase from $17 billion in 1994, according to a survey by the American Pet Products Association in Greenwich, Connecticut. If you love animals, and you're good with them, you can tap into this market for full-time, part-time, or seasonal work in the following roles:

✔ **Pet sitter:** As vacationers head off for school breaks and summer frolic, someone's got to tend to those members of the family that can't fit (or fit quietly) in the suitcase. As a pet sitter, you're generally self-employed, so you'll have to drum up business on your own. After you're established locally as reliable, you should have no trouble filling open slots.

Consider joining the National Association of Professional Pet Sitters (www.petsitters.org) or signing up with a national franchise operator such as Fetch! Petcare (www.fetchpetcare.com) or Pet Sitters International (www.petsit.com).

✔ **Pet shop owner or operator:** If you have a head for business, a love of animals, and expertise in caring for a wide range of critters from fish and reptiles to cats and dogs, you can tap into the fast-growing pet care industry and blend your work with your passion by running a local pet store.

✔ **Pet groomer:** Primping a pooch (or cat) runs the gamut from bathing, brushing, and cleaning ears and to clipping coats and trimming nails. You've got to be detail-oriented and in good physical condition. You may work out of a kennel, pet shop, your own home, or even a mobile grooming van. The National Dog Groomers Association of America (www.nationaldoggroomers.com) offers certification as a groomer and can provide a list of state-licensed schools.

✔ **Dog walker:** Expect to walk in all kinds of weather at least twice a day. The trek can take a degree of fitness and physical strength, depending on the size and demeanor of your charges. Walking more than one dog at a time is not unusual, if you have the strength and dexterity. This word-of-mouth business can be bolstered by good relations with veterinarians, pet shop personnel, and groomers. DogWalker.com (www.dogwalker.com), an online directory of dog walkers around the country, offers educational resources for those starting out.

✔ **Veterinary technician:** If you love animals and have an aptitude for science and the willingness to go back to school to ramp up the necessary skills, you've got a great chance of landing a job as a vet tech — especially if you live in a rural area. Veterinary technicians usually have a two-year associate's degree in a veterinary technology program. In 2013, 217 veterinary technology programs were accredited by the American Veterinary Medical Association (www.avma.org).

Furthering Your Research

Look to these sites to locate jobs that are available in the industry of your choice:

- ✔ **AnnualReports.com** (www.annualreports.com) allows you to search their database for free electronic files of annual reports. This is a great way for you to better understand the firm's mission, key accomplishments, and problem areas over the past year.

- ✔ **CEOExpress.com** (www.ceoexpress.com) offers links to newspapers and periodicals in a range of industries. It's a way to stay abreast of events that impact companies and industries. There is a 14-day free trial. Afterwards, the fee is $29 for the first year.

- ✔ **Google.com** (www.google.com) has an alert function you can set up for a particular company you're interested in so you can receive links to the latest news.

- ✔ **Highbeam.com** (www.highbeam.com) is an online library and research tool that provides access to more than 6,500 publications, including newspapers, magazines, journals, transcripts, and reference titles, and more than 80 million articles from trade journals and more, and is updated daily. Archives dating back over 25 years. A monthly subscription currently costs $29.95 a month.

- ✔ **Job-Hunt.org** (www.job-hunt.org) offers a comprehensive list of useful job-search resources and services on the web.

- ✔ **LinkedIn.com** (www.linkedin.com) is a powerful tool for researching a company and its employees. Use the company search feature.

- ✔ **Vault.com** (www.vault.com) allows job seekers to read employee surveys on companies and read message boards for sharing job-search information for a nominal fee. The mission is to provide the inside scoop on what it's really like to work in an industry, company, or profession.

- ✔ **ZoomInfo** (www.zoominfo.com) is a business information search engine used to quickly find information about industries, companies, people, products, and services.

Digging Up Leads in Lesser-Known Markets

Large, growing job markets and big employers are big targets for job seekers. You may achieve greater success by targeting smaller employers and lesser-known markets. Smaller employers, especially start-ups, may have a greater need for people with more life skills and wisdom — those who can hit the ground running and have no trouble filling in when duty calls. In this section, I steer you in the direction of these smaller, lesser-known markets that collectively represent a huge job market.

Seeking jobs in small businesses

Companies with fewer than 500 employees create two of every three new jobs, according to the U.S. Small Business Administration. Adjust your job-search strategy accordingly:

- ✔ Search the web for "fastest growing companies" followed by the name of your city and state.

- ✔ Check out the local edition of the *Business Times* (www.bizjournals.com) for information on local companies.

- ✔ Read your local newspaper's business section for news about start-ups and growing businesses. Nearly every local newspaper has a corresponding website you can subscribe to.

- ✔ Check company information on ReferenceUSA (www.referenceusa.com). You'll need a valid library card from a subscribing library to gain access to ReferenceUSA through your library's website. This database contains 24 million businesses in the United States, including a special section with 4 million new ones, where job openings may be less competitive than in established companies.

- ✔ Search LinkedIn's company directory after you identify a small business that interests you. You may well find someone in your network who works at that company. (See Chapter 10 for more about LinkedIn.)

- ✔ Scan your college's and even high school's alumni directory to see who has started a business.

- ✔ Talk with officers at local organizations, including Rotary Club, Kiwanis International, Lions Club, the Chamber of Commerce, the League of Women Voters, and so on. Ask which local businesses are new or growing.

✔ Look at the lobby directories in office buildings in your town, walk into any businesses that appeal to you and see if you can befriend the receptionist to help you connect with a hiring manager there. If you're open to working in a storefront, walk right in the door and introduce yourself.

Finding openings at start-ups

How do you find a job at firms that may have only a handful of team members and no budget to spend on hunting down candidates? Here's how:

✔ **Network.** Most entrepreneurs are too busy to post jobs and aren't interested in playing that game to track down the best candidates. They fill their open slots by asking people they know, the people their friends refer to them, and the candidates they meet through their personal and professional networking efforts.

✔ **Look for start-up events in your town.** With a little investigation, you can find innovation labs and networking groups, all focused on start-up companies. Search the web for your city followed by "start-up group" to find networking events for local start-ups. Go to a few events and always ask people you meet for other events you should be attending. Search on Meetup (www.meetup.com) to find start-up events near you.

✔ **Connect with entrepreneurs in your area.** When you attend networking events, connect with the big names you meet there. Look for people you can ask to do an informational interview and offer to buy coffee in return for his or her advice about how to navigate the start-up community and find the company that's the best fit for you.

✔ **Get to know a start-up recruiter.** Use LinkedIn to find a recruiter (see Chapter 10), or ask the people you meet at networking events. These recruiters are typically familiar in the start-up community. They'll know which companies are hiring. This takes some relationship building but can produce results.

✔ **Cold call start-ups.** Read the local business journals or search online for start-ups in your area. Call the CEOs of those companies directly. Explain why you're interested in meeting with them, and tell them why you're crazy about their mission and why you'd be a great fit for the company. Start-ups love hearing from people who are passionate about their mission.

✔ **Tap into start-up-specific websites and job boards.** Here are several to get you started:

- CrunchBase (www.crunchbase.com)

- StartUpHire (www.startuphire.com)

- VentureFizz (www.venturefizz.com)

- VentureLoop (www.ventureloop.com)

Pursuing positions with nonprofits

One lesser-known job field that's picking up a head of steam is the nonprofit arena. According to the 2015 Nonprofit Employment Practices survey by Nonprofit HR, a human resources consulting firm, 50 percent of the 362 nonprofits it canvassed say they expected to create new positions in the next year, up strikingly from just 19 percent in 2009. The greatest job growth will be in direct services to the public that require counselors, social workers, and intake coordinators. These positions are followed by program managers, fundraising/development workers, and personnel in education and community outreach.

The ability to hit the ground running is your calling card. Not having to shell out time and money for training is a real selling point for a nonprofit with pressing needs, tight deadlines, and perhaps a small budget. Having a genuine passion for the nonprofit's mission along with the skills they need puts you head and shoulders above the competition.

To find openings in the nonprofit sector, visit the websites of the nonprofits you're interested in. For a broader selection of nonprofits and jobs at nonprofits, check out these websites:

- The Bridgespan Group runs the online Nonprofit Jobs Center (www. bridgespan.org/Nonprofit_Jobs.aspx), which now has about 330 positions, including paid part-time and full-time jobs.

- The Chronicle of Philanthropy Job Search (www.philanthropy.com/ jobs) has hundreds of fundraising, programming, and other positions listed.

- Commongood Careers (www.commongoodcareers.org) is a headhunter for nonprofits looking to hire management-level types. Under the Find a Job tab, you can apply directly for openings with its clients.

- Encore.org (www.encore.org) is a go-to site for anyone interested in starting an encore career with social purpose. Click on Job Leads, then Job Listings and Encore Career Finder to search by field and location. Here, you'll also find links to other nonprofit job boards and a smorgasbord of videos and articles about nonprofit job hunting.

- The Foundation Center (www.foundationcenter.org) is a premier site that is chockablock with philanthropy information and news.

- Idealist.org (www.idealist.org) offers an extensive job board with more than 10,000 jobs currently posted. You can search by job function, such as fundraising, marketing, or accounting. You can also drill down to sort for part-time or full-time positions or contract work, and even salary and education requirements.

✔ Nonprofit Professionals Advisory Group (`www.nonprofit professionals.com`) works with nonprofits looking for specific candidates to fill positions and posts those on the site, but the team also offers a fee-based service, aimed at job seekers transitioning to the nonprofit world, that includes career coaching, job-search strategy, and résumé and interview help.

✔ The NonProfit Talent Match (`www.nonprofittalentmatch.com`), powered by The NonProfit Times, *the* trade publication for nonprofit managers, helps "connect people who want to make a difference to the jobs that do."

✔ The Philanthropy News Digest jobs board (`www.philanthropynews digest.org/jobs`) lists opportunities at foundations and nonprofits. Recently, there were 722 listings in the database.

Chapter 6

Joining the Growing Ranks of the Self-Employed

In This Chapter

▶ Making a living as a contract worker

▶ Building a business and hiring yourself to run it

▶ Doing a world of good while supporting yourself as a social entrepreneur

▶ Getting up to speed on the franchising biz

*I*f you're like many workers in the United States, your American Dream is to be your own boss and set your own hours. If you've ever freelanced, owned your own business, or worked on contract, you know how silly that notion really is. Instead of being your own "boss," a self-employed worker has dozens of bosses. They're just called something else, such as "customers" and "clients." "Setting your own hours" means choosing between working 60 to 80 hours whenever you want during the week instead of working five 8-hour days.

Still, the dream is alluring. You become the master of your own destiny, sinking or swimming according to your talents, skills, and vision. Although you do face the risk of your enterprise going belly up, you don't have to worry about landing a job; you simply hire yourself. And you're a lot less likely to get fired or laid off.

If I haven't scared you off yet, and you're still interested in flying solo, you've come to the right place. In this chapter, I present four approaches to becoming your own boss: finding gainful employment as a contract worker, starting your own business, working as a social entrepreneur, and buying a pre-fab business (a franchise).

Working on Contract

Part-time and contract staffing is on the rise. Recently, the big online job site CareerBuilder released a Harris Interactive survey of more than 3,000 hiring managers and human resource professionals, showing that more than a third of U.S. companies are operating with smaller staffs than before the recession. To keep business trucking along, these companies hire contract or temporary workers. It's an easy way for employers to get great, experienced staff and save money at the same time. That can be good news for you.

Being a contractor has its downsides, of course, such as, typically, no health insurance and no paid holidays or sick leave.

Getting sold on the idea

I'm a big fan of contract work, especially for people who are retired or are considering a job or career change, for several reasons:

- ✓ **It gives you something to do if you're not currently employed.** Don't discount this. Having a sense of purpose improves your mood and attitude.

- ✓ **It gets you in the door.** It may lead to full-time work with an employer eventually. Don't miss the opportunity.

- ✓ **It brings in some cash.** You can make your experience a plus. Employers are typically willing to pay you generously, providing you have the chops and can solve their problem or meet their need quickly. It lets them bypass the hand-holding and learning curve stage that a younger, less experienced but lower-paid worker may require. And when you're making money, you feel better about yourself. You feel valued, more confident.

- ✓ **It provides an opportunity to test drive different jobs.** With a short-term "dip in the pool" assignment, you can find out whether this is something you really want to do. Do the job first: moonlight, apprentice, volunteer. If you can get paid for it, go for it. That's the only way you'll know whether the new career is all you dreamed it would be.

- ✓ **It builds your professional network.** Nurture relationships with coworkers during your assignments. You never know where contacts may lead you.

- ✓ **It secures for you new and up-to-date references for future employers to contact to find out about what you've been up to lately.**

- ✓ **It pads your résumé with current experience.** It's a great way to fill the gaps in your résumé.

> ✔ **It sharpens your skills.** You know the mantra: Use it or lose it.
>
> ✔ **It gets you psyched about a work project without the pressure of long-term expectations.** No job is forever, anyway. This one may be shorter than most, and that can be tremendously liberating.

Consider yourself the CEO of your own small business, even if you have a full-time job. Your primary employer is simply your largest client. I always did side jobs when I had a full-time position. That prepared me for my current self-employed status and gave me a ready list of clients.

Hone your yarn spinning. Even if the assignment was the pits, and that's always possible, find a clever way to use the experience in a positive way. It can be a great example of your work ethic or your ability to helicopter in and solve a problem, or it can fill a professional need for a company. Make the time spent part of your personal career story. Exercise your poetic license.

Lining up contract gigs

Lining up contract gigs isn't all that different from finding a job, except that you now must find *jobs,* plural. Your former employer may become your first and biggest client, and then you can expand out from there, perhaps working for your former employer's competitors, clients, and vendors (assuming you don't have an agreement not to do so). To expand your clientele, network, search the job boards, and let people know that you're looking for projects or temporary assignments. You may also want to tap temp agencies. Another way to expand is to add services, if you have additional skills that weren't needed in your previous position but that your clientele would be willing to pay for.

When you're engaged in a project or temporary assignment, collect names and contact information for all the people you work with. One project or temporary assignment often leads to others.

You can drum up additional work online by using service marketplaces that connect freelancers with clients. Setting up an account is free, but you usually pay the marketplace a percentage of your earnings. Here are a few sites you can use to hawk your services:

> ✔ **Elance** (www.elance.com) is for freelancers in all fields, including writers, editors, graphic designers, translators, marketing specialists, and web developers. Elance keeps 8.75 percent of whatever you earn.
>
> ✔ **Fiverr** (www.fiverr.com) is another freelancer marketplace like Elance. Fiverr keeps $1 for every $5 gig you sell.

- **Freelancer** (www.freelancer.com) enables clients to post projects they need done and allows talented freelancers to bid on them. Freelancer generally collects 3 percent of all payments from clients and 10 percent from the freelancer.

- **Guides.co** (www.guides.co) is a service that "connects people who know with people who want to grow." You create a multimedia guide with text, images, audio, video, and so on, and interested members can purchase your guide. When they do, you receive 95 percent of the proceeds.

- **Guru** (www.guru.com) helps businesses connect with freelance workers in more than 160 fields of expertise.

- **HourlyNerd** (www.hourlynerd.com) is an online, on-demand freelance marketplace connecting MBA graduates and students with businesses looking for a flexible, cost-efficient way to address business challenges. Those who work for HourlyNerd can make as much as $300 an hour. Many of the companies are seeking marketing, funding, or strategic planning advice. HourlyNerd charges the client 15 percent and the contractor 5 percent.

- **Skillshare** (www.skillshare.com) connects teachers in all fields with students interested in those fields, so if you have valuable skills and a knack for teaching those skills to others, check out Skillshare. Compensation is based on the number of students enrolled in your courses. You're also paid a referral whenever someone clicks your unique teacher referral link and becomes a member.

These types of marketplaces generally value older workers, says Jeff Williams, CEO of Bizstarters (www.bizstarters.com), a company that provides coaching and training to older entrepreneurs. "If you can deliver the solution, your age is not important." The keys to success: a solid knowledge about a specific subject, a knack for consulting, and an ease with selling services online.

If you plan to make contract work your full-time occupation, I recommend that you build a strong brand, as explained in Chapters 9 and 10. A strong brand presence helps you build your clientele by establishing you as an expert in your field and someone who can be trusted. Prospective clients want to know the person they're hiring before they sign you to a contract.

Running your contracting operation as a business

When you work as a contractor, you're a business, and you need to run your operation as a business. Here are some of the business chores you must attend to:

✔ **Become a legitimate business entity.** Check with the Small Business Administration (SBA at www.sba.gov) in your area to find out what you need to do in terms of registering your business with the state and obtaining a business license and permits to operate in your area. You also need to determine whether you want to operate your business as a sole proprietor or as a corporation, such as a Limited Liability Company (LLC), S Corporation, or C corporation. Certain legal protections and tax benefits and responsibilities are associated with each. Consult an attorney and tax specialist to find out more about your options.

✔ **Withhold and pay estimated quarterly income taxes.** Independent contractors are required to pay quarterly estimated income taxes to the federal government, the state, and perhaps even the county and city in which they live. Consult a local tax expert to find out more about your tax obligations, get assistance estimating the amounts you're obligated to pay, and find out when and where to send payments.

✔ **Pay attention to the paperwork.** You'll need to keep a detailed record of payments received and expenses, including travel expenses (mileage, restaurant and hotel receipts, and so on). In addition, unless you get all your work through a third party, such as Freelancer, you'll need to invoice clients for payments and perhaps provide them with receipts. You may also need to draw up a standard contract (with the assistance of a contract attorney).

✔ **Check your insurance.** Add a rider to your homeowner's or renter's policy to cover any business equipment and supplies. You may also need liability insurance, just in case a client decides to file a lawsuit against you. Each state has rules about insurance that can be offered to home-based outfits. Talk to your insurance agent to assess your needs.

Avoiding common pitfalls

Not everyone makes it as a contract worker. Some workers perform better in a standard workplace setting where nearby coworkers provide social interaction and hold one another accountable just by being in close proximity. To boost your success, consider these suggestions:

✔ **Set and keep a regular work schedule.** A schedule serves two purposes. First, it helps to ensure that you work a set number of hours per week. Second, it prevents work from bleeding into the rest of your life.

✔ **Set a monthly financial goal.** If you need $30,000 a year to survive and $60,000 to live your desired lifestyle, add 30 percent or more to cover income taxes and expenses. That's $39,000 to $78,000 you need to gross, which represents $3,200 to $6,400 a month.

✔ **Know what you're worth.** Research the going rate for what you do. Many contract workers have websites where they post their rates. Contact other contract workers in your field and discuss rates. If they're reluctant to share, tell them that you're looking into entering the field and you don't want to undercut others on price; they should be more cooperative after hearing your concern.

✔ **Don't agree to a fixed price for unlimited work.** Be very specific about how much work you're going to do for X dollars. Otherwise, you either find yourself earning about $1.75 an hour or upsetting clients who feel as though you're changing the terms of the agreement. Setting a fair price is a huge challenge, because many times you enter into a project not knowing the amount of time involved. If you can charge by the hour, that's usually best.

✔ **Calculate a day rate.** Some clients hire contractors for three- to six-month assignments and require them to work onsite like a standard nine-to-five job. If you're working in a client's office, I recommend charging a day rate, for instance $500 to $600 per day. Some clients will pay overtime by the hour above that amount.

✔ **Track the time you spend on projects.** By tracking your time and knowing the total paid for a project, you can calculate your hourly wage and adjust your quotes for projects accordingly.

✔ **Expect and plan for tech crises.** If you're working remotely, make sure you have an in-house or on-call tech support person to assist you if you encounter a technical glitch or have a question.

✔ **Find or start a professional group for people in your line of work.** A group provides a forum for human interaction that's essential for your mental and emotional well-being. In addition, you may need to talk shop with others to vent frustrations with clients and share advice on how to overcome common challenges.

Launching Your Own Business

In 2009, the Ewing Marion Kauffman Foundation report "The Coming Entrepreneurship Boom" predicted that the United States would soon see an entrepreneurship boom, "not in spite of an aging population but because of it." Entrepreneurs age 55 to 65 accounted for 26 percent of all start-ups last year, up from 15 percent in 1996, according to the Kauffman Index of Entrepreneurial Activity.

According to the State of Entrepreneurship 2015 report released by the Kauffman Foundation, which specializes in studying and promoting entrepreneurship, many Boomers (born between 1946 and 1964) who became entrepreneurs during the information technology revolution in the 1980s and 1990s are today's serial entrepreneurs.

Data shows that these 50- and 60-year-old entrepreneurs have started more businesses in the last ten years, while in the meantime, the rate of business creation among 20- to 30-year-olds has slowed. With life expectancy rising, Boomers continue to be an important economic force for years to come as the Foundation concludes:

- ✔ Boomers have been, and will continue to be, an entrepreneurial generation.

- ✔ As they work longer and live longer, Boomers also will be entrepreneurs for longer periods of time.

- ✔ The aging of Baby Boomers will create numerous challenges and entrepreneurial opportunities — and Boomers will be the ones who start companies to capitalize on them.

- ✔ The promise of lifetime employment has declined dramatically for people age 35 to 64 over the past 50 years.

- ✔ With older generations living longer, healthier lives, they're likely to continue starting new businesses and mentoring young entrepreneurs.

- ✔ Transaction costs and the barriers to entry have fallen for entrepreneurs of every age.

If you're ready to become a member of one of the greatest generations of entrepreneurs in the United States, read on. In this section, I help you prepare for what's ahead so you don't get discouraged by unrealistic expectations, and I cover the fundamentals of getting your business up and running. (For additional guidance, check out *Starting a Business All-in-One For Dummies,* published by Wiley.)

Managing your expectations

Opening a business takes a lot of time, energy, drive, and commitment, especially in the initial stages. Expect to work long hours away from friends and family unless, of course, you're launching a family business or partnering with friends. Juggling the whole work-life balance thing when work is your life is tremendously difficult. Work seems to be embedded in every nook and cranny.

As with most endeavors in life, however, substantial investment often leads to substantial rewards — the joy of pursuing your passion; potentially more time with friends and family and more money to enjoy it; enough money to help friends, relatives, and others in need; a chance to make the world a better place; the health benefits of remaining physically and mentally active; and much more. And with years of business and life experience and an expansive professional network, you're far better equipped than a 20- or 30-something to start a business.

I interviewed hundreds of entrepreneurs and profiled some of their success stories in my book *What's Next?: Finding Your Passion and Your Dream Job in Your Forties, Fifties and Beyond* (Berkley), and I'm always struck by their confidence, tenacity, and hope. No one questions how challenging starting and running a business can be, but for most, the reward is an inner payout that blows right past the struggles and sacrifice.

Ready? I'll get around to business planning and that sort of thing later in this section, but here are my quick tips to get you over the first speed bump:

- ✔ **Don't think that you're too old to start your own business.** The Kauffman Foundation reported that the median age of founders is 39 — right at the midpoint of a typical professional career — and 69 percent are 35 or older. Nonprofit entrepreneurs tend to be older on average than their traditional counterparts. The average age for nonprofit founders is around 53, according to a study, Profiles of Nonprofit Startups and Nonprofit Entrepreneurs, by David M. Van Slyke, professor of Public Administration at Syracuse University and Jesse D. Lecy, assistant professor of public policy at Georgia State University.

- ✔ **Get comfortable with salesmanship or team up with someone who already is.** Sales is a key ingredient for success. Your confidence is only part of the battle; the other part is marketing yourself as you move along from those heady first few months or even years.

- ✔ **Brace yourself for greenhorn blues.** Moving into a new arena requires psychological preparation. You're the boss now and probably making a few mistakes. A supportive partner or best friend may be all the shoring up you need, but don't ignore the possible emotional setbacks you may experience as you work through the transition phase.

- ✔ **Make mistakes with grace.** Face it, the older you are and further along on your professional success ladder, the harder it is to accept criticism and responsibility for screwing up. Your ego just isn't as nimble and forgiving as it once was. Accept that trying new things means learning from your mistakes along the way. You'll be in a healthier, stronger place to move ahead. Doing things poorly is just another step toward doing them well.

Coming up with a business idea

When you're looking to start a business, opportunities are endless, but you need to pick one idea and make sure it's the right fit for you and your future customers or clientele. In this section, I explain various approaches to discover a business idea that's right for you. As you peruse your options, use the following criteria as test strips to determine whether the business idea has legs:

✔ The idea is going to be something you enjoy working on (because you're going to be doing it a lot).

✔ The idea serves a need that's not being met or solves a problem that's not being addressed satisfactorily.

✔ People want or will want the product or service you're selling. You can often gauge the marketability of a product by looking at its benefits. If it's going to solve a huge problem or save the buyer a huge amount of money, they'll want it. In other cases, you may need to perform market research; for example, without giving away your brilliant idea, talk to as many potential customers as possible to gauge future demand.

✔ You can offer the product or service for a price that customers or clients are willing to pay and that produces a sufficient profit to make it worth your efforts. Do your homework to estimate costs for manufacturing the product or making the service available, marketing it, delivering it, covering overhead, and so on. After you deduct the costs, is the profit that remains worth your efforts and the risk you're taking? Do some additional market research to find out how much prospective customers would be willing to pay for such a product or service.

✔ The idea is within your risk tolerance. If it's not, you're going to be a nervous wreck until the business turns a significant profit, which may take months or even years.

Now that you have a few benchmarks for judging ideas, you're ready to start brainstorming ideas to judge. Get your pen and paper handy and read on.

Looking to your current occupation for ideas

One of the easiest, quickest, and least risky business ideas is to keep doing what you were doing as an employee but doing it as a contractor. (See the earlier section "Working on Contract" for details.) But that's not the only option for transitioning from employee to business owner in your own field. You could start a business that serves the needs of your industry in other ways, perhaps by inventing a product or service that solves a common problem your former employer had but never managed to solve. Or perhaps you thought of a way to use the service or product your former employer sells to make money in a different way.

As an expert in some aspect of the industry or field you're already in, you have the knowledge to innovate in that industry or field, so that's the first place to look for new business ideas.

Turning a hobby into a profit

Turning a hobby into a business may really pay off, but doing so can take a while. That's the finding of a recent study that looks at entrepreneurs who start a business based on a personal pursuit. In the study, published in the

Journal of Business Venturing, these entrepreneurs lagged behind other founders in the first few years of developing their enterprises. But they caught up after 45 months in terms of pace. In the end, the hobby-to-business founders were more likely than others to produce revenue, achieve a profit, and have a deep commitment to their business.

So look to your hobbies and pastimes for business ideas. Are you musically inclined? Do you like to garden, bake, do crafts, write, take photographs, or play games? Whatever it is you do, you may be able to turn it into a money-making venture. Just try not to ruin your avocation by making it your vocation, to borrow a play on words from Robert Frost.

Cashing in on your natural gifts

Some things can't be taught. They just come naturally to you. We're all born with a distinctive set of talents that are as singular as fingerprints. These aren't skills that we learn along the way or passions discovered over the years. These are inborn gifts. It's the way your voice sounds, for instance, or your athletic prowess, or your inner mechanical capability.

If you aren't certain of what you have a knack for, ask friends, relatives, and colleagues. They may point out things you simply take for granted. Think about what you've been good at since you were a kid. If you're uncertain, though, several organizations, including the Rockport Institute (www.rockportinstitute.com), provide career-testing programs that can help you assess your natural talents. And AARP's LifeReimagined.org offers interactive programs that help you identify your interests, values, goals, and purpose.

Here are a few jobs where you can follow your talent to make money. These jobs may offer flexible hours and can be on a full- or part-time basis:

- **Voice-over actor/artist:** If you've been blessed with a deep, resonating timbre, or perhaps a smoky, husky purr, it might be time to put it to work. The need for voice talent is rising, thanks to the increase in online multimedia websites and audiobooks. The variety of possible gigs ranges from commercials to web videos, audiobooks, documentaries, business and training videos, telephone messages, and applications. Last year, the freelance website Elance (www.elance.com) touted voice acting as one of the fastest-growing fields, with a threefold increase in job postings on the site.

- **Organizer:** If you're great at and enjoy organizing offices, kitchens, bathrooms, garages, sheds, and other spaces, consider creating a business that offers your organizational skills to others. Your skills can come in particularly handy for retirees who are seeking to downsize. You may even offer additional services, such as selling property on eBay and through various other means.

✔ **Medical equipment maintenance and repair:** Were you the kid who always took things apart in the garage for the sheer fun of putting them back together? From wheelchairs to gurneys, if you've got the fix-it gene, this is a fast-growing job that plays right into your innate mechanical ability. Employment of medical equipment repairers is projected to grow 31 percent from 2010 to 2020, according to the Bureau of Labor Statistics (BLS), much faster than the average for all occupations. You can start your own business or work for someone else.

✔ **Calligraphy artist:** Harness your power of penmanship. In the digital world, where the electronic signature is becoming status quo, those who can create flowing cursive writing with smooth coordination and fine motor skills are few and far between. You can use your dexterity to create fonts and scripts for company logos, wedding invitations, place cards and menus, among other word-based undertakings. You probably won't get rich, but there's work for someone who practices the antique art of calligraphy.

✔ **Seamstress and tailor:** Sewing like a pro requires a mixture of sharp hand-eye coordination and artistic flair. The job boils down to dexterity and details. And, truth is, for many people, simply threading a needle is maddening. Old-fashioned sewing has become a fading art, even though finding someone who can perform the job with panache has been in steady demand. Nearly half of all seamstresses and tailors are self-employed, according to the BLS.

✔ **Senior fitness trainer:** The nitty-gritty: If you're a natural athlete, working out is in your blood. That's why teaching active adult exercise classes might just be your dream job. More fitness clubs and gyms across the country are offering classes catering to the silver-hair set, according to fitness industry experts. Overall, employment of fitness trainers and instructors is expected to grow by 24 percent from 2010 to 2020, faster than the average for all occupations.

Getting help

While starting a business carries a ring of independence, you have a better chance of succeeding if you reach out for help. Here are some resources you can tap for help in starting a business:

✔ AARP's Guide to Encore Entrepreneurship (www.aarp.org/StartaBusiness) is part of a collaborative effort between AARP and the Small Business Administration (SBA) to connect entrepreneurs with the resources needed to start or expand a small business. Through videos, quizzes, articles, and webinars from the AARP/SBA Encore Entrepreneurship Series, the site covers topics such as writing a business plan and raising money.

- AARP's Life Reimagined (www.lifereimagined.org) has a number of ideas to help plan your next career move to become a business owner.

- The Association of Small Business Development Centers (www.americass bdc.org), a joint effort of the Small Business Administration (SBA), universities, colleges, and local governments, provides no-cost consulting and low-cost training at about 1,000 locations.

- The Kauffman Foundation's FastTrac Boomer Entrepreneur program (www.fasttrac.org/entrepreneurs.aspx), in collaboration with AARP, is piloting specialized ten-week courses in both English and Spanish in select cities. Up to 20 applicants will be accepted in each course.

- Lawrence N. Field Center for Entrepreneurship at the Zicklin School of Business at Baruch College offers a free, online, open-source entrepreneurship curriculum intended for people over 50. It includes help with developing business plans, obtaining loans, gaining access to business start-up incubators, and meeting mentors to serve as sounding boards. For more information, visit www.blogs.baruch.cuny.edu/field center/.

- SCORE (www.score.org) is a nonprofit that provides education to entrepreneurs. At SCORE, working and retired executives and business owners donate their time and expertise free of charge in person or online.

- Senior Entrepreneurship Works (www.seniorentrepreneurship works.org) is a nonprofit organization designed to engage, empower, and connect would-be entrepreneurs over the age of 55.

- The Small Business Administration (www.sba.gov) has loads of information about starting and managing a business. In fact, in the menu bar near the top of the home page is an option called Starting & Managing. Mouse over that option to access links to pages that cover nearly every aspect of starting and managing a business, from thinking about starting a business to paying taxes and hiring employees.

- The SBA website has a section specifically for 50-plus entrepreneurs at www.sba.gov/content/50-entrepreneurs. Also check out AARP's small business site www.aarp.org/startabusiness.

- Startup Nation (www.startupnation.com) is packed with practical information from quality sources relevant to starting, managing, and growing a business. In addition, it encourages and enables small-business owners and people seeking to become small-business owners to connect with and learn from one another.

Find a mentor. Connect with someone who started a business similar to yours and ask the person to be your mentor. Try finding someone in your existing network who fits the bill. If you can't find someone you're already connected with, track down candidates online. Many of the resources listed in this section are good places to start looking. PivotPlanet (see Chapter 3) lets you connect with expert advisers via one-on-one video and phone conferences, for a fee. Look for an entrepreneur mentor who has the following qualities:

✔ Knowledge and confidence in the skills you lack

✔ Business acumen and a successful track record in starting and running a business — someone who's walked the walk and succeeded

✔ Practical, honest, and supportive all at the same time

If you're planning to launch a major business venture that requires financing possibly through investors, consider assembling an advisory board — a diverse group of three to eight individuals who have a proven track record in various areas of starting and running a business. By diversity, I mean some men, some women; some older and some younger; conservative players and risk takers; creative and practical. They can guide you and may lead you to investors and customers.

To find prospective board members, tap your network of people who have experience with your type of business (and maybe some who don't) and invite about three to five of them to join your board. Then, conduct either virtual or in-person meetings with them on a periodic basis to discuss two to three issues of key importance. Board members are typically compensated by a certain percentage of equity in the company (0.25 to 2.0 percent is common). But you may find friends and other associates willing to offer their expertise pro bono.

Writing a solid business plan

Writing a business plan before launching your business is essential for two reasons: process and product. The process of writing the plan forces you to consider key factors to achieving success and helps you define your vision. The product (the finished plan) provides a road map of how to get from point A to point B. Although you may need to take some detours along the way to get around roadblocks, having a plan in place keeps you on track. The product is also necessary if you need to apply for a loan or other financing.

There's no strict model to follow, but in general, a simple plan should be about 20 pages and contain the following sections:

✔ An **executive summary** that explains what your business will do, who the customers will be, why you're qualified to run it, how you'll sell your goods and services, and your financial outlook.

✔ A **detailed description** of the business, its location, who your management team is, and what your staffing requirements are. Also include information about your industry and your competition.

✔ A **market analysis** that targets your customers more specifically (demographically), including age, gender, and where they live. The analysis also describes your sales and promotional strategy to reach them.

✔ A **realistic forecast** of start-up outlays — cost of raw materials, equipment, employee salaries, marketing materials, insurance, utilities, and fees for attorneys and accountants — along with projections for gross and net annual profit.

Search the web for "business plans." You may even want to narrow your search for business plans in a specific industry or for a specific type of business, service, or product. You'll find plenty of examples. Another great resource is *Business Plans Kit For Dummies,* by Steven D. Peterson and Peter E. Jaret (Wiley).

Financing your enterprise

For most businesses, securing capital is the biggest obstacle. Research the start-up costs for your business and develop a plan with your financial advisor to ensure that you'll have the funds you need. Here are some sources of financing to explore:

✔ **Personal savings:** Most start-ups are financed with an entrepreneur's own money.

✔ **Loans from banks and credit unions:** For many who want to start a business, the local bank is frequently a first stop for financing, but don't hold your breath; many banks won't approve loans for start-up businesses. In the off-chance you find a bank that will, you'll need a clean credit record, an excellent credit score (720 or higher), a solid business plan, and probably a good chunk of your own change invested in the business.

✔ For more about securing a small-business loan, check out BusinessUSA (www.business.usa.gov), the federal government's site for entrepreneurs seeking small-business loans. An SBA-guaranteed bank loan can lower your down payment and monthly payments. To find a bank offering one of these loans, check the Local Resources section of the SBA's website as well as the site's loans and grants search tool.

✔ **Home equity credit lines or loans:** If you've built up some equity in your home, a home equity line of credit is a fairly easy route to gain access to cash, and interest is generally manageable. Lenders typically let you borrow 75 to 80 percent of your home's value, minus the amount of money you still owe on the mortgage. With a line of credit, you borrow money on an as-needed basis up to the amount of the approved loan.

✔ With a home equity line of credit, you're putting your house up as collateral. If you can't make the monthly payments or pay the loan in full when it becomes due (typically 10 to 15 years down the line), you risk losing your home.

✔ **Friends and relatives:** Members of your inner circle may be willing to lend you cash interest-free or at a low rate. Put everything in writing to avoid misunderstandings that may arise over the loan's terms, including repayment dates.

✔ **Equity investors:** Equity investors may back you in exchange for equity or partial ownership. The SBA's Small Business Investment Company program (`www.sba.gov/category/lender-navigation/sba-loan-programs/sbic-program-0`) can offer leads. These investors typically fall into two groups:

- *Angel investors* are high-net-worth individuals who generally invest $25,000 to $100,000 and may consider investing in a good idea. Visit AngelList (`www.angel.co`) to get in touch with an angel investor.

- *Venture capitalists* are also high-net-worth individuals, but they're more likely to invest more, require much more than just a good idea, and perform much more due diligence. In many cases, they band together to form a venture capital firm to pool their investments.

Both types are typically swamped by requests, extremely careful with their money, and prefer growth-oriented sectors, such as technology and bioscience.

✔ **Crowdfunding websites:** A relative newcomer in start-up financing is *crowdfunding,* virtual fundraising campaigns intended to typically raise relatively small amounts of money from donors who are not repaid. For details, visit crowdfunding sites, including Kickstarter (`www.kickstarter.com`), Gofundme (`www.gofundme.com`), and Indiegogo (`www.indiegogo.com`).

✔ **Crowdlending websites:** *Crowdlending* is a variation on the crowdfunding theme, but in this case, people expect to get their money back. Crowdlending sites include Fundingcircle.com (`www.fundingcircle.com`), Onevest (`www.onevest.com`), Accion (`www.accion.org`), and Kiva Zip (`zip.kiva.org`). Many crowdlending sites specialize in making no- or low-interest microloans (up to $25,000) to impoverished individuals who want to start businesses. The SBA also issues microloans up to $50,000. In general, interest rates range from 8 to 13 percent.

✔ **Economic development programs:** You'll need to do some legwork for this type of financing, but it could be well worth your time. Getting your firm certified as a woman-owned business, for example, can help you qualify for money that's only available to companies with that designation. Certification can also help you land government and big-business clients. For example, Michelin North America, based in Greenville, South Carolina, has provided $1 million in low-interest financing — loans range from $10,000 to $100,000 — to certain businesses, including women-owned firms, in parts of South Carolina.

✔ **State and local economic development agencies:** Some states and municipalities provide funding for economic development that's available for starting specific businesses in certain locations. Check the SBA's online directory and contact the office in your area to see whether any money is available and find out restrictions on its use.

✔ **Grant programs:** The SBA operates a network of nearly 100 Women's Business Centers around the country. They provide state, local, and private grant information to women eager to start for-profit or nonprofit businesses. Grants.gov (www.grants.gov) lists information on more than 1,000 federal grant programs. BusinessUSA (www.business.usa. gov) is another great resource to find out about federal government financing for businesses.

Here are a couple financing sources to steer clear of:

✔ **Credit cards:** Avoid using personal plastic at all costs. Most cards carry high double-digit interest rates, which is an outlandish price to pay for starting a business.

✔ **Retirement savings:** Don't put your future financial security at risk. Not only will you owe income taxes by taking money out, you'll lose the tax-deferred compounding and, if you're younger than 59½, you'll owe Internal Revenue Service withdrawal penalties. Please don't do that. No business is worth it. Furthermore, if the business fails, and your nest egg goes with it, the loss comes at a point in your life when it will be tough to rebuild that retirement fund.

A new twist is *rollovers as business start-ups* (ROBS), which raise the risks a bit higher, according to some experts. With this approach, business owners use their retirement funds, such as 401(k) assets, to finance or expand a business without incurring taxes or penalties. The account is rolled over into a new retirement fund. And that new retirement fund, in effect, becomes a shareholder in the start-up. It's legitimate, according to the Internal Revenue Service, but it's complicated. And if not set up perfectly, it could result in penalties and a big tax bill.

Here are seven tips for people who are keen to launch businesses and who need to attract money to their start-up (with input from Jeanne Sullivan, a noted venture capitalist, who I consulted for a NextAvenue.org column):

✔ **Hone your story.** You need one or two lines that sum up your product or service. The key is to be able to get that company story out of your mouth in a clear, succinct, short pitch. You'll also want to include a clear example of how a customer would use your product or service.

✔ **Know your market.** To get a solid grip on the potential size of your customer base, ask yourself: How big is it? Is it crowded? What niche are you trying to serve?

✔ **Be able to reel off your business's current finances and financial needs.** It's basic math — adding, subtracting, and percentages. Investors want to see that you're accounting for all the costs and not just dreaming of the profits.

> Brush up on the lingo. You need to be able to answer questions such as "What are the capital needs of the business over time?", "What are the gross margins?", and "What's your break-even timeframe?"

✔ **Prepare for show and tell.** If you're selling a product, make sure you have a prototype and get it in the hands of early pilot customers. Then you'll have something real to discuss with an investor.

✔ **Have a strategy for hiring your team.** Outline the key people you need over the next 18 months and recruit them — knowing that they may work for you now for equity or part-time until you get some funding.

✔ **Surround yourself with an advisory board — a brain trust.** Your advisers can be formidable references for you with investors. (See the earlier section "Getting help" for more about assembling an advisory board.)

✔ **Prepare to work harder than you ever have**. Most small-business owners work over 60 hours a week, according to a new survey by small business loan provider Kabbage. Prepare for the inevitable setbacks.

If all this sounds overwhelming, don't let that get you down. Based on what I've heard from the 50-plus founders I interviewed, you'll only wish you'd done it sooner.

Becoming a Social Entrepreneur

A *social entrepreneur* is a person who creates a business venture with the goal of making the world a better place. With more and more people over 50 seeking meaningful employment and facing a job market that makes it tough for workers over 50 to get hired, social entrepreneurship is becoming an attractive option for the 50-plus crowd.

In this section, I explain the ins and outs of getting started and making it as a social entrepreneur. But first, I want you to answer five key questions.

Before you head down the path of making a living by doing good deeds, answer these five questions:

✔ **What social problem or need are you truly passionate about?** The first step is finding an unmet need or a problem that's yet to be solved. Selecting your area of focus must come from your heart, from what you genuinely care about, so think carefully about your mission.

✔ **What's your plan for cracking the problem or meeting the need you've identified?** An innovative idea or creative approach to meeting the need or solving the problem is essential. Consult with several people who share your passion. The idea is to put something on paper that's adequate to show possible advisors, financers, and colleagues what you have in mind.

✔ **Do you have the skills and conviction required?** Gut check time. To run a successful operation, you need to be a CEO, CFO, marketing and sales specialist, and more. How good are you at rallying the troops, motivating others to join your cause and contribute their time, talents, and energy? Do you have the eagerness and energy to work long hours, perhaps with little or no pay for weeks or months on end?

✔ **Are you comfortable engaging with the public and asking for help?** As the founder of a nonprofit, you're typically the face of the organization. That means you need to be prepared for public exposure. In addition, you must be comfortable asking everyone in your network for support — friends, relatives, community members, and so on.

✔ **Can you obtain the funds?** Do you already have (or know how you can secure) the monetary and in-kind donations needed to support the organization for the foreseeable future?

Although its primary goal is to do good instead of make a boatload of money, a social entrepreneurship is still a business. Follow the guidance in the earlier section "Launching Your Own Business" to establish a firm foundation for your venture to give yourself the best chance of achieving your goal.

Making a nonprofit start-up to-do list

To start off on the right foot, take the following steps:

1. **Research the field you're entering and develop a detailed plan for getting from point A to point B.**

2. **Obtain first-, second-, and thirdhand knowledge of how nonprofits operate.**

   • **Firsthand:** Work with other nonprofits if you haven't done so already. Volunteer so you know what you're getting into and the challenges involved.

   • **Secondhand:** Talk with people who've started nonprofits to glean their perspectives and experience.

   • **Thirdhand:** Read up on nonprofits and take workshops on how to get started.

3. **Complete the IRS paperwork to establish a nonprofit entity.**

   IRS publication 557 (`www.irs.gov/pub/irs-pdf/p557.pdf`) contains information on all the organizational categories and instructions on qualifying for and applying for 501(c) status.

4. **Secure the funding to launch your nonprofit and sustain it for the foreseeable future.**

   See the earlier section "Financing your enterprise" for details, but ignore the parts about using your own money and borrowing against your personal assets. Don't put any of your personal assets at risk.

Here's some additional advice:

- ✔ **Don't underestimate the burnout factor.** Starting this kind of venture typically demands long hours, low or no pay (for some time), and the final responsibility for your project's success falls to you and you alone. And don't hold your breath for all the backslapping for a job well done. It may be years before your organization's work is acknowledged, if it ever is.

- ✔ **Be aware of your time commitment.** As founder, you may play a huge and active role in the early days, but eventually you'll need to have a plan in place to step off the stage. Making room for a new generation of leaders to take the reins is never easy, but it's critical to sustaining an organization over time.

- ✔ **Be careful not to lose your own identity in that of the nonprofit.** With all the time, energy, and passion that go into starting and nourishing a nonprofit, drawing the line between yourself and the organization can be harder than you think. This kind of work is personal and takes passion. Learn to make the space between.

Lessons from The Pink Fund

Molly MacDonald is founder and CEO of The Pink Fund, a nonprofit that provides financial aid to breast cancer patients. I interviewed her for my column that runs on PBS's NextAvenue. org. The 63-year-old breast cancer survivor offers the following ten tips to others who are eager to launch nonprofits around causes that are dear to them:

- ✔ **Start out by volunteering your time.** You may have to work for nothing for the first year.

- ✔ **Go slow.** Some people will applaud your mission but will hang back before offering funding until they see that you're successful.

- ✔ **Invite a well-known speaker to an event.** Bringing in someone with a following could gin up interest in your nonprofit when you're just starting out and under the radar.

- ✔ **Create a vision board to inspire you.** That's a collage on a big white poster board with

(continued)

(continued)

images and magazine cutouts that home in on your dreams and goals for your nonprofit.

✔ **Use your connections to get the word out through the media**. MacDonald got one of her former employers, the *Detroit Free Press,* to run a story on her effort, and more than a dozen other newspapers picked it up.

✔ **Seek out nonfinancial donations or barter for services**. The Pink Fund's office space, legal work, brochure, and website are all donated. Even its logo was designed by one of MacDonald's friends in exchange for a table.

✔ **Make sure your financials are in good shape**. Run a lean organization, keep impeccable records, file your taxes on time, and have a treasurer who advises you on how to spend money and stay within your budget.

✔ **Develop an intern program**. It saves some costs and gives interns work experience for ten weeks or so.

✔ **Use social media relentlessly**. Follow people on Facebook, Google+, LinkedIn, and Twitter to network and tap into their collective knowledge.

✔ **Network, network, network**. Attend community events and volunteer to speak at local Rotary Clubs and similar organizations. You never know who you'll meet or where your networking will lead.

You can read Molly MacDonald's story along with expanded tips at `www.kerryhannon.com/?p=4214`.

Getting help: Organizations that support social entrepreneurs

When you're starting a nonprofit, you're not alone. Many people have traveled the path, and almost everyone wants you to succeed. After all, you're striving to make the world a better place. One of the first steps is to get schooled in how to become a social entrepreneur and how to start a nonprofit. Here are several resources to check out:

✔ The Bridgespan group (`www.bridgespan.org`) offers information and guidance along with support and networking opportunities to help you get started.

✔ The Chronicle of Philanthropy (`www.philanthropy.com`) provides information and advice for leaders of philanthropic enterprises. You can also use this site to recruit people who want to work for a nonprofit.

✔ CommonGood Careers (`www.commongoodcareers.org`) recruits for nonprofit careers at management level.

- Encore.org (www.encore.org) is a go-to site for anyone interested in a career with social meaning and purpose; it includes a list of nonprofit job opportunities.

- GuideStar (www.guidestar.org) is a leading source on nonprofit organizations.

- Idealist (www.idealist.org) provides leads to more than 10,000 job opportunities nationwide in the nonprofit sector. This is a great place to go to recruit volunteers and interns.

- Independent Sector (www.independentsector.org) has research and resources of over 600 charities, foundations, corporations, and individuals.

- The National Council of Nonprofits (www.councilofnonprofits.org) is a network of state and regional nonprofit associations serving more than 20,000 organizations.

For more about starting a social entrepreneurship, check out *Social Entrepreneurship For Dummies,* by Mark Durieux and Robert Stebbins (Wiley).

Exploring Franchising Opportunities

Many boomers eyeing a second career fancy the idea of running their own business. Yet the risk and work involved in starting a business from scratch can be daunting. One way to ease into entrepreneurship is to purchase a franchise. Many franchises provide a full range of services, including site selection, training, product supply, marketing plans, and even assistance in obtaining financing.

Evidence of franchises' persistent popularity: Currently in operation are more than 780,000 franchise businesses, up from 736,114 in 2011, according to the International Franchise Association.

But franchising can be a tricky and expensive road. An initial investment ranges from tens of thousands of dollars up to $500,000. And it's not unusual to hear franchisees gripe about ongoing royalty and advertising fees. For example, to own a Subway franchise store is an estimated $116,000 to $263,000 in the United States. On top of that, however, franchisees pay fees of 12.5 percent of gross sales (minus sales tax) every week to corporate headquarters: Eight percent is for franchise royalties, and 4.5 percent goes to advertising. That's a lot of bread.

In this section, I shed light on franchising opportunities and offer advice on how to get started and what to watch out for.

Don't rush in

One of the biggest mistakes franchisees make is to hurry into business without doing enough research and soul-searching to determine whether franchising is right for them or whether a certain franchise is really a good match. Don't let the fear of missing out on a golden opportunity drive you to make a rash decision.

Take your time to evaluate your options and research franchises you may be interested in buying, including talking to other franchise owners, particularly owners of the same franchises you're interested in. Find out what they like and dislike about the franchise. For more about reality-testing a franchise opportunity, see the later section "Do your due diligence."

Do a self-assessment

Buying a franchise is a huge time and money commitment. You're putting tens or even hundreds of thousands of your own dollars on the line and will be working 60 or more hours every week to make your franchise a success. Before making that commitment, answer the following questions:

- **Is this concept, product, or service something I'm passionate about?** The answer had better be yes, because passion provides the drive to help you overcome the inevitable setbacks and frustrations.

- **Am I prepared to work hard?** Although the franchisor provides you with a ready-made business, its success is entirely up to you. You need to show up and work hard to satisfy your customers and attend to all the details of running a business. The franchisor won't do that for you.

- **Am I customer-focused?** To succeed, you need to be honest, fair, personable, service-oriented, and customer-focused. If you're not, you're more likely to drive away customers than attract them.

- **Am I optimistic and confident?** Optimism and confidence are contagious and convey to customers and clients your belief in the products and services you're selling.

- **Do I have the skills to run a business?** Franchisors are looking for people with transferable business skills such as sales, marketing, management, communication, customer service, and an ability to balance the books.

- **Am I a quick learner?** The learning curve is steep. You need to be able to read and follow instructions and "catch on" to the way the franchise wants the business run.

- **Am I willing to follow orders?** As explained next, franchisors make the rules, and franchisees follow them. If you're not comfortable with that, you may be better off starting your own business.

Accept that you don't call the shots

Franchising is a cookie-cutter approach to expanding a business. It's important to realize that regardless of the sales pitch, you're not really your own boss. You must follow the formula. There's little wiggle room for innovation. Franchises depend on the by-the-book execution of a business plan. For the most part, you have to be willing to do what you're told. And if you don't, you could lose your right to own the franchise.

Franchise guidelines may cover site selection, marketing materials, signage, employee uniforms, bookkeeping procedures, sales area, which vendors you use, and more. If you're independent and like to call the shots, franchising may not be your thing.

Do your due diligence

When researching franchise opportunities and narrowing the field, perform your due diligence to select a franchise that's likely to succeed and meet your goals. To perform your due diligence, take the following steps:

1. **Gauge demand for the franchisor's products or services.**

   Is there a need in your community that's not being met or a problem that's not being addressed that the franchise is uniquely positioned to meet or solve?

2. **Assess potential competitors.**

   Are other businesses addressing the same need or problem successfully within your community or online? What makes the franchise you're considering that much better that potential customers would choose it over what's already available? If the franchise has competitors and isn't significantly better than them, cross it off your list.

3. **Evaluate brand recognition.**

   Does the franchise have a strong brand presence and a good reputation in your community for delivering quality products and services? Do people talk about a desire to have that particular brand available locally?

4. **Search the web for complaints about the franchise.**

   Visit the franchise's website and find it on Facebook, LinkedIn, and Twitter, and read what others (customers and franchisees) post about it. Search the web for the company's name followed by "complaints" or "rip-off" to find out what customers and perhaps former employees and franchisees have to say about the franchise. Check also with the Better Business Bureau or local consumer protection agency for any complaints that have been filed.

5. Find out how long the franchise has been in the franchising biz.

A long track record proves that the franchise is doing something right.

6. Find out how supportive the franchise is.

Support often comes in the form of training and advertising. In addition, some franchises may offer financing to get up and running. If you get the feeling that the franchisor is more interested in its own wealth at the expense of franchisee success, cross it off your list.

7. Obtain and read the franchisor's disclosure agreement.

It provides contact information for previous purchasers in your region, audited financial statements, a breakdown of start-up and ongoing costs, and an outline of your responsibilities and the franchisor's obligations. Pay close attention to the pages in the document showing franchisee turnover. Names and phone numbers of former and current franchisees in your area should be listed.

Check whether the franchise you're exploring has the SBA's stamp of approval (`www.sba.gov/content/franchise-registry-approved-brands`). SBA-approved franchises are ones whose disclosure agreements have been reviewed and accepted by the SBA.

8. Contact current and former franchise owners.

Ask them what they like and dislike about the franchise and what they think could be done better. Contacting former franchisees may take some legwork, but the key is to find out why they're no longer in business.

Interview franchisees in person. Chances are that they'll be more forthcoming in a face-to-face meeting. Be aware that some may have signed confidentiality agreements that prevent them from talking to you.

Consult an accountant or attorney with experience in franchising to help you gauge the entire franchise package, including costs, projected profits, tax implications, and your ability to sell the franchise later, if desired.

Be sure you have enough money

How much can you afford to lose? Do you have a financial cushion or another source of income to cover your living expenses for a year or more? If not, pump the brakes. Create a budget and figure out how much you will need to live on while your start-up gains traction.

Although some franchises break even quickly, most take 12 months or longer before a newcomer can draw a salary. The initial fee for a franchise is clearly stated in the disclosure documents, but newcomers often underestimate operating costs.

Consider getting a loan

Many franchisees take out a loan to cover initial investment and start-up costs. You may want to try a bank where you've been a longtime customer or one that's familiar with the franchise field.

Applying for a preapproved franchise loan is often easier and quicker. To find the green-lighted list, go to the Franchise Registry (www.franchise registry.com) or to FRANdata.com (www.frandata.com). You can search by name if you have a certain franchise in mind or by industry. Plan on a down payment of 20 to 30 percent of the loan amount.

Check out additional resources

For more information and guidance on buying and running a franchise, check out these resources:

- ✔ American Franchisee Association (AFA at www.franchisee.org) is a national trade association of franchisees and dealers with more than 7,000 members.

- ✔ American Association of Franchisees & Dealers (AAFD at www.aafd.org) has developed fair franchising standards for franchisors and franchisees to adopt.

- ✔ Blue MauMau (bluemaumau.org) presents accounts of the ins and outs of franchising.

- ✔ The Federal Trade Commission's (FTC's) Franchises, Business Opportunities, and Investments page at www.ftc.gov/tips-advice/business-center/selected-industries/franchises,-business-opportunities,-and-investments features links to several relevant areas on the site.

- ✔ Read the Federal Trade Commission's (FTC's) "Buying a Franchise: A Consumer Guide" (www.ftc.gov/tips-advice/business-center/guidance/buying-franchise-consumer-guide), which is available on the web or as a downloadable PDF. It's a 16-page booklet that's well worth the time required to read it.

- ✔ International Franchise Association (IFA at www.franchise.org) is a great place to go to find out more about franchising and specific franchise opportunities.

- ✔ Small Business Administration's (SBA) Franchise Businesses page at www.sba.gov/content/franchise-businesses provides a good overview of franchising.

- ✔ Unhappy Franchisee (www.unhappyfranchisee.com) features stories of franchises gone wrong. What a way to end a section on franchising, eh?

For more information and guidance on starting and running a franchise, check out *Franchising For Dummies,* by Michael Seid and Dave Thomas (Wiley).

Chapter 7

Dealing with Special Circumstances

*F*inding a job can be tough, but the challenge may be even greater if you compound your age with other factors, such as a disability or an extended leave of absence from the workforce. Fortunately, these special circumstances often come with some additional support to help level the playing field. In this chapter, I help you find those resources. I also cover other special circumstances, including returning to the civilian workforce after military service and working abroad as an expat.

Looking for Civilian Work as a Veteran

After you've served in the military, you'd think that employers would be tripping over themselves to hire you. After all, you served your country, you're obviously a team player, you probably received specialized training, you traveled, you've gained valuable life experience, and you have a track record of "sticking with it." The reality, however, is that many employers are reluctant to hire veterans for several reasons:

✔ **Fear/stigma:** Some employers fear that veterans have higher incidents of post-traumatic stress disorder (PTSD) and suicide than the general population or have other undisclosed physical or mental illnesses that may compromise their ability to perform the required job duties.

✔ **Misplaced beliefs:** Some employers mistakenly believe that veterans require closer supervision and more direction than other candidates, because they've been accustomed to "following orders."

✔ **Inability to recognize transferrable skills:** Employers may not understand how artillery experience makes you qualified for their current openings, for example.

✔ **Concern over future deployments:** Unless you're in active reserves, this shouldn't be a concern, but some employers who see "veteran" on a job application may automatically assume that there's a possibility you'll be called to serve, and they'll need to scramble to fill your position.

As employers find out more about the value of hiring veterans, they're becoming more open to the idea, but you should still keep these points in mind as you apply for jobs and send out résumés. You may need to do more to help prospective employers understand how your job skills, experience, and character transfer to the position and meet the employer's needs.

In the following sections, I point out additional resources that can help you transition from military service to the civilian workforce.

Getting help through American Corporate Partners

The nonprofit veterans mentoring program American Corporate Partners (www.acp-usa.org) is dedicated to assisting veterans in their transition from the armed services to the civilian workforce. With the mentoring guidance of business professionals nationwide, ACP offers veterans tools for career growth through mentoring, career counseling, and networking opportunities. Much of the advice is parlayed via an online bulletin board where HR experts and seasoned professionals give advice in response to specific workplace and education questions posed by military vets of all stripes and ages.

ACP's mentoring program is open to all currently serving and recently separated veterans (including members of the Reserve and National Guard) who have served on active duty for at least 180 days since September 11, 2001. ACP's mentoring program is also open to spouses of veterans killed on duty and spouses of severely wounded post-9/11 veterans.

Unlike traditional "wisdom of the crowd" sites such as Yahoo! Answers or Ask.com, the volunteer contributors on ACP's bulletin board are highly credentialed and vetted beforehand. IBM employees created the website's online bulletin board and app on a pro bono basis.

ACP also pairs specific vets with corporate execs in more traditional mentor-protégé relationships. Although the initial effort was started by IBM, employees from corporations such as Alcoa, Bloomberg, Disney, PNC, UPS, and Yum! Brands now participate.

Checking out job sites for veterans

As a veteran, you can certainly take advantage of all the job-search websites and apps presented in Chapter 5, but several job-search sites are devoted exclusively to helping veterans, including the following:

- ✔ **FedsHireVets** (www.fedshirevets.gov) is a one-stop resource for veterans and their family members to find out more about jobs with the federal government. Here, you can find out whether you're eligible for Veteran's Preference, which gives veterans an edge over non-veterans. You must still apply for the position at USAJobs.gov (www.usajobs.gov). For more about finding and applying for federal jobs, see Chapter 5.

- ✔ **Hire Heroes USA** (www.hireheroesusa.org) has a team of former military and business professionals that teach veterans self-marketing skills and provide each veteran dedicated career coaching and workshops. The site also contains a link to the Hire Heroes USA job board (jobs.hireheroesusa.org), where you can search for jobs by title, key words, company name, and location. The organization partners with more than 200 veteran-friendly companies.

- ✔ **Hire Veterans** (www.hireveterans.com) enables you to search for jobs, post your résumé, and find out about job fairs for veterans. Employers and recruiters are encouraged to post jobs and search for résumés to find veterans to fill positions.

- ✔ **Military.com** (www.military.com) is the largest military and veteran membership organization, connecting service members, military families, and veterans to government benefits that include career and educational opportunities.

- ✔ **MilitaryHire** (www.militaryhire.com) enables you to post your résumé, so you can be discovered by employers and recruiters looking to hire veterans. This site also provides a job-search tool and career resources.

- ✔ **U.S. Department of Labor Veterans' Employment and Training Services** (www.dol.gov/vets) features links to find a job, look into apprenticeship opportunities, find out about programs and services, and obtain special assistance if you're a female veteran.

- ✔ **U.S. Department of Veterans Affairs Employment Services** (www.ebenefits.va.gov/ebenefits/jobs) provides résumé builders, career-assessment tools, and job banks. If you need additional training, you can find out about education and training programs and support for veterans.

- ✔ **Transition Assistance Online** (www.taonline.com) is a resource for transitioning service members, reservists, guardsmen, veterans, and their spouses from active military duty to the civilian workforce. It provides content on the transition process and related topics, along with a full service job board. All services for job seekers are free.

- ✔ **VetJobs** (www.vetjobs.com) is a leading military job board, sponsored by the Veterans of Foreign Wars (VFW). VetJobs is for all transitioning military, veterans, Department of Defense (DOD) civilians, and their family members. The VetJobs Employment Assistance section provides career advice and assessment tools and prepares a candidate for the job search and interviewing process.

Confronting the unique challenges of a female veteran

If you're a female veteran, you qualify for special assistance. Check out Joining Forces Mentoring Plus (www.joiningforcesmentoringplus.org), a group tailored to women veterans, military spouses, and caregivers of wounded warriors. The Business and Professional Women's Foundation is the organization behind the mentoring program, which provides unlimited free online career development tools and resources to participants. Advice from Joining Forces can help you translate your military skills into the next step in your career.

The organization has a particularly impressive toolkit for women. The group does everything from tracking down ways to pay college tuition for learning new skills to identifying successful female mentors who'll hone your career objectives and package your talents so you can find a great job or start a successful business. Mentors can help a female vet revamp her résumé, negotiate salaries, and identify training programs.

Knowing where to look

Success in finding the job you want often hinges on where you look. In addition to checking out the websites mentioned earlier in this section, look for career fairs and networking opportunities and check out veteran-friendly employers.

The Military Officers Association of America (www.moaa.org) hosts military career fairs around the country and has a job board on its website as well as an interactive tool to help you prepare for interviews and tips for tracking down the job you want. It also has a LinkedIn Career Networking group. The events and information are available to active duty, retired, former and National Guard/Reserve servicemembers of all ranks and their spouses and government employees.

At these career fairs, for example, job seekers have the opportunity to meet local, national and international employers, including Lockheed Martin, Amazon, JPMorgan Chase & Co., the National Security Agency, Shafer Corp., the Department of Veteran Affairs, and many more. And they feature several career-planning seminars to help military personnel tackle the challenge of transitioning to work life after the military. The seminars include

- ✔ Network Your Way to Employment
- ✔ Federal Job Application Preparation
- ✔ LinkedIn Best Practices
- ✔ Be Your Own Boss! Exploring Entrepreneurship

Some private companies have launched initiatives to hire more veterans, including AT&T; BAE Systems, Inc.; Bank of America; Blackstone; Boeing; Cisco Systems; Citi; Comcast; CVS; Deloitte; DuPont; Frontier Communications Corporation; General Electric; Google; Hewlett Packard; Home Depot; Honeywell; Humana; The International Franchise Association; JPMorgan Chase; Johnson & Johnson; LinkedIn; Lockheed Martin; McDonald's; Microsoft; Navistar; Oracle; Orkin; Prudential; Raytheon; Safeway; Sears; Siemens; Starbucks; Target; Unilever; U.S. Bank; UPS; Visa; Walmart; Waste Management, Inc.; Wells Fargo; and Xerox.

You can find a long list of companies that have committed to hiring veterans at www.whitehouse.gov/joiningforces/commitments.

Looking for Work When You Have a Disability

If you have a disability, you need to deal not only with the disability but also with employers who may disregard you because of it even when you're the best candidate for the position. Some studies estimate that unemployment among those with disabilities is as high as 80 percent. Yet many people with disabilities overcome the challenge by proving to at least one employer that they have what it takes to do the job.

In many ways, finding a job when you have a disability is like finding a job when you don't. You still have to use your skills to your advantage (Chapter 2); network (Chapter 3), search the job boards (Chapter 5), tailor your résumé to the position (Chapter 8), establish a strong, positive online persona (Chapters 9 and 10), submit job applications (Chapter 11), and ace your interviews (Chapters 12 and 13). In other words, you need to master the fundamentals.

Project confidence and optimism to overcome any misconceptions that prospective employers may have regarding your attitude. You need to connect with the decision makers personally, so they see past your disability.

Tracking down assistance

Seek assistance from organizations dedicated to helping people with disabilities find and keep jobs. Support is available at the national, state, and local levels and often includes education, training, and any physical and occupational therapy you may need to prepare you for the workforce. Here are a few resources to start your search:

- ✔ **ABILITYJobs.com** (www.abilityjobs.com) brings employers and job seekers with disabilities together. When you reach the home page, click the Job Seeker link and follow the trail of links to the job seekers area, where you'll find links to post your résumé, view job postings, set up job alerts, and create a job seeker account.

- ✔ **American Foundation for the Blind** (www.afb.org) is the place on the web to start your job search if you're blind or visually impaired. Mouse over Living with Vision Loss, near the top of the page, and click For Job Seekers to access the employment page. Here, you'll find links for creating a profile, registering with CareerConnect, exploring careers, making connections, finding a job, connecting with a mentor, and getting help with interviewing skills, résumé building, and disability disclosure.

- ✔ **CareerOneStop** (www.careeronestop.org) is sponsored by the U.S. Department of Labor's Employment and Training Administration to help U.S. citizens find the training and resources they need to pursue a career. Scroll down and click Workers with Disabilities to access a page that serves as your starting point. From here, you can find out more about the Americans with Disabilities Act, job-search resources, interview tips, insight on when and how to disclose a disability, job accommodations, vocational rehabilitation, and more.

✔ **disABLEDperson.com** (www.disabledperson.com) is a huge job board specifically for people with disabilities and the companies seeking to hire them. Here, you can search for jobs, browse jobs by category and location, set up job alerts, and find plenty of informative articles to help you in your job search.

✔ **Getting Hired** (www.gettinghired.com) is a job-search website dedicated to people with disabilities and employers looking to hire them. Here, you can search for a job by job title or key words, location, and category. The site also features a Career Tools section with articles, a career assessment, job recommendations, and interview training.

✔ **National Industries for the Blind** (www.nib.org) "and its associate agencies work to deliver quality products and services by employing thousands of eligible, visually impaired Americans." Here, you'll find job listings, a résumé builder, links to state resources, and much more.

✔ **RecruitDisability.org** (www.recruitdisability.org) lets you search for jobs by job title, key word, and location; browse jobs by category; build and post your résumé; set up job alerts; compare salaries based on industry, function, location, and more; and read plenty of articles to help with your job search.

✔ **SourceAmerica** (www.sourceamerica.org) bills itself as the leading source of job opportunities for people with significant disabilities. The organization and its partners provide training to people with disabilities, help them find jobs, and enable them to be successful at work. It is one of only two nonprofit agencies established to assist with the AbilityOne Program, a Federal program designed to provide employment opportunities to people who are blind or have other significant disabilities.

✔ **Think Beyond the Label** (www.thinkbeyondthelabel.com) lets you search for jobs by key word, job title, industry, and location and sort your search results by date. Click Jobs and then Jobseekers — Get Resources to find additional information to help with your job search.

✔ **USAJobs.gov** (www.usajobs.gov) is *the* place to go to find out about and apply for jobs with the federal government. See Chapter 5 for more about finding and applying for government jobs. Visit www.opm.gov/ policy-data-oversight/disability-employment for details about getting a job with the federal government when you have a disability.

Don't overlook state and local resources. Search the web for <your state> or <your city> or <your county> followed by "jobs disabilities" or "jobs disabled" to find links to state and local resources.

Being defined by your ability, not your disability

Kate Williams, 72, is blind, due to a progressive congenital eye disease that began to slowly erode her vision at 47. "It was devastating to me," Williams told me when I interviewed her for my NextAvenue.org column. "But I realized that I just had to learn to do things differently if I wanted to keep working." Today, Williams runs an employment program at Lighthouse for the Blind and Visually Impaired in San Francisco, California, to help people who are blind find jobs. "I have an opportunity to let people know that life is not being defined by your disability, but your ability," Williams told me.

Here are Williams' eight recommendations for people who are blind or have visual impairments:

- Start with a positive mindset. "You have to get out of the 'I can't do it. I'm not capable' mentality."

- Pinpoint a company where you really want to work. "Then, network to find someone you know who works there or has a connection."

- Skill up. "It's your responsibility to become qualified for the job with the right certifications and training."

- Find a mentor. "It's best if you can connect with someone who is blind and doing a job that interests you. The American Foundation for the Blind is a good resource."

- When relevant, disclose your disability to a potential employer. "My opinion is that you should always let your interviewer know in advance, after the interview date is set."

- Make eye contact. "You have to connect with your interviewer. That's not so easy when you're blind. So I teach them to 'look at the voice.'"

- Watch your body language. "Blind people tend to rock or sweep with their bodies. This movement makes people uncomfortable. And blind people often talk with their hands moving constantly, usually look down, or are stooped. Repeat to yourself: 'Shoulders back, head up.' This gives you a look of confidence and shows how you feel about yourself."

- Tap into the federal government job board. "Go to USAJobs.gov and then click on the link for individuals with disabilities. You can set up a profile and receive job alerts for jobs specifically for [people who are] disabled."

Williams won the Purpose Prize — awarded to Americans age 60 and older who are making an impact in 2014. Purpose Prizes are given by Encore.org, a nonprofit that's building a movement to tap the skills and experience of those in midlife and beyond who are improving their communities and the world.

Williams had one parting tip. "If you have a guide dog, make sure you give him a bath the night before you go on an interview." For the full story, visit `www.kerryhannon.com/?p=4174`.

Considering how employment may affect your disability benefits

If you're receiving Social Security disability benefits (SSDI) or Supplemental Security Income (SSI), you need to look into how employment may affect your benefits and Medicaid coverage. Special rules make it possible for people receiving SSDI or SSI to work and still receive monthly payments as well as health insurance coverage. However, the rules differ for each program. See www.socialsecurity.gov/pubs/EN-05-10095.pdf for a detailed explanation of the rules for each program.

Relaunching a Career Placed on Hold

Many women (and increasingly men) decide to step out of the workforce to stay home and raise their kids or care for a relative. A decade hence, when they want to return to the workforce, they often discover that doors aren't swinging open. Why? Several reasons:

- Technology has changed radically in the past decade. Odds are the job you had is handled a lot differently these days.

- Even with a strong economy, it takes a 55-year-old worker almost a year to land a job after losing one, according to the U.S. Bureau of Labor Statistics.

- Age discrimination is alive and well. Like it or not, this ugly phenomenon is a fact at many companies. A recent AARP survey found that nearly one in five people age 45 to 74 believe they didn't get hired because of their age.

- The corporate world values work experience, and no matter how you spin the story about your PTA service and volunteer work, staying home with the kids doesn't qualify as work experience in the eyes of many employers. You need to showcase the experience in a positive way. You can show how you can prioritize work issues or delegate tasks. Now is the time to get creative!

It's usually easier to get a job if you never left the workforce entirely. If not, here are some tips to help you return to the workforce:

- **Pump up your networking.** Yes, this really works. Networking isn't necessarily going to land you a job tomorrow; it's a process of developing contacts gradually. (See Chapter 3 for details.)

Show interest in what other people are up to and learn from them. When I'm at a networking event, I spend twice as much time listening as talking, with a goal of meeting at least three new people and getting their contact information.

✔ **Freelance or contract to get back up to speed.** Become a freelancer or contract worker (see Chapter 6), at least for the time being, to refresh your skills, get current and relevant job experience and references, and expand your professional network.

✔ **Add skills and certificates.** Not up on the latest technology or changes in your former field? Sign up for classes and make an investment in your future. A specialized professional certificate from a community college or trade association (with classes that you can take in person or online) may be the card you need to punch. Learning Advisor (`www.learning advisor.com`), powered by Kaplan in partnership with AARP's LifeReimagined.org, offers information about certificates, degrees, and scholarships. (See Chapter 2 for more about skill building.)

✔ **Dive into the social media pool.** Get comfortable with and use LinkedIn, Twitter, and Facebook. Employers expect it. (See Chapters 9 and 10 for more about using social media and networking in your job search.)

✔ **Look for jobs at small companies.** Small companies and businesses can't always afford to lure top-level talent with sweet benefits like stock options, 401(k) plans, and generous health insurance, so they may be thrilled to snag someone as sharp as you.

✔ **Volunteer.** Meaningful volunteering can be an excellent way to eventually land a job. You can demonstrate your skills helping out at a nonprofit and then tout your accomplishments when applying for a paid position. You may even wind up getting hired at the organization where you volunteer. A few recent surveys have shown that volunteering helps job candidates find work.

A networking success story

Here's an example of how networking paid off for one opt-out married mom: Sandy Shaw, now the vice president of corporate partnerships at the nonprofit Points of Light.

Shaw had a successful finance career but called it quits at 40, spending the next 15 years raising her two sons and volunteering in their schools. When her eldest son went off to college last year, she decided to look for a job with meaning and began networking with friends and former colleagues, widening that circle daily. She pledged never to end a phone call or leave a meeting without a new person to get in touch with. Six months later, Shaw landed her current job. It pays less than what she once made, but she loves it.

The moral of the story: Start networking now and keep at it until you find the job you want.

Working Abroad in Retirement

I write a lot about people who retire but continue to work part-time as a financial safety net and for the mental and social engagement, retirees who have made work a pillar of their retirement. Those who work abroad provide a twist on this theme.

Lots of these retired-but-working Americans are heading abroad to live and work. They've opted to use this chapter of their lives to put down stakes in a foreign town, where they can get jazzed about a new culture, find romance perhaps, and slow down the pace of their lives. Often, the move is a financial win, too, because it's cheaper to live in many overseas spots, particularly those in Latin America.

To join the ranks of the semi-retired workers living abroad, consider the following strategies:

- **Shop for a job that's in your wheelhouse.** You may accept contract assignments from former employers and other clients, essentially working out of your home — telecommuting gone global. You can also explore a range of jobs that involve teaching English, working as a translator or a tour guide for English-speaking tourists, or working on staff at a hotel where English-speaking travelers congregate.

- **Consider virtual jobs.** Generally speaking, if you have something you like to do online, you can do it from anywhere in the world with good Internet access. You don't have to pick a place to live based on whether you can find a job there. I recommend that you tap into what you've done all your life and turn it into a business you can do online.

- **Start your own brick-and-mortar business.** Many expats start small businesses such as art galleries, bistros, bed and breakfasts, retail shops, and real estate agencies.

- **Do your homework**. *International Living* magazine, which focuses on retirement abroad, offers a guide to the leading countries to open a business. It indexes factors in areas such as visas, setting up bank accounts, living expenses, local taxes, and language hurdles. In the most recent survey, Panama topped the list, followed by Belize, Ecuador, Columbia, Costa Rica, Nicaragua, and the Dominican Republic.

- **Go for an extended visit.** Spend six months or a year where you're thinking of starting your working retirement. Don't take a lot of dough with you, and don't jump to buy property straight away. You want to make sure the community is favorable to letting you actually do what you have in mind. Take the time to meet other like-minded expats and learn from their experience. Find an expat to mentor you if you can.

✓ **Know the local employment laws.** Find out whether you need a work permit for the job you want to do and make sure the country allows foreigners to do the job; some countries allow only nationals to perform certain services, such as providing medical treatment. Also, gauge the competition for the job you want to do; it's all about supply and demand.

✓ **Be open-eyed about the drawbacks.** Your Internet connection might flicker in and out at times, and the electricity may zap off for six hours at a time. Siesta time? Your bank may even shutter its doors at odd intervals.

✓ **Don't get tripped up by taxes.** The U.S. government requires U.S. citizens living and working abroad to file an annual tax return with the IRS.

I recommend that if you're going to work overseas and earn even a small salary, you spend the bucks to hire a tax adviser who is an expert in international tax issues. That's because tax laws for Americans living overseas can be confusing. Both the United States and your country of residence could try to tax your earned income while living abroad.

✓ **Report your foreign bank accounts to Uncle Sam.** Faithfully filing your 1040 with the IRS is not enough. If you hold a total of more than $10,000 in all your foreign accounts (and living abroad, you well might) you must also file Treasury Form 90.221, known as an FBAR, with the U.S. Treasury by June 30th of each year. And don't think you can safely ignore this obscure requirement. The financial penalties for not filing are stiff. Plus, the Foreign Account Tax Compliance Act means foreign banks must report information on U.S. account holders.

✓ **Tune in to business cycles.** Businesspeople who cater to tourists need to be prepared to ride the waves of the seasonal fluctuations in tourism. And uncertainties in the supply chain are not unusual when conducting business abroad. Moreover, you normally don't have access to credit.

✓ **Hire a translator**. Don't go it alone. Even if you're fluent in the language, hiring a bilingual assistant or advisor, who can pilot you through the operating challenges, is strategic. Of course, you want to hire someone who is trustworthy, so take your time and properly vet candidates. Importantly, to help you negotiate transactions with both employees and suppliers, that person really must have a grip on the business lingo. Business terminology can be quite different from that required for general conversation. Be careful not to sign a business contract without a legal advisor or terrific translator guiding you.

✔ **Learn proper etiquette for business relationships.** Slow down. Some deals don't get done until you've had a meal together. Breathing even a word about a financial transaction can't begin until you've had a lengthy repartee about someone's family or health. It's a total relationship, not a wham bam get down to business world in many places.

✔ **Study up on currency ins and outs.** Conducting business in dual currencies can pose quite a challenge. You may choose to operate only in U.S. dollars or on a cash basis, for instance, depending on your situation.

Tango dancing in Buenos Aires

When my friend Nancy turned 60, she became the "it" girl, she says. She took up tango dancing, lost weight, bought some cool high-heeled shoes, and felt really alive for the first time in years.

Then she took the next step. She moved to Buenos Aires. She bought a beautiful condo there and now tangos a couple of nights a week. She considers herself retired from her successful career as a financial journalist and book editor. As an expat, however, she still pulls in earnings from contract ghostwriting and editing assignments for book publishers in the United States.

It's seamless. She can talk to her clients via Skype. She emails and zaps copy back and forth electronically. Plus, the time zone is the same, so no one really even knows where her office is located.

Nancy has plenty of company these days. While the exact number of people retired overseas is not easy to pin down, around 350,000 American retirees receive Social Security benefits in countries other than the U.S., according to the Social Security Administration's annual statistical supplement. (And, of course, that doesn't count those baby boomer expatriates who aren't yet eligible for Social Security or have postponed taking it.) Most choose to live in European countries (German, Italy, and the United Kingdom are popular) or in Canada or Mexico. In recent years, though, an increasing number of Social Security checks have been sent to retirees in Central American countries, including Costa Rica and The Dominican Republic. Those numbers could swell as baby boomers hit their retirement years and go global in search of adventure and slimmer living expenses.

Part III
Marketing Yourself

Six Essential Qualities of a Promising Candidate

- **Self-starter:** Demonstrate that you're capable of working independently, able to get along without lots of supervision, and are great at managing your time and keeping a project on track.

- **Techie:** Show you're up to speed with technology and willing to learn.

- **Problem solver:** Showcase your ability to identify and solve a problem.

- **Communicator:** Show your ability to understand and clearly present ideas and information.

- **Innovator:** Confirm your ability to develop and pitch new ways of doing things and navigating challenges.

- **Lifelong learner:** Express your willingness to accept new ideas and information and your eagerness to learn new things and improve yourself.

Visit www.dummies.com/extras/gettingthejobyouwantafter50 for a bonus article with great tips on writing an eye-catching cover letter.

In this part . . .

- ✔ Pump up your résumé to make your experience an asset rather than an obstacle and write a cover letter to match.

- ✔ Build a strong online presence via LinkedIn, Facebook, Twitter, and your very own website to establish yourself as the go-to guy or gal in your field and tap your personal and professional networks for leads.

- ✔ Harness the people-power of LinkedIn to expand your professional network, get recommendations and endorsements, and find jobs that may not be posted anywhere else.

- ✔ Complete and submit job applications that don't make you look ancient and are less likely to get tagged and bagged by automated screening technology.

Chapter 8

Rehabbing Your Résumé and Cover Letter

*N*early every job worth having requires a résumé and a cover letter as part of the application process. These few pages are often your only shot at getting your foot in the door and landing an interview, so making sure these docs are not only good but better than the hundreds or thousands of other résumés and cover letters the organization is likely to receive is key.

Every résumé and cover letter combination is unique, or at least it should be, so I'm not about to stifle your creativity by presenting a formula (as if any such thing exists). And, because creating a résumé when you're over 50 brings its own set of challenges, I provide some résumé guidelines to follow, along with a few do's and don'ts, so you can speak to the needs and expectations of the organization you're applying to in whatever creative way you choose.

Constructing a Winning Résumé

Your résumé is your calling card, often serving as your only opportunity to make a good first impression. It needs to capture the essence of who you are and what you have to offer an employer. The trick is to boil all that down into a clear, sharp, and engaging two-dimensional presentation. Challenging, yes, but doable. It's called editing. Think of your résumé as your highlight reel.

A great résumé is at the heart of any successful job hunt. But the older you are, the trickier it can be to create a résumé that's not only concise but also detailed enough to do your years of experience justice. In the following sections, I show you how it's done.

Covering the six essential qualities of a promising candidate

When you're job hunting, the first step is to be certain that your résumé clearly trumpets the qualities that most employers view as non-negotiable these days. Of course, each position has its unique requirements, but these six universal qualities are the ones you must showcase.

Show, don't tell. Don't use the terms introduced in the following sections, such as *self-starter* or *tech savvy,* on your résumé or cover letter. Employers see these terms so often that they've become cliché. Instead, demonstrate through concrete examples that you embody these qualities.

Self-starter

One reason employers value experienced workers is that they don't need a lot of hand-holding and can hit the ground running. You need to demonstrate that you're capable of working independently, able to get along without lots of supervision, and are great at managing your time and keeping a project on track.

When describing your work experience, use words such as *managed, led, executed,* and *delivered* and describe instances when you took the initiative or completed a project with little or no supervision. For example, "Interviewed machine operators and developed multimedia training programs that reduced training time for new hires by 25 percent." Statements like this *show* rather than *tell* that you're a self-starter.

Techie

One of the biggest concerns employers have about older workers is they aren't up to speed with technology and perhaps are unwilling to learn. Prove them wrong. Here are a few ways to show that you're tech savvy:

✔ **Include your email address as part of your contact information at the top of your résumé.** Better yet, use a personal branded email address, such as kerry@kerryhannon.com, instead of a generic email address, such as kerryhannon@gmail.com or kerryhannon@hotmail.com. Yes, many employers discriminate based on the domain name of your email provider, and it could prevent you from landing an interview. See Chapter 9 for details on how to get a branded email address.

✔ **Mention in your résumé any experience with computer hardware and software, especially any hardware and software indicated specifically in the job description for the position you're applying for.** For example, AutoCad, QuickBooks, or WordPress.

✔ **Work teleconferencing and webinar technologies into your résumé, including Cisco WebEx, join.me, Google+, GoToMeeting, and TeamViewer.** Experience with any of these teleconferencing and collaboration technologies demonstrates that you're a team player who can work remotely while staying connected.

✔ **Maintain an active LinkedIn presence (see Chapter 10) and list your personal LinkedIn URL on your résumé just below your email address.** Prospective employers can then see for themselves how active you are in relevant industry and professional groups.

✔ **Showcase your personal blogging or website.** If you have your own blog or website, include its URL on your résumé, so prospective employers can check it out. Even if they don't visit, the URL shows that you're tech savvy enough to create an online presence.

Problem solver

Employers see employees as either problems or problem solvers, and you definitely want to be in that second camp. When describing your professional accomplishments, add at least one that demonstrates your ability to identify and solve a problem. For example, you may describe an instance when you noticed that several customers had the same complaint and you recommended a change in your company's policies or procedures that improved customer satisfaction. Perhaps you found a way to cut the time required to perform a certain operation or a way to cut costs.

When you're able to demonstrate that you're a problem solver, you also show prospective employers that you're more about solving problems than trying to find someone to blame.

Communicator

Regardless of the position you're applying for, employers want people who can communicate effectively. You need to demonstrate an ability to understand and clearly present ideas and information. In terms of your résumé, your ability to communicate is demonstrated mostly through the organization and writing on the résumé itself. Here are few tips to make sure your résumé reflects your ability to communicate:

✔ Tailor your résumé to the organization and job description to demonstrate your ability to understand the organization's needs based on what you read. (See the later section, "Tailoring your résumé for specific openings and circumstances," for details.)

✔ Organize your résumé to present the information in a way that makes it easy for the reader to capture your work experience quickly. Aim for sharp, clear job titles, and easy to follow lively narratives of your job responsibilities. For example, you managed X project or led the team that introduced a new product.

✔ Carefully proofread your résumé to eliminate errors. Better yet, have a friend or colleague read it for you and suggest corrections and improvements. An error-free résumé demonstrates attention to detail and commitment to quality, along with showing that you can express yourself clearly in writing.

Innovator

Most employers are looking for candidates who are creative thinkers. You need to be able to develop and pitch new ways of doing things and navigating challenges. When describing your experience or skills, be sure to include at least one instance when you invented a new idea or a way of doing something. Perhaps you read customer posts online that inspired an idea for a new product or service, or maybe you read something about a competitor that opened up new opportunities for your organization. Try to think of any ideas you may have had that either made or saved your organization time or money or improved it in some way.

Lifelong learner

Having a high-school diploma or a college degree is a definite plus, but if you earned those in the '70s or '80s, that's history. If possible, include more recent education, training, or certifications. Presenting yourself as a lifelong learner demonstrates that you're humble enough to accept instruction, open to new ideas and information, and eager and willing to learn new things and improve yourself.

Revealing the seven secrets to making your résumé pop

A résumé revamp can help you stand out from other applicants in the screening process. Here are seven ways experienced job seekers can get their résumés noticed.

Keep it short and simple

Your résumé has about five minutes to convince an employer that you're worthy enough to advance to the next step in the vetting process, according to a 2014 Society for Human Resource Management (SHRM) Résumés,

Cover Letters and Interviews Survey. (And according to some studies, a lousy résumé has only about six seconds.) To improve your odds of surviving the first cut, keep your résumé short and simple:

- **Limit yourself to two pages.** Anything longer will probably go unread. In certain circumstances, you can go as long as three pages, but make your résumé only as long as needed to highlight your qualifications.

- **Select a traditional font.** Times New Roman, Calibri, and Arial are all good choices. Stick to a 10- to 12-point size, and use black type against white paper for the body of the résumé. Consider going larger for your name (up to 15 points) and your contact info (up to 12 points).

- **Go easy on text enhancements.** Use boldface type, italics, and underlining sparingly and consistently, and avoid using any of them together.

- **Choose a common file format.** Save your résumé as a Microsoft Word document that can easily be viewed on most computers. Also saving it in PDF form is wise to prevent format corruption when uploading as part of an online application. Most job postings will state what type of format is preferred.

Include your contact information

Place your name and contact information and the title of the job you're applying for at the top of your résumé. Here's what you should include at the top of your résumé and in what order:

- **Your full name.** Use your first and last name. Refrain from using a middle initial or middle name unless it's part of your professional identity.

- **The city and state in which you live.** Recruiters want to know what town you live in so they can estimate your commute time. Omit your street address for privacy reasons.

- **Your email address.** Consider getting a branded email address, as explained in Chapter 9.

- **Your phone number.** Include only one phone number, the number where you're most likely to answer.

- **Your personal LinkedIn URL and blog or website address, if you have one.** Including your LinkedIn URL and blog or website address makes it easy for recruiters and hiring managers to find out more about you online. (See Chapter 10 for details.)

- **The position for which you're applying.** Below your contact information, add the specific title of the job for which you're applying — for example, type "Objective: [employer's job title]"

Cull your professional experience

Just because you've been gainfully employed for 30 or 40 years doesn't mean you have to include all those years on your résumé. When listing your work experience, focus on what you've been doing for the past 10 to 15 years.

Although most job seekers use the traditional chronological or reverse-chronological résumé format, there are alternatives. You might, for example, highlight your specific skills first, focusing on those that are most transferable to the job you're looking for.

In a skills-based résumé, you do, of course, include your employment history — but that goes at the bottom of your résumé. This type of approach can be advantageous if there are gaps in your work history of a year or more, or if you're switching careers or industries and your previous job titles don't correspond.

The top three or four key broad skill categories mandatory for the job you're targeting will help you to pick what to include in this Skills Summary section. In your bullets, you expand with precise achievements or experiences. You will mention companies here, but you don't have to be too specific about the specific position.

Following the skills section, you'll have a concise work chronicle section. Include the company name, your job title, employment dates, and the city and state of the organization. Include volunteer positions or internships in this section. Related experience doesn't just have to be paid positions.

Think advertisement, not obituary. No one wants, or needs, to read every one of your employment entries over a three- to four-decade career.

When presenting your professional experience in reverse chronological order, start with your most recent position. Include the following details for each organization you served:

- ✔ Start and end dates (month and year)
- ✔ Organization's name and what the organization does or did
- ✔ Position(s) you held and major accomplishments at each position (see the later section "Tell your story with gusto," for details)

There's no need to distinguish between paid and unpaid work-related skills on your résumé. Include any volunteer work that suggests you have management skills. Being in charge of a gala fundraising event, for instance, converts to sales and marketing chops. Holding a board position shows leadership ability. Also, if you work for a family business, you don't need to mention that it's a family business on your résumé.

Package your earlier experiences into one nice, tidy paragraph at the end of your résumé's Experience section. Include only the work history that's relevant to the job you're applying for now, and omit dates. Here's an example suggested by Susan Whitcomb, author of *Résumé Magic: Trade Secrets of a Professional Résumé Writer.*

> **Prior Experience (Commercial Development, Business Development and Technology):** During tenure with Ecolabs, promoted through positions in Food Business Development, Industrial Commercial Development; Applied Research and Commercial Development for Performance Materials; and Applied R&D. Initially recruited from UCLA as Research Chemist for Shell Oil.

Plug the gaps

If your employment history has any gaps, fill them in; otherwise, prospective employers may think you're hiding something. Try plugging any gaps with educational experiences. Maybe you traveled, performed community service, added a degree, or pursued other educational opportunities. Include a one-line explanation, such as "Caregiving" or "Volunteer for Habitat for Humanity" to fill in for any extended periods of unemployment. Otherwise, the gap is a major red flag that something is wrong with you even if that's far from the truth.

Reaping the benefits of volunteering

Extended unemployment, coupled with age discrimination and other barriers, can add to the challenges older workers face in finding a job, as the AARP Public Policy Institute report "The Long Road Back: Struggling to Find Work after Unemployment" found. One excellent way to plug gaps in your résumé, add to your skill set, gain valuable experience, and perhaps even find your way back into the workforce is to volunteer.

Meaningful volunteering can be an excellent way to eventually land a job. You can demonstrate your skills helping out at a nonprofit and then tout your accomplishments when applying for a paid position.

By putting your volunteering on your résumé, you avoid that blank phase of unemployment. To the degree that you can be out in the world applying your skills, volunteering benefits you as well as those you serve.

If you were out of the workforce for caregiving duties, you can market that, too. You were skill building. Perhaps you were a "project manager," supervising a team of other caregivers — from nurses to doctors and physical therapists. Maybe you were a "researcher" tracking down the best doctors and medical care. You may have been a "financial manager" in charge of bill paying and insurance claims. Use strong action verbs to describe your caregiving, or other, experience and skills: *directed, enabled, facilitated, hired, supervised, controlled, coordinated, executed, organized, planned, implemented, spearheaded, navigated, negotiated, secured,* and *resolved.*

Tell your story with gusto

As you populate your résumé with job experiences, focus on quantifiable benefits you delivered to your previous employers. You want to say, for instance, that you grew sales by 25 percent or that you completed a project four months ahead of schedule. Résumé-writing pros refer to this as telling your CAR story — *challenge, action,* and *result.*

Talk about a problem you faced, what you did to solve it, and the specific tangible result of your efforts; for example, "Researched market and identified opportunity for a new service, adding a revenue stream that increased profits 15 percent." As much as possible, make your CAR stories relevant to the job you're applying for.

There is no *I* in résumé. Technically speaking, your résumé is all about you, but what employers really want to know is what you can do for them as reflected in what you've done for past employers. Keep yourself out of your résumé as much as possible, and never use the word *I*. For example, instead of saying, "I managed," just use action verbs in a bullet point: "Managed X project, Oversaw, Created, Designed, Initiated" and so on.

On the other hand, don't be too formal in your writing. Show a little personality and let reviewers hear your voice and the pride you take in your accomplishments. Include relevant metrics and anything that has made you look like a star, including exceeding national or corporate standards and winning awards.

Highlight additional education and training

If you've had any specialized education and training over the years, include a section for it on your résumé. By adding recent training, education, and certifications, you highlight your commitment to professional development, show that you're current with industry and management trends, and demonstrate an eagerness to learn new things.

Interests, hobbies, activities, and professional memberships can also help you get noticed or even reveal that you're physically and intellectually active. That can be a great way to subtly address any concerns an employer may have that, as an older worker, you don't have the stamina for the job. A shared interest may also create a personal connection with the person reading your résumé.

Be mindful of automated screening systems

If you're submitting your résumé via an online portal, tweak it to ensure that it makes it past any automated screening system. Here are some tips:

✔ **Save your résumé as a .doc or .txt file.** These programs are the most universal and are easy to upload. Use .pdf files when it's listed as preferred or when you want to keep your formatting intact.

✔ **List the names of your employers first followed by the dates you worked there.** Some screening systems reject résumés that present the date before the employers.

✔ **Add key words and phrases that match those used in the job description of the position you're applying for.** For example, if the job requires knowledge of "Microsoft Office" or "excellent communication skills," make sure those key words and phrases appear in your résumé. If the job requires someone who has "managed" a team, use *managed*, not *directed* or *operated* or any other synonym.

✔ **Don't embed charts or images that the screening system can't read.** Keep it simple — text only. But be sure to include hyperlinks or addresses to sites where additional information can be found, such as to your LinkedIn profile or your website, if you have one.

Before submitting your résumé online, check the site to see whether it contains any guidelines, and, if it does, read those guidelines and follow them exactly.

Avoiding the top seven résumé turnoffs

Knowing what *not* to include in a résumé is almost as important as knowing what *to* include. Remove these résumé red flags right now:

✔ **The "Career Objective" section:** Employers don't care about your objectives. They care about theirs. Career objective statements are old-fashioned. Hiring managers say they're immaterial for the initial screening process. It's all about what the company needs, not what you want. You'll have a chance to talk about yourself during the interview.

✔ **College or high-school graduation dates:** The fact that you graduated high school or college is important. When you did isn't. Not only are these dates immaterial, but they also age you.

✔ **Outdated tech skills:** Being a certified WordPerfect trainer in the 1980s is about as useful now as once knowing how to operate an elevator in the 1950s.

✔ **Too much personal information:** If you wouldn't want it on the front page of your local newspaper, skip it.

✔ **"References available upon request":** If you advance in the process, you'll be asked to provide references. For now, this information just takes up valuable space.

✔ **Quirky job titles:** Although these can be a conversation icebreaker at a networking event, on your résumé, an offbeat title can be a turnoff and inappropriate for a more traditional company. A bigger drawback is that the title could eliminate you from a recruiter's search criteria. "Wordsmith," for instance, is unlikely to show up in an Applicant Tracking Systems Search for the specific keyword "editor." "Happiness activist" won't turn up in a search for an experienced "activities director."

✔ **Misspellings and grammar mistakes:** Proofread, proofread, proofread. Take the time to check your résumé carefully. And then take someone else's time to recheck it. If you wrote it, you're probably too close to it to catch the errors. Read it out loud.

Bending the truth

The pressure to stand out in a sea of applicants may tempt job seekers to be less than honest on their résumés and when interviewing, but is it worth the risk? Fifty-eight percent of hiring managers said they've caught a lie on a résumé; one-third (33 percent) of these employers have seen an increase in résumé embellishments post-recession. The most common lies include

✔ Embellished skill set (57 percent)

✔ Embellished responsibilities (55 percent)

✔ Dates of employment (42 percent)

✔ Job title (34 percent)

✔ Academic degree (33 percent)

✔ Companies worked for (26 percent)

✔ Accolades/awards (18 percent)

The nationwide survey, which was conducted online by Harris Poll on behalf of CareerBuilder from May 13 to June 6, 2014, included a representative sample of 2,188 hiring managers and human resource professionals across industries and company sizes.

Half of employers (51 percent) said they would automatically dismiss a candidate if they caught a lie on his/her résumé, while 40 percent said it would depend on what the candidate lied about. Seven percent said they'd be willing to overlook a lie if they liked the candidate.

Moral of the story: Don't lie on your résumé. Telling the truth gives you a better chance of finding the position that's the right match for you and the organization.

Airbrushing your résumé

After you've built a solid résumé, take some time to perfect it by highlighting your distinctions and scrubbing it clean of any imperfections. Of course, nobody's perfect, but your résumé should enhance your best features while concealing any blemishes.

Highlighting distinctions

The old saying, "Play to your strengths" applies to résumé writing. Your résumé should place your distinctions front and center and shine the spotlight on them:

- **Use a personal headline instead of a career objective.** Your personal headline describes who you are or who you want to be; for example, Digital Marketing Executive, Senior Financial Analyst, or Information Systems Administrator. Use your current title or the title of the position you're applying for.

- **Play up your experience in the industry.** Employers and recruiters prefer specialists over generalists. They're more likely to choose someone who has deep knowledge and experience in their industry over someone who dabbles in various industries. So if you're experienced in the industry, play it up.

- **Provide links to a portfolio of your expertise.** Hiring managers want to know that you're on top of your game and can deliver the goods. What better way than to show them? Presentations and documents attached and available to download from your LinkedIn profile are a great way to do just that. You can add a line that directs the reader to your portfolio on LinkedIn. (See Chapter 10 for more about using LinkedIn to market yourself.)

Omitting imperfections

Prospective employers don't expect a résumé that provides full disclosure. They're well aware that the purpose of your résumé is to highlight your qualifications and accomplishments, so feel free to omit less flattering details, including the following:

- **Jobs that lasted fewer than six months:** These in-and-out jobs make you look like a flight risk at best and a bad bet at worst. If you can't stay with a company for more than a year or two, it might be a sign that you get bored too easily or that you have trouble fitting into the company culture. Take the opportunity to shorten your résumé by omitting these short-lived jobs. Be upfront about these jobs, though, if asked about them in an interview.

✔ **Gaps in employment:** If the gap is fewer than six months, don't worry about that. However, if you lost a job and decided to take a break to travel, opted out of the job market for a number of years to raise your children, or have been unable to find work for nearly a year, you have some explaining to do. Recruiters and hiring managers want to know what you were up to during that time. See the earlier section, "Plug the gaps" for ideas on how to fill in these dead zones.

✔ **Unrelated jobs:** If you work in a field unrelated to one you worked in a decade ago, consider excluding the details of that previous work experience. Include only the years and industries in which you worked, but not the specific employers and positions.

✔ **Lower-level jobs:** For jobs you held several years ago that are in the same field but don't reflect your current level, keep descriptions brief.

Tailoring your résumé to specific openings and circumstances

Every résumé you submit should be tailored to the specific organization and position you're applying to. Open your generic résumé and use the Save As feature in your word processor to save the résumé under another name so you can make changes without affecting the original. After you research the organization and read the job description for the position that interests you, create your custom résumé as explained in the following sections.

Targeting a specific opening

When you're applying for a specific position, pay close attention to the qualifications and responsibilities described in the job ad, and adjust your résumé accordingly. For example, if the employer asks for "strong Excel and report-writing skills," tuck these key expressions somewhere in the narrative of your past work experience. If the firm is looking for a "sales associate" with "a strong customer focus," then include this phrase two or three times. If a firm is hiring a "communications manager" who is "proficient in the use of web technology, social media tools, and metrics" and "understanding of department budgeting," pop these phrases in your story. The aim is to sprinkle the key words into your description of your work experience.

Don't go overboard with key words to the point where they sound forced. You may need to perform significant revisions so that the key words and phrases flow naturally.

Getting found on a job board

When posting your résumé on a job board, use key words and phrases to help potential employers and recruiters find the talent they need. Put yourself in the shoes of prospective employers and recruiters and ask yourself which key words and phrases they're likely to enter when searching for someone with your skills and experience or to fill the type of position you're looking for. Then add these key words and phrases to your résumé. You can work key words into your personal headline, your experience section, or even your education and training section.

Adjusting for a career change

When you're looking to change careers, play up your skills, not your positions. Cast a wide net. Look at your skill set and past experience as transferable to many different challenges and fields. Think of this approach as redirecting or redeploying your skills. Although you may need to list past employers, you can tweak your résumé to focus less on positions and more on the skills needed to do the jobs.

Look inside yourself and answer some important questions: What am I best at? Ask friends and colleagues, too. They may notice skills that you take for granted, such as problem solving, conflict resolution, or an ability to work a crowd. What skills have you gathered in your previous positions that would be helpful in another job? You're not reinventing your work; you're redeploying your skills. You *can* transfer skills and experience you've gained from your primary career into a different industry or position. Scan your past for clues to your future. Think about how your skill set may be transferable to other fields, and then show how those skills the employer is looking for are right in your wheelhouse and easily tapped for your new field.

Jumping ship

Retired Navy Captain Don Covington, who became the company manager for the Big Apple Circus in his mid-50s, told me: "When you think about it, the military and the circus are not that different." What he meant is that the leadership and management skills honed in his naval career translated to moving a circus troupe of 100-plus from town to town.

As you transition to a different industry or position, think more about how you can use your skills to address an organization's needs instead of trying to target a position that may not be a good fit. You'll probably discover that you're qualified to perform many jobs you never imagined you'd be good at. Be sure your résumé showcases those skills you possess that are pertinent to the job you're applying for.

Returning to the workforce after an extended absence

If you're returning to the workforce after an extended absence, you have no option but to come clean about it and try to explain what exactly you were doing during that time. (See the earlier section "Plug the gaps" for details.)

Even though life experience and volunteer gigs are valuable, they're not the equivalent of formal training and job experience. When you're returning to the workforce after an extended absence, try to highlight any education and training you pursued during that time. If you didn't receive any specialized education and training, now is the time to start. Head to Chapter 2 for guidance on getting the training and skills you need to remain competitive in the job market.

Making use of key word searches

Key words are the industry-specific terms necessary to get attention. By placing them in your résumé, you can get more attention. Try these techniques:

- ✔ Sprinkle key words throughout the résumé.
- ✔ Use them when referring to job titles, accomplishments, experience, skills, education, career objectives, and training.
- ✔ Use the exact key words and language that the employers uses in the job posting.

Filming a video résumé

Video résumés are gaining in popularity among job seekers, employers, and recruiters. Although they're no replacement for a traditional résumé, a quality video résumé serves as a nice accompaniment to a cover letter and résumé, sets you apart from the crowd, helps you build rapport with prospective employers before they have a chance to meet you, and provides you with another opportunity to demonstrate your mastery of modern technology.

Not all jobs warrant video résumés. But if you're in a line of work where all eyes are on you — sales, public speaking, tourism, or fundraising, for instance — a video résumé is a chance to show off your personality and your skills. It also shows a future employer that you're not intimidated by technology.

You can create your video résumé by using your own video recording software. Here are some suggestions to get you started:

✔ **Buy a good quality HD webcam.** Don't film your video résumé with your smartphone, unless you think that would be effective in your field. Your webcam should include the video-recording software you need to produce your video résumé.

✔ **Star in your video.** Although some individuals have used animations, slide shows, and other creative approaches effectively, you're usually better off simply speaking to the camera, assuming, of course, you're good at it. However, if you have an idea for a super-creative video that's guaranteed to impress, go for it!

✔ **Report to wardrobe.** Dress professionally as if you were going to an in-person interview. These videos are traditionally shot from the waist up, so slip into your full costume to set the mood. Style your hair. Ladies: Use a little extra lipstick and makeup because the camera can wash you out. Go easy on the jewelry. Men: Make sure ties are straightened and shirts are pressed. Watch for stray hairs drifting about on your collar.

✔ **Prepare your pitch and rehearse.** Review sample videos, and write a script. You don't have to memorize it, but outline your talking points. Practice what you're going to say. This isn't a long segment. Think of it as a 60-second commercial, a sound bite with some snap to it. It can run longer but certainly no longer than three minutes. Begin by introducing yourself with your full name, say what you do, and briefly describe the type of position you're seeking. Speak clearly, confidently and conversationally — not too fast but with a punch of energy. (This is excellent practice if you ever have to do a video interview, as explained in Chapter 12.)

✔ **Check the set.** You don't want any background noise, such as a barking dog. Be aware of what's behind you. Some healthy plants or fresh flowers in a vase are good. A bookcase makes a great background, but screen it for any trashy novels. You may opt for a wall hanging that says something about you, such as a framed award you've won. A photo of you actually doing the kind of job you're seeking is another possibility.

✔ **Sit in the light and speak to the camera.** If you're using a laptop with a built-in camera, set the computer so that the lens is at eye level. You want light on the front of your face. If your room has a window, face it, or put a small light on the desk in front of you. Gaze straight into the camera as if you're looking into your interviewer's eyes. Talk directly to him or her — your choice of gender.

✔ **Pay attention to your body language.** No hair twirling around your finger, lip biting, squinting, or excessive blinking. Don't slouch. Try to appear animated and energized. Feel free to smile, as long as you can smile without it seeming fake.

✔ **End on a strong note.** End your video with something simple like, "Thank you for considering me for the job." Smile, and keep looking into the camera until you stop recording.

✔ **Take two . . . or three.** Plan to run through a few practice taped sessions. Ask your friends or family to critique the video. Save the version you like to your desktop. If you're really good with video-editing software, you may be able to assemble the best segments into a single video.

✔ **Distribute it — selectively.** You may want to upload your video on YouTube to provide easy access to it, but upload it as Unlisted, so it's more likely to be viewed only by those people you tell about it. Include a link to your video résumé in both your paper and online résumés. Put it up on your own website, if you have one. Send the link to your networking contacts. Upload it to your LinkedIn profile and any other job boards that support videos.

Knowing where to go for résumé-writing help

If your résumé isn't getting the response you desire, consider hiring a certified résumé writer. You may be highly qualified to perform tasks that few people on this earth can do and simply fall short when it comes to résumé writing or specifically writing your own résumé. Boomers spend zillions of hours trying to perfect their copy and still can't get noticed by an employer or recruiter.

You can find certified résumé writers through Career Directors International (www.careerdirectors.com) or the National Résumé Writers Association (www.thenrwa.com). Fees range from $300 to $1,500 or more. You can deduct the cost of preparing and mailing your résumé from your federal taxes. If you're a college graduate, check with your college career center to see whether it offers free résumé services. Another option is to seek the assistance of a career counselor, coach, or consultant to help you write your résumé as well as help you hone your job-search skills and strategies. You can also check out www.aarp.org/work for résumé examples and best practices.

Writing a Killer Cover Letter

The importance of the cover letter varies by organization. Many large organizations, including corporations and universities, forgo the cover letter and use automated systems to process résumés and match candidates to needs within their organizations. For others, the cover letter is a key component of the application and is used as an acid test to determine how well a candidate understands the needs of the organization and can communicate in writing. For these organizations, your cover letter is the key that opens the door for your résumé.

Unless the job posting states otherwise or you're submitting your résumé on a site that includes no option for including a cover letter, always include a cover letter with your résumé. This is your chance to sell yourself! A well-crafted cover letter demonstrates what you bring to the organization and why you're the best candidate for the job. It showcases your skills, experience, and achievements and highlights their relevance to the organization's needs.

In this section, I explain the do's and don'ts of writing a persuasive cover letter.

Do your homework. Read the job description of the position you're applying for. Research the industry and your prospective employer. Visit the company's website. Visit the websites of the company's top competitors. Visit Glassdoor, Manta, and ZoomInfo where you can dig up additional information. Find out who your supervisor is likely to be and look up the person on LinkedIn. If you need to get past a hiring manager, try to find out who that person is and look her up on LinkedIn. The more you know about your audience, the better able you are to appeal to that individual on a personal level.

Drafting your cover letter

Structuring or outlining your cover letter is the first order of business. Having an outline in place ensures that you present your message in an organized way and cover all the essentials. Your cover letter should be no longer than one page and typically organized by using the following three sections:

- ✔ **Introduction:** In the first paragraph, tell the employer what job you're applying for, why you're applying for it, and (if applicable) who referred you. For example, "Your need for a detail-oriented person with years of experience in strategic communication is precisely what I am in a position to offer and is timed perfectly for my decision to pursue my goal of working for [organization name]."

  Avoid boring, overused opening lines, such as "I am writing to submit my résumé for the position of. . . ."

✔ **Body:** Briefly describe your skills in a way that matches your skills to the needs of the organization. Use this opportunity to highlight training, education, and skills mentioned in your résumé that are particularly relevant to the position you're applying for and the organization's needs.

Try writing an *elevator speech* — a pithy 30-second summary of who you are, what you do, and what you'd like to do professionally. Doing so will make you feel more confident in your job search, and you can use elements of your elevator speech in your cover letter.

✔ **Conclusion:** In the last paragraph, tie in your résumé and express your eagerness to meet with the person to discuss your qualifications and the organization's needs in greater detail. For example, you may write something like, "For additional details, please refer to my résumé (attached). I look forward to the opportunity to meet with you in person to discuss the position and my qualifications in greater depth."

Be specific without going into too much detail. Think of your letter as a carefully planned appetizer that whets the reader's appetite for the main course — served up in your résumé.

Fine-tuning your cover letter

After drafting your cover letter, print it, read it closely, and revise it to optimize its impact. Here are a few suggestions on how to fine-tune your cover letter:

✔ **Address your letter to a specific person, not just a title or department.** You may need to do some research or call the organization to find out the name of the person who's in charge of filling the position or screening applicants.

✔ **In the first paragraph, refer to the specific position you're applying for,** including a reference code if the job description provides one.

✔ **Include key words and phrases in your cover letter that match those used in your résumé,** just in case the organization uses an automated system for screening cover letters and résumés.

✔ **Write short paragraphs or use a bulleted list to present details.** Leaving plenty of white space makes your cover letter more inviting and easier to read.

✔ **Be clear, direct, and terse.** For example, instead of writing, "As was mentioned in the job description for this position, your company is in need of a team-oriented individual with a background in marketing and communications. As you can see from the details in my résumé, my qualifications make me perfectly suited to that position," write something like this, "Your company needs a team player with experience in marketing and communications. I am that person."

✔ **Share your cover letter with friends who will give you their frank reactions.** Does your letter feel intriguing? Does it make the reader want to know more about you? If not, revise it in light of the feedback you receive.

✔ **Purge your prose of spelling and grammar errors.** Proofread your cover letter several times and have someone else proofread it as well.

Avoiding common mistakes

After reviewing hundreds of cover letters and résumés and speaking with dozens of people in human resources and others in charge of screening applicants, I developed the following list of common mistakes you should avoid when writing a cover letter:

✔ **Don't send out a generic cover letter regardless of position.** Instead, tailor each cover letter (and résumé) to the specific position.

✔ **Don't waste space on phrases such as "I am writing to . . . ," "Let me introduce myself," and so on.** Get to the point.

✔ **Don't merely repeat the contents of your résumé.** Instead, highlight your skills and achievements that address the organization's needs and qualifications for the position.

✔ **Don't call attention to your age by citing your 20, 30, or 40 years of experience.** Instead, use words like *extensive* or *significant* to describe your experience.

✔ **Don't include your salary requirements unless the organization specifically requests this information.** Save the salary discussion until you're close to being offered the job.

For additional guidance in structuring and writing cover letters, check out *Writing Resumes and Cover Letters For Dummies,* by Amanda McCarthy and Kate Southam (Wiley).

Lining Up Your References in Advance

A prospective employer is likely to ask for professional references to confirm your previous employment and to get a sense of what kind of employee you are. They may also ask for personal references to get a bead on the kind of person you are outside of work. Some employers may ask for the exact number of years you've known someone and in what capacity — for example, a previous manager or coworker you've known for more than five years.

Prior to applying for any openings, choose four or five people willing to serve as references. Here are some suggestions for picking and contacting references:

✔ Create a list of possible references by reviewing those you've worked with and even volunteered alongside. Bosses, coworkers, professors, and former customers and clients are good choices, but be certain they think favorably of you or are at least neutral about your job performance with their organization. Keep in mind that many employers have policies that reference checkers can only focus on verifying facts and managers must refer requests to the HR Department. So what you're asking for may require someone to break from the "official" policy.

✔ Contact your references before you hand over their contact information to see if they're willing to vouch for you. You might need to refresh your reference's recall about the job you held while working with them. If your potential reference is on board, then ask what times and what phone number is best for someone to reach him.

✔ When listing a previous employer, confirm with human resources that all information in your personnel file is accurate.

✔ Give your reference some background on the potential employer, why you're interested in the position, and why you think your skills are a good fit. Forward him a copy of your résumé and the job description, so he's prepared.

✔ Let your references know every time you share his contact information with a prospective employer.

✔ Each time your reference supports you with a new prospective employer, take the time to send him a thank-you letter or at the very least an email message. It's good manners and will keep the good juju flowing.

✔ If you land the job, call or email your reference, and thank him again. You might even spring for a lunch or a cup of coffee and pass along your new contact information.

Do employers actually contact references?

After hearing stories of con artists with only high-school educations landing jobs as airline pilots or doctors, you may start to wonder whether employers ever really check an applicant's references or credentials. Research shows they do.

According to a Society for Human Resource Management (SHRM) survey, more than eight of ten human resource professionals said that they regularly conduct reference checks for professional (89 percent), executive (85 percent), administrative (84 percent), and technical (81 percent) positions. And here's what most of them want to know:

- ✔ Dates of employment — did you really work the dates you said you did?

- ✔ If it's a former boss, would she hire you back?

- ✔ What are your strengths and weaknesses, and how might they apply to the job at hand?

If you know that a reference check will be an electronic one, let your references know and review how they might check those boxes. It's human nature to answer more coldly when responding to an electronic questionnaire. When asked to rate a person's reliability on a scale of one to five, a reference might check four, thinking that's an honest appraisal, but that four can sink your chances of landing the job. Let your references know of the risks so they can take those risks into consideration when entering their responses.

Chapter 9

Creating a Strong Online Presence

In This Chapter

▶ Gauging the value of establishing a brand presence online

▶ Becoming master of your own domain

▶ Harnessing the power of social networking and media

The best way to land the job of your dreams is to network. In the old days, that involved meeting face-to-face with colleagues and customers, attending conferences, becoming involved in philanthropic organizations, mentoring and being mentored, and mingling with others in social and professional circles. That old-school networking is still very effective, but online networking is becoming increasingly important. Now, prospective employers and recruiters are more likely to get to know you online long before they ever meet you in person. You build your reputation online, and that reputation plays two key roles in determining whether you get the job: being well known gets you discovered, and demonstrating your knowledge and skills gets you hired.

In this chapter, I explain how to build a *personal brand*, using numerous online tools. "A personal brand is what you stand for and what makes you special," says Dan Schawbel, the author of *Promote Yourself: The New Rules For Career Success* (St. Martin's Press). "It's composed of values and your mission." Your personal brand is also the way you portray yourself to your professional world, whether it be via your résumé, your LinkedIn profile, or the way you dress and whose tweets you retweet on Twitter or what you like on Facebook.

Here, you discover how to establish a home base by obtaining your own branded domain and creating a website or blog, reinforce it with a branded email address, and link to it from social networking sites, including LinkedIn, Facebook, and Twitter. You find out how to get involved in online communities in a way that builds a good, solid reputation. And you discover secrets to avoid the most common pitfalls.

Recognizing the Importance of Building a Personal Brand

Job seekers young and old often fail to realize the importance of personal branding. They assume that the only two things they need to do to land a job is to create a great résumé and cover letter and then ace the job interview. Unfortunately, that's not the case. Employers and recruiters *will* search for you online, and whatever they find out about you, good or bad, will help them decide whether you're worth pursuing. A strong, positive personal brand shows recruiters and employers that you have the following qualities:

- **You're tech savvy.** Having your own domain name and perhaps your own personal website or blog; being active in social networks on LinkedIn, Facebook, and Twitter; and contributing valuable information and insight in your areas of expertise demonstrate that you're not afraid of technology, and you know how to use it.

- **You're energetic.** Building and maintaining a brand presence on the web and in social networking circles requires time, effort, and endurance. These qualities help address any possible employer concerns that as an older worker you lack the stamina to do the job.

- **You're sociable.** You're engaging, polite, and gracious. You get along with others and are likely to get along with coworkers. Even better, if you have connections with people younger than you and demonstrate a willingness and ability to learn and take direction from them, you address another concern that employers often have regarding older workers — that they may run into trouble with a younger supervisor.

- **You're a professional.** A photo of yourself well dressed and properly groomed goes a long way toward showing employers and recruiters that you have a positive self-image and respect others. Ensuring that all content you post is tasteful and free of any serious errors shows that you pay attention to details.

Include a photo of yourself as part of your profile on LinkedIn, Facebook, and other social networking sites. According to LinkedIn, recruiters are 11 times more likely to click on a profile that has a photo than one without.

- **You know your stuff.** You can join professional groups on LinkedIn and participate in discussions to demonstrate your knowledge of and commitment to the industry in which you work or plan to work.

Being involved in various online communities further develops your online identity and delivers additional benefits for job seekers, including the following:

✔ You can check out job postings that may not be advertised anywhere else.

✔ You can reconnect with coworkers from previous jobs and with friends, family members, schoolmates, and others you've lost touch with who may now be working in industries or for companies you'd like to join.

✔ You throw your name in the hat, giving employers and recruiters the opportunity to discover you.

✔ You can find out more about industries and organizations that interest you and research some of the key people in those industries and organizations. Knowing a little about a company or a specific person at the company can be very helpful when you're preparing a résumé or cover letter or preparing for an interview.

Even if you do nothing to establish an online persona, you're probably mentioned online somewhere. By playing an active role in building your persona, you have much more control over what others find out about you. When an employer or recruiter searches for you by name, what you posted about yourself and posted as yourself is much more likely to pop up at the top of the search results than something someone else posted about you.

For more about personal branding best practices, check out *Personal Branding For Dummies,* by Susan Chritton (Wiley).

Launching Your Own Website

The centerpiece in your online branding efforts is a website, blog, or combination website/blog, and it's not very difficult, expensive, or time-consuming to build and maintain. You can get a personal website/blog up and running in less than an hour and spend about a half hour a week updating it. After you have it up and running, you can link to it from LinkedIn, Facebook, Twitter, Google+, and other accounts, driving traffic from those services to your personal website and raising your site's profile in the process.

In the following sections, I walk you through the process of setting a goal for your website/blog and launching it. Where you go from there and how powerful this new marketing tool becomes are limited only by your imagination and dedication.

Appreciating the value of a website and blog

If you are planning to join the ranks of the self-employed or are searching for a job at your dream company, a website and blog are key components to your personal brand. Here's why:

✔ Your website/blog provides you with an opportunity to reveal more to prospective clients, employers, and recruiters than you can on sites you don't own. You can post articles to demonstrate your knowledge of and insight into the industry, share a portfolio of your work, and even include testimonials from past clients, supervisors, and coworkers.

✔ You reveal an added dimension of your personality. Everything from the design of your site to the colors you choose and what you share reflects on who you are as a person and as a professional.

✔ Approximately 71 percent of those surveyed by WorkplaceTrends.com say that having a website is either very important

or important in helping build their personal brand, and 70 percent believe that employers are reviewing their online brand before they're interviewed.

✔ If you're self-employed as a consultant or freelancer or you have a job where showcasing your work is the primary way you sell your services (for example, as a writer, photographer, graphic designer, or landscaper), a website/blog is an essential marketing tool.

✔ Nearly half of the people who maintain a personal website or blog cite job offers as a benefit, in addition to professional recognition and networking opportunities. A whopping 61 percent say they've received a job offer because of their personal blog.

One thing is certain. Depending on the kind of position you're looking for, having a website where you can be found online will attract employers and recruiters.

According to a study from branded.me and .ME Registry, which operates the .ME domain name, 42 percent of people say they've grappled with (or failed) to launch their own personal website because it takes too much time to manage. That's not my experience. Once you set up your website, it can be very easy to navigate and update. I generally spend no more than a half an hour a week adding to and editing mine.

Setting a goal

Before you build a website, consider the goal you expect it to accomplish. A website for promoting a business differs significantly in both form and content from a blog whose goal is to build a person's reputation as an expert in a particular field. Your goal influences every other choice you make regarding your website/blog, so give it some careful thought.

People have different goals for their website, but for me it's a way to gather all my work in one place, from my articles, books, videos, and radio and TV appearances to articles for which I've been interviewed as an expert voice. When someone is looking to book a writer or speaker on a topic area I specialize in, I want my name to pop up at the top of the search results, and I want my website to convince whoever visits it that I'm the person they want to hire. To add a more personal touch, I share pictures of my pets, which helps promote my brand. Sharing pet photos may not be appropriate for people in more rigid lines of work, but it fits with my goal.

Your website/blog doesn't need a lot of bells and whistles. You can launch a single-page website detailing your professional background and interests — kind of like a spotlighted résumé — and build on it later.

Choosing a domain name

Your domain name is your name tag and address on the web. It's where people go to find you. Mine is `kerryhannon.com` — my name followed by .com. Spend some time thinking about the domain name you want to use, because transitioning to a new domain later weakens your brand presence, making it difficult for people to find you. When choosing a domain name, consider the following:

- ✔ **Use your name, business name, or a pseudonym you want to become known as.** For personal branding, I recommend using your full name and adding a middle initial or some other distinguishing letter(s) if you have a common name. For example, if your name is taken, you may add the kind of work you do; for instance, kerryhannonauthor.com.

- ✔ **Stick with .com.** The last part of a domain name, the *top-level domain*, can be .com, .net, .info, or even .guru. Choose .com, which is more common. If someone is looking for your site and has only the name of your site without the top-level domain, they're more likely to guess that it's .com than .net or something else.

- ✔ **Keep it short and easy to say, spell, and type.** Your domain name can be as long as 59 characters, but that's a mouthful and can be hard to remember, let alone type! The goal is for your domain name to be passed along easily by you and by others.

- ✔ **Stick with letters of the alphabet.** Remembering and typing hyphens, asterisks, numbers, and other characters is difficult.

- ✔ **Consider your email address.** For branding purposes, I recommend that you use your domain name as part of your email address (see the later section, "Obtaining a Branded Email Address"). Keep this in mind when choosing a domain. It could influence your decision.

> ✔ **Make sure the name is obtainable on social sites.** When picking your domain, check Facebook, LinkedIn, Twitter, and so on to see if you can use it there, too. Using the same name for all your online properties reinforces your brand.

When displaying your domain name on business cards, stationery, email, and other items you distribute, feel free to adjust the capitalization of your domain name to make it easier to remember; for example, KerryHannon.com. When someone enters your domain name into a web browser, capitalization doesn't matter. Keep in mind, however, that capitalization does matter for anything after the domain name; for example, `www.dummies.com/store.html` opens the Dummies bookstore, but `www.dummies.com/Store.html` results in an error message.

Registering your domain and choosing a hosting provider

After choosing a domain name, check a domain registrar or hosting service to see whether the domain you want is available. Here are a few of the many services you can search and ultimately use to register your domain name and host your site:

- ✔ `Bluehost.com`
- ✔ `FatCow.com`
- ✔ `GoDaddy.com`
- ✔ `HostGator.com`

Visit any of these sites and you're greeted by either a search box where you can enter the domain you want to search for or a link you can click to access the domain search form. Enter the domain you want (without .com) and click the button for executing the search. In a few seconds, the site displays a list of available domain names that match what you searched for and a list of alternatives in case the name isn't available.

Expect to pay two fees: a domain registration fee that generally ranges from $10 to $20 annually and a hosting fee, which is typically about $6 to $10 per month for a basic package. Most services advertise a much lower starting price and, if you pay your hosting fee annually, will drop the domain registration fee.

Before buying a domain name, think about where you want it hosted. All the hosting services mentioned earlier in this section are reputable firms, but you may want to search for them first to see what others have to say about them and to compare costs. It's more convenient and sometimes cheaper to have your domain registered with the same service that hosts your site. You can always transfer your registration, but that's a hassle.

Building your website/blog

When you sign up (and pay for) a hosting service, it provides you with a number of different tools for creating a website, blog, or combination website/blog. I recommend that you use an easy to use website/blog platform such as WordPress. Other platform options include Blogger.com, Joomla.org, and Typepad.com. WordPress (www.wordpress.com) is popular, so you can find plenty of information and videos on how to use it, it has thousands of templates available for controlling the look and feel of your site, and it's flexible. You can use it to create a website, a blog, or a combination website/blog, or you can start with a website and easily add a blogging component later or vice versa. Search your hosting provider's site for instructions on how to install and use WordPress.

When choosing a template for your WordPress site, I recommend purchasing a professionally designed template that's billed as a *responsive* design. A responsive design resizes to any screen, from a computer screen down to a smartphone display. With more and more people navigating the web via mobile devices, a responsive design is essential.

If you need something more complex than a personal website or blog, consider hiring a professional to help. For example, if you're opting to become a self-employed retailer selling products, consider hiring a professional to help you set up your online store. If your needs are more modest, you should be able to handle it yourself or get a friend or a local high-school or college student to help you. When I was starting out, I paid a web consultant $100 a month to monitor and add to my site on a regular basis. Now with WordPress, I can handle all the duties myself without breaking a sweat.

If you have the time to post content regularly to your site, I recommend that you create a combination website/blog. Regular blog posts boost your site's ranking with search engines, making you a bigger target for recruiters and prospective employers. The website component enables you to host several static web pages that require little or no maintenance.

When populating your site with pages, consider including a few of the following pages:

✔ **Your bio:** A bio should be a couple of paragraphs long and include your full name, job title (or one you're seeking), a photo of you, and any credentials. In essence, this is a brief description of you. You may also include a sentence or two about your professional interests, volunteer work, and hobbies.

Don't chintz on the photo. Dress up and have a professional photo taken of yourself.

- ✔ **Your résumé:** Create a page that displays your résumé, and on that page include a link to a printable PDF version of your résumé. Most word processors allow you to save documents as PDFs. You may want to remove any detailed information about yourself on the résumé web page, such as your phone number, but include that information on the PDF to make it easier for employers and recruiters to contact you.

- ✔ **An email contact form:** Some WordPress themes include an option to create a page with a contact form on it. This lets visitors complete and submit the form to contact you via email. Don't include a link for your email address, because it'll get picked up by spammers. If your WordPress theme doesn't contain an option for creating an email contact form, you can add such a feature via a WordPress plugin.

- ✔ **A portfolio or gallery page:** If you have any work you can showcase on a webpage that's relevant to the work you're wanting to do, post it on your site and include a portfolio or gallery page that presents your work or contains links to other documents that represent what you do. If you're stumped, visit personal websites and LinkedIn pages of others who do similar work as you do and read what they've written to describe their work and skills.

- ✔ **A testimonials page:** If people you worked with or for are willing to share testimonials about you, create a testimonials page and invite them to post something about you.

  Always ask and get permission before posting a testimonial or any other content from someone else. It's best to ask people to post content themselves and provide them with the address to the testimonials page where they can do just that.

Include in your web design, typically in the header or in a sidebar, links that people can click to follow you on LinkedIn, Facebook, Twitter, and other social sites where you're active. (Check out "Practicing online etiquette," later in this chapter, for tips on acting appropriately in the online world.) Again, the WordPress theme you use may have such a feature, and if it doesn't, you can find a WordPress plugin that adds this functionality.

Fine-tuning your site

Prior to revealing your site to the world, have one or more people review your site's design, usability, and content. Choose reviewers who read closely and are able to spot errors and those who are likely to provide honest feedback. If nobody in your inner circle fits that description, you may want to hire a proofreader or copy editor to review your site. Ask for feedback regarding tone as well. You can easily come across as being flippant or overly formal and serious without realizing it. Having an objective third party give your site the once-over gives you a more objective perspective.

After receiving feedback, return to your site and enter corrections and improvements. Another great aspect of WordPress is that making changes is as easy as opening and editing a text document.

Check your site on a desktop computer, tablet PC, iPad, smartphone, and any other Internet-enabled devices you can get your hands on to make sure your site looks good and functions properly on a wide range of devices.

In this brief section on launching a website/blog, I've merely touched on the steps required to give you a preview of what's involved. To find out more about creating and managing a website/blog with WordPress, check out *WordPress For Dummies,* by Lisa Sabin-Wilson (Wiley).

Obtaining a Branded Email Address

Your domain name registration and hosting service comes with an additional perk — the ability to create branded email addresses. For example, if your domain name were dummies.com, you could have email addresses such as billy@dummies.com, cindy@dummies.com, linda@dummies.com, and so on. And these cost nothing extra!

I'm not about to get into the details of creating and managing email accounts on a hosting service. You can search your hosting provider's help system for instructions. What I am going to tell you is to do it. Dump your old yourname@gmail.com and yourname@hotmail.com addresses and other such addresses and use your branded email address for *all* professional correspondence. Doing so sends a clear signal to employers, clients, recruiters, and others that you're tech savvy, and every email message you send reinforces your personal brand. Your branded email also looks more professional; you don't look like a hobo who had to set up shop on a borrowed email server.

Here are a few additional tips for making the most of your new branded email address and account:

- ✔ **Include your email address at the bottom of every email you send.** Better yet, use your email program's signature feature to add it for you. Search your email program's help system for "signature" for instructions.

- ✔ **Add your new, branded email address to all your marketing materials,** including your business card, résumé, cover letters, and stationery.

- ✔ **Use your branded email address exclusively for professional and personal email and never when registering on websites.** This cuts down on junk mail you may receive via your branded email account.

✔ **You can continue to use your favorite email servers, such as Gmail, to send and receive email,** if you have a good reason for wanting to do so. Search the help system of the email server you use to learn how to set it up to send and receive email for your branded email account.

✔ **As you make the transition to your new email account, consider having email forwarded from your other accounts to your new account.** Search the help system of your old email accounts to find out how to set up email forwarding. (You may also be able to enter email forwarding settings on your hosting provider that pulls email from these other email accounts.)

Acquiring Social Media Street Smarts

Most professional job searches these days are at least started on the Internet. Yes, the big job boards are worth trolling, but if you're a serious job hunter, you need more information than just a job posting — you need to dig deeper to research and network before you blindly shoot off a résumé. And that's where online networking sites can step up your game.

Online networking sites make it easier for recruiters to learn about you and for you to find out more about companies that interest you — both essential ingredients to landing a job. For workers over 50, an online presence is also a way to show potential employers that you're not intimidated by technology — something they're wary of when considering an older worker for a job today.

If you've recently lost your job or aren't at ease with online networking, learning the new rules of job hunting can take some ramping up, as I explain in this section.

Tracking down an inside connection

My friend Bill, who has been actively looking for a full-time position for months, called to tell me he had seen the "perfect" job at a great company posted on a job board. Problem was, he wasn't sure he knew anyone working there who might be able to get his virtual résumé noticed. "Without a real connection, it's like sending a message in a bottle, or shooting an arrow in the air," he told me.

He used his LinkedIn account to run a search and see if he knew anyone at the firm. Bingo. He did. He sent a quick email to his connection asking for help. Within a half-hour, he received a note back and got the ball rolling.

Creating a profile

Immediately after registering for any online networking site — LinkedIn, Facebook, Twitter, you name it — create a profile. Better yet, type up a profile on your computer and save it as a separate document. If you don't already have a great photo of yourself, get one and store it in the same folder as your profile. Now, all you have to do is copy and paste to create profiles on the different networking sites you join. And, because you're copying and pasting, you're ensuring that your profile is consistent wherever people happen to track you down.

That said, every networking site has its own profile feature that enables you to enter different types and amounts of information. On all of them, of course, you can include a photo, your name, and perhaps most importantly your website/blog address. Others may allow you to enter your birthday, work history, education, relationship status, and so on. Because of this, I cover profiles in greater detail in sections about specific networking sites. I cover Facebook and Twitter later in this chapter and LinkedIn in Chapter 10.

Foolish consistency may be the hobgoblin of little minds, but strategic consistency is an essential component of branding. It's how you burn your image into the brains of the people you want to impress.

Practicing online etiquette

As with any other form of communication, you must abide by certain standards of etiquette when expressing yourself online. Here are a few good manners to put into practice:

- ✔ **Read at least twice as much as you post, especially when you first join a discussion.** Get a feel for the group dynamic and the unwritten rules in a discussion group before posting anything. You'll be less likely to inadvertently step on someone's toes.

- ✔ **Be nice.** No cussing, ranting, raving, or engaging in other behavior that's likely to make people think less of you. Don't post anything you don't want recruiters or prospective employers to see.

- ✔ **Give more than you take.** Asking for advice is fine, but look for opportunities to contribute something valuable to a discussion, something that helps the other participants.

- ✔ **Stick to the topic.** At best, wandering off topic makes you appear as though you lost focus or can't follow a discussion. At worst, it makes you look rude and self-absorbed.

✔ **Don't engage in personal attacks.** Disagreeing with someone respectfully is fine. Attacking the person with emotionally charged language or sarcasm is unacceptable. If you feel angry, don't post anything. You can always post something later, after you've calmed down, and by then, you will probably have thought better of it.

✔ **Don't share tasteless jokes.** Just because you think something's funny doesn't mean others will. Being funny online is difficult and risky.

✔ **Add something of value.** Don't just chime in with agreement or disagreement. If you're inspired to post something, make sure it adds to the discussion.

✔ **Be concise.** This is not your personal soapbox. Save that for your blog, and even then consider keeping your posts brief. Lengthy posts lack impact and probably won't be read past word 500 anyway.

✔ **Don't type in ALL CAPS,** because it is the equivalent of shouting. It's also just more difficult to read.

✔ **Enter every discussion as a gracious guest, not as a rowdy party crasher.** In other words, you want to be polite in your language as if you were talking to someone in person.

Following companies you're interested in

Organizations and their representatives are more likely to be interested in you if you show a genuine interest in them, and one small way you can do that is to "follow" or "like" them on networking sites, including Twitter, Facebook, LinkedIn, Google +, and Pinterest. Following an organization not only shows you care about the organization, but it also keeps you informed about what the organization is up to and perhaps even what's going on in the industry. This information comes in handy when you need to submit a résumé and cover letter or prepare for an interview.

Assuming you already have LinkedIn, Twitter, Facebook, Pinterest, and Google+ accounts, take the following steps for any organization you're interested in working for:

1. **Search for the organization on LinkedIn, Twitter, Facebook, and Pinterest and click any links that may help narrow your search.**

2. **If the organization's name or picture appears, click it.**

3. **Select the option to like or follow the organization.**

4. **Create a Google News alert for the organization.**

   See the later section "Incorporating Google in Your Job Search" for details.

After you choose to follow or like an organization, take advantage of the following features:

✔ Visit an organization's page on LinkedIn, and notice off to the right a How You're Connected panel that displays people you're already connected to at that organization.

✔ After you "like" an organization on Facebook, anything posted by that organization pops up in your Newsfeed.

✔ After you "follow" an organization on Twitter, its tweets appear in your Twitter feed. Some large organizations, such as IBM, have numerous divisions you can choose to follow as well.

✔ Search Twitter for job feeds and follow the ones you like, such as `twitter.com/jobsintech` and `twitter.com/hrcrossing`. Every day, thousands of jobs are posted on Twitter, often long before they appear on more traditional job boards. See the later section "Incorporating Twitter in Your Job Search" for additional guidance.

Protecting and repairing your online reputation

According to a CareerBuilder survey, more than two in five hiring managers who currently research candidates via social media said they have found information that caused them to pass over an applicant. To improve your chances of getting hired, find out what's on the web about you, take steps to remove any potentially harmful content, and make sure everything you post sheds a positive light on you or is at least neutral. In this section, I show you how.

Know what's already "out there" about you

Run a background check on yourself. Conduct an online search for your name and follow the top 10 to 20 links to see what's posted about you. Remove anything that may reflect poorly on you. If you can't remove it yourself, contact the site manager and request to have it removed.

Review everything on your Facebook Timeline, and remove anything you don't want employers or recruiters to see. Check out posts you're tagged in and untag yourself if the post contains any content, including photos, that may reflect poorly on you. Review photos you've posted on Facebook or other sites that may cast a shadow on your persona. (See the later section "Reppler and SimpleWash" for tools to help you evaluate the appropriateness of content on your Facebook Timeline.)

On Twitter, you can review mentions on your @profile and discover tweets by others that mention you. If you can't remove an unflattering comment or photo, you can at least prepare a response should a potential client or employer mention it.

Create a Google News alert for your name to be notified via email whenever anything newsworthy is posted about you (or someone with your same name) online. See "Harnessing the Power of Google" to find out how to create a Google News alert.

Be discreet

"Image is everything," as Andre Agassi coolly said in his successful ad for Canon cameras. Posting inappropriate photos and comments will come back to haunt you. Don't post a picture that shows you quaffing a pint of ale or wearing goofy clothes, even on Halloween. Don't post a comment that hints at bias by race, religion, gender, or age, even if it's meant in good fun or teasing. And never take a jab at an ex-employer or boss.

Take control

One of the most important steps in repairing and protecting your online reputation is to post more positive content from and about yourself than anyone else posts about you. Remaining active online with your own website, blog, and social media and networking accounts almost guarantees that when someone searches for you by name, links to content you posted or authorized rise to the top of the search results.

Keep at it. Post fresh content regularly to remain relevant in the eyes of Internet search engines. Creating a positive online persona and an expansive professional network is not accomplished with a one-time media blast. It's something you build over months and years of trickling content to the web and interacting in positive ways with others.

Go easy on personal and opinionated posts

Before posting anything, review it closely to make sure it promotes or at least doesn't distract from your brand. Be particularly careful about sharing too much information, going overboard with self-disclosure, or expressing what you really think about sensitive subjects, such as politics and religion.

Share yourself

Although you need to be careful about what you post, you don't want to be so tight-lipped that prospective employers can't find out anything about you online or come to think that you're not playful or creative. Hiring managers do look for a squeaky clean professional image, but they also want to get a sense of what makes you tick and your level of comfort and engagement on social media channels.

Calculated posts on your Twitter account, LinkedIn, Google+, Pinterest, and other such sites craft a fuller picture for potential employers. From me, you'll find a well-written feature story by the likes of *The New York Times* sports writer Joe Drape will pop up from time to time. I've been known to retweet items about my hometown of Pittsburgh, Pennsylvania's sports teams, ones that say what a great city the 'Burgh is to live in. I also periodically pop up in pictures of where I'm traveling and foods I savor. Can you say Café du Monde beignets?

These posts taken together can help someone understand who I am and decide whether I'm a good fit for their company culture. It also might give a hiring manager an icebreaker for interviews. I had a great interview with someone who became a new client after we both commented over pictures of our Labrador retrievers that we had posted on Facebook. I'm not sure how dogs fit in with personal branding, but they've always seemed to work well for me.

Tout your accomplishments

Bragging online is not in bad taste, if it's properly presented. For instance, there's a place on your LinkedIn profile to add all those sweet nuggets from professional recognitions and awards to volunteer activities and speaking engagements.

On LinkedIn, post recommendations for colleagues and other people you know. Whenever you recommend someone as having a particular skill or expertise, LinkedIn notifies the person, and that individual is likely to reciprocate.

Protecting your privacy

Every social media and networking channel has privacy settings you can adjust to share more or less about yourself and, in some cases, restrict what other people share about you. I strongly encourage you to check and adjust your privacy settings to suit your comfort level. With most services, you can click an icon in the upper-right corner of the opening screen to open a menu that includes a Privacy Settings option. On Pinterest, you click your name in the upper-right corner of the screen to view your page and then click the menu button in the upper-right corner of the resulting page and click Account Settings.

The available privacy settings vary depending on the service, they tend to change over time, and they're too numerous to cover in this short section, so I encourage you to explore them on your own. For details, check the service's help system.

Engaging with the community

"People don't care how much you know until they know how much you care" is a quote commonly attributed to President Theodore Roosevelt and John C. Maxwell that applies to online communities. Although I encourage you to use social media and networks as a powerful tool for finding and landing that dream job, landing a job shouldn't be the force motivating you to connect with others. If it is, you're almost destined to come across as a desperate, self-serving individual that few, if any, people want to associate with.

Instead, approach these channels as opportunities to join and share with a community of like-minded people. Look for ways to contribute valuable content. Show an interest in what others in the community post. Think first about what you can do to help someone else before thinking about what they can do to help you. Make yourself useful, and people will seek you out . . . and perhaps even offer you that dream job.

Harnessing the Power of Search Engines

While there are other search engines such as Bing and Yahoo! Search, Google is one of the most powerful job-search tools on the planet. You can search for your name as part of your ongoing image-management campaign, search for organizations and key personnel to find out more about them, set up Google News alerts to keep posted of late-breaking news about an industry or a specific organization, and use Google+ to expand your personal and professional network. Here's how:

- **Research organizations and key personnel.** Go to `www.google.com` and search for an organization you may be interested in working for. Click the link to the organization's website, and you'll find loads of information about the organization and what it does. Most organizations have an About page where you can find valuable information about the company, its leaders, its mission statement, and more.

- **Expand your network connections.** Go to `plus.google.com`, where you can join Google+, Google's answer to Facebook. Although Google+ isn't as popular as Facebook, it may provide you with information about and opportunities to connect with professionals who aren't on Facebook.

- **Create Google News alerts.** To be notified whenever a certain organization or individual is mentioned in a newsworthy article, create a Google News alert for the organization or individual. Go to `news.google.com`, search for the organization or individual by name, scroll to the bottom of the page, click Create alert, and follow the on-screen cues to create a news alert for the organization.

✔ **Google yourself.** Go to www.google.com and search for your name to find out what's been posted about you and any other people who share your name. This is an important part of managing your reputation online. See the earlier section, "Know what's already 'out there' about you" for details.

Visit www.google.com/intl/en/about/products to find out more about the many Google tools that can help you find a job or run a business. Google features its own web browser (Chrome), document sharing software, website analytics, an online calendar for scheduling, social networking (Google+), and even a tool (Picasa) for editing and sharing photos.

Tweeting Your Way to Your Next Job

I'm a Twitter fan for many reasons, but one selling point is that it doesn't require a personal introduction or recommendation, which you need with LinkedIn. Just by following other Twitter users, you can get the scoop on organizations and people you may wind up interviewing with or tapping for mentoring advice. You can also share ideas and tips with other job seekers and pros. As you follow others and post interesting tweets, you build your own following and create your own personal network.

I chat daily with Twitter friends whom I've never met or worked with, but we share ideas and information and send private messages. We help each other out. In my case, they might suggest sources for stories I'm reporting or point me toward research on a topic.

In the following sections, I explain how to register for a Twitter account, how to use it specifically to increase your exposure to employment opportunities, and how to showcase your online savviness.

Registering for a Twitter account

The first order of business is to register for a Twitter account. Head to twitter.com, and you're greeted with a screen that lets you sign in or sign up. In the New to Twitter? box, enter your name, email address, and the password you want to use to access the service. Click the Sign Up for Twitter button and then follow the trail as Twitter steps you through the process of entering a username and getting other preliminaries out of the way.

Although you can change your username at any time, as long as the username you want isn't already being used, I encourage you to choose your name carefully to reinforce your online brand presence and then keep that name, so your future Twitter followers won't lose track of you.

If you have a smartphone, get the Twitter app for your phone, so you can remain connected when you're on the road. Twitter prompts you to sign up for apps as part of the registration process.

Building an attractive profile

Shortly after registering with Twitter, click the Profile and Settings button in the upper-right corner of the Twitter page, click View Profile, click the Edit Profile button, and use the resulting screen to add a profile photo, a brief description of who you are and what you do, your city and state, and your website/blog address. Make your changes and click the Save Changes button.

Choose a good quality head shot with only you in the photo, not your significant other, your pet parakeet, or any other animate or inanimate object, unless, of course, such accoutrements are appropriate for the culture in which you're seeking employment.

Brushing up on Twitter etiquette

Twitter doesn't have many formal rules and regulations, but users generally expect you to abide by these unwritten guidelines:

- ✔ Tweet at least once a day. Tweets are no longer than 140 characters, so tweeting daily requires little effort.

- ✔ Keep Tweets longer than one word so that your followers can understand you.

- ✔ Respond to Twitter followers when you can add value to the conversation.

- ✔ Don't tweet to an individual. Instead, use the Messages feature to contact the person directly.

- ✔ Don't thank people publicly for following you. It's a lovely gesture, but some users find it annoying.

- ✔ Use a hashtag (#) before any key words in your tweet (no space between # and the word), so your tweet shows up in twitter feeds for users who are interested in the topic. Don't use more than two hashtags in a tweet. If a key word is two or more words, close up the spaces between the words, for example, #dummiesjobs.

- ✔ Whenever you're referencing another Twitter user, type @ followed by the person's username (no space after @), so the person knows you mentioned her.

Focusing on industries, companies, or professions

To use Twitter as a tool for exploring employment opportunities, choose one or more industries, companies, or professions you're interested in, tweet about them regularly, and follow others who tweet about them. You can use the Search box at the top of any Twitter page to find tweets by and about specific industries, companies, and professions you're interested in.

How many followers you have is less important than what you can learn from those you follow and the value you add to conversations. Tweet relevant, original content, and Twitter users who are active participants in the industry, company, or profession are likely to take notice.

If you mention an influential member of a particular community in a tweet, type @ followed by the person's *Twitter handle* (username) in the body of the tweet. The recipient will see the tweet in his Twitter notifications. If he has the Twitter app installed on his smartphone, he will be notified instantly. This is one way to get noticed by an employer or recruiter.

Plugging into job feeds

Twitter has dozens of job feeds for specific companies, industries, and locations. Conduct a Twitter search to find relevant job feeds. For example, search for "microsoft jobs," and you find several feeds for jobs at Microsoft, including @MicrosoftJobs, @MicrosoftJobsUS, and @MicrosoftJobsNL. Search for "jobs chicago," and you find @JobsChicago, @ChicagoWebJobs, and @Jobs4CHI.

Try searching with and without spaces between the key words to get different results. Also, instead of executing the search, simply type your key words into the Search box and wait. A drop-down menu appears with several of the top job feed matches for what you typed.

Certain Twitter apps can also help you in your job hunt. Check out TweetMyJobs at `www.tweetmyjobs.com/job-seeker`, where you can choose to have targeted job openings delivered directly to you via email or Twitter or to your smartphone. All you do is type a description of the job title you're interested in or the skills you have, along with the city, state, and zip code of where you prefer to work; choose the desired delivery method; and click Send Me Job Matches.

Following the right Twitter users

When you first sign up and before you start tweeting regularly, be selective when choosing Twitter users to follow, so you become associated with the right crowd and don't dilute your inner circle with users who are irrelevant to meeting your goals. Start slowly, following people you know and who know you. Then, as you start tweeting regularly, follow more people based on your interests or the companies you're curious about.

In addition to following individuals on Twitter, follow the organizations that interest you professionally, especially those you'd like to work for.

For valuable advice in finding and landing the job you want, consider following one or more of the experts listed here:

Job Search

@Absolutely_Abby

@AlisonDoyle

@AvidCareerist

@CareerAttract and @KevinKermes

@CareerRocketeer

@CornOnTheJob

@David_Shindler

@DawnRasmussen

@dorothydalton

@eExecutives

@HeatherHuhman

@JacobShare

@JobHunterCoach

@JobHuntOrg

@JoshuaWaldman

@KatCareerGal

@Keppie_Careers

@PhyllisMufson

@Social_Hire

@Tonyrestell

@undercoverrec

@YouTern and @YouTernMark

Résumés, Cover Letters, and More

@jobjenny

@SandraJTResumes

@JulieWalraven

@LisaRangel

@ResumeExpert

@resumeservice

@rezlady and @ITtechExec

@ValueIntoWords

Career

@AARPMoney

@Beverlyejones

@careersherpa

@dailymuse

@encoreorg

@DorieClark

@MaggieMistal

@ManageAmericans

@MeghanMBiro

@MHynesPDX

@WorkCoachCafe

@NextAvenue

Recruiters

@animal

@ChrisRussell

@JimStroud

@levyrecruits

@RecruitingBlogs

@StacyZapar

Human Resources

@CyndyTrivella

@realevilhrlady

@hrbartender	@LifeReimagined	@USNewsCareers
@new_resource	@megguiseppi	@WetFeet_Career
@SabrinaLBaker	@PeterSterlacci	@BI_Careers
@SteveBoese	@WalterAkana	**Over 50 Job Search**
@tombolt	**Big Guys**	@KerryHannon
@ThisIsLars	@Glassdoor	@CareerPivot
Personal Branding	@Flexjobs	@NancyCollamer
	@Coolworks	@JobhuntOrg
@DanSchawbel	@MonsterCareers	

Use Twitter lists to keep your personal and professional conversations separate. To view your lists, click the Profile and Settings button in the upper-right corner of any Twitter page and click Lists. Scroll down the page and click Create New List. Type a name and description for the list, choose to make it Public or Private, and click Save List. Follow the on-screen cues to add Twitter users to your list. To view tweets from only those users on the list, click the Profile and Settings button, click Lists, and click the desired list.

Tapping the Power and Reach of Facebook

With 1.39 billion monthly users, Facebook is more than four times the size of LinkedIn, which has 332 million members. For that reason alone, Facebook is an essential component of your personal branding campaign and an excellent tool for networking your way to your next job. If you're inclined to start a job search by asking people you know, you're more likely to find these folks tuned in to Facebook than to any other social venue. In short, if you don't have a Facebook account, head over to Facebook.com and register. In this section, I explain how to create a Facebook account and leverage its power to find your next job.

In addition to helping you expand your personal and professional network and get connected with people who can help you find and secure employment, Facebook can open the doors to great conversations during a job interview.

Gaining a competitive edge

A recent survey by Jobvite, the leading social recruiting and applicant tracking system, found that older job seekers are not using social media and mobile job apps enough to find out about jobs and to apply for them. When Jobvite asked: "Which of the following resources did you use that directly led to finding your current/ most recent job," only 3 percent of those 55 and older and 5 percent of those age 40 to 54 said "social network." By contrast, 19 percent of respondents 18 to 29 did. Only 10 percent of survey respondents age 40 to 54 said they use Facebook to find connections and network.

The social network numbers for older workers don't make sense today, when you consider that 73 percent of recruiters hire through social networks and 93 percent say they view applicants' social profile before making a decision.

But then again, this can be good news for you. By building a strong online persona, especially on the top social media and networking channels, you gain a competitive advantage over a significant majority of job seekers who fail to tap into these valuable resources.

Creating a Facebook account

To create a Facebook account, visit www.facebook.com, complete the Sign Up form, click the Sign Up button, and follow the on-screen prompts to get started. Facebook sends you an email message, and you need to confirm your email address before you can do much more on Facebook. After you confirm your email address, Facebook prompts you to flesh out your profile with education and work history along with other details and find people you already know on Facebook. Simply follow the prompts. If you get stuck, click the icon in the upper-right corner of any Facebook page and click Help.

If you have a smartphone, get the Facebook app for your phone, so you can remain connected when you're on the road.

Editing your Facebook profile

In your eagerness to get started on Facebook, you may have omitted important profile data. Take the time to edit your profile and flesh it out with additional details. To edit your profile, click your name or picture in the navigation bar at the top of any Facebook page and click the Update Info button near the middle of the resulting page. The About page appears. Focus on the following areas:

Do I need a Facebook page?

On Facebook, you can create a page to promote a business, service, product, or even yourself, which makes pages an excellent choice for businesses. If, however, your focus is on personal branding, posting to your Timeline or Newsfeed as yourself is more likely to help reinforce your online brand presence in the eyes of search engines. So you're probably better off posting status updates about your work and connecting with people and organizations on Facebook as yourself rather than as a page.

Pages do have one great benefit in that the page enables you to keep your personal and professional status updates separate, but generally speaking, the drawbacks outweigh the benefits.

✔ **Work and Education:** Include all employers you worked for over the past 10 to 15 years, omitting any places you worked for fewer than six months. Add professional skills along with any colleges you attended and the high school from which you graduated.

✔ **Contact and Basic Info:** Add the address of your website/blog. Linking to your website/blog improves its search engine ranking. You may also want to include your email address to make it easy for people to contact you, but if you don't want to share your email address, people can contact you by using Facebook's Message feature.

Click the section you want to edit in the left panel. To add an entry to a section (for example, to add a workplace to the Work and Education section), click the link to add the entry and follow the onscreen cues. To edit an existing entry, mouse over it, click Options, click Edit, and then enter and save your changes.

Whenever you choose to create or edit an entry, a privacy icon appears, initially labeled Public, Friends, Only Me, or Custom. Click the icon and choose the desired privacy setting to permit access to everyone (Public) or restrict access to certain people.

Checking your privacy settings

Before you start to open up on Facebook, check your privacy settings to determine what you're set up to share and with whom and to adjust the settings to share more or less, depending on your preference. To access your privacy settings, click the icon in the upper-right corner of any Facebook page, click Settings, and then click Privacy in the navigation bar on the left. For most content, you have the following options:

- ✔ **Public:** Share with anyone on or off Facebook.
- ✔ **Friends:** Share only with people you befriended on Facebook.
- ✔ **Only Me:** Visible only by you.
- ✔ **Custom:** Share with specific friends or groups of friends or not share with specific friends or groups of friends.
- ✔ **Selected Groups:** You can create groups, such as Family, Friends, and Coworkers, add specific Facebook friends to each group, and share selectively with those groups.

Following the organizations that interest you

Soon after you flesh out your profile, search for organizations where you'd like to work. When you find an organization, click its link to pull up its page and click the Like button. This adds the organization to your list of Likes on your Timeline. When you choose to like an organization, the +Follow button next to the Liked button becomes active. Click the +Follow button so content that's posted by the organization will appear in your Newsfeed when you click the Home button in the navigation bar at the top of any Facebook page.

If you want to keep up with an organization's status updates on Facebook, you must choose to both Like and Follow the organization.

Posting status updates and comments

As with most social media and networking sites, you need to post content regularly on Facebook to reap its benefits and remain relevant in the communities to which you belong. Facebook makes it easy to post status updates and to comment on content your friends post. To post a status update, click Home in the navigation bar at the top, click What's on your mind?, type your status update, and click Post or press Enter. You can also post photos or videos.

If a status update appears in your newsfeed and you want to add something to the discussion, click Comment, type your comment, and press Enter.

As on Twitter, you can type a hashtag (#) before a key word in a status update or comment on Facebook to turn the key word into a link that you or others can click to see related posts. You can also search for hashtags in the Search box at the top of any Facebook page, but you'll see only those posts you're authorized to view.

Enhancing Facebook with specialized apps

Facebook wasn't planned for professional networking and job searching. Subsequently, seeing what companies are in your network and creating a more vigorous professional presence isn't natural to Facebook. That's why several companies have developed Facebook applications designed to fill this void. In this section, I highlight a few of the more useful and popular Facebook personal branding and job search apps.

BranchOut

BranchOut analyzes your Facebook friend network to help you identify all your professional connections, including your friends and your friends' friends, providing access to three million available jobs. With more than 800 million profiles, BranchOut is the largest professional networking service.

To use BranchOut, go to `branchout.com`, click in the People or Jobs box, type the name of the person or the job title you're looking for, select a category to search, and click the Search People or Search Jobs button. The first time you use the service, it requests that you log on to your Facebook account so it can get the information it needs to do its job, including accessing your friend list, email address, work and education history, and your friends' work and education history. Assuming you're okay with that, click Okay.

BranchOut displays the relevant jobs matched by title, location, and company name. BranchOut analyzes your friend network and provides the inside track through your network to the job, if such a path exists. For example, when you search for people by company name, you see which of your friends or your friends' friends work at that company. This inside track may provide greater accessibility to the decision makers.

GlassDoor

GlassDoor holds a growing database of 6 million company reviews, CEO approval ratings, salary reports, interview reviews and questions, benefits reviews, office photos, and more. Unlike other jobs sites, all this information is entirely shared by those who know a company best — the employees. Add to that millions of the latest jobs — no other community allows you to see which employers are hiring, what it's really like to work or interview there according to employees, and how much you could earn.

To use GlassDoor, visit www.glassdoor.com; choose to search Jobs, Companies & Reviews, Salaries, or Interviews; enter the key words to describe what you're looking for, enter the location (city and state), and click the Search button. You're not required to share your Facebook account or friend list, but by choosing to integrate GlassDoor with your Facebook account (and giving it access to your friend list), you gain a few additional perks, such as seeing which of your Facebook friends work for a particular company you're looking into, so you can find an inside track to the job.

GlassDoor is also available via its mobile app on iOS and Android platforms.

Reppler and SimpleWash

Reppler at www.reppler.com and SimpleWash at www.simplewa.sh are Facebook Timeline scanning tools that scrutinize your pictures and timeline posts for tone, appropriateness, and any signs of someone hacking your account. To use either tool, simply log in with your Facebook account and give it a few minutes to scan your Timeline. Repeat the scan every couple of weeks to make sure your Timeline is still clean.

Chapter 10

Marketing Yourself on LinkedIn

*W*hether you're job hunting or shaking the bushes for contract work, LinkedIn is *the* professional networking place to be. On LinkedIn, you can reconnect with old colleagues, expand your professional network with friends and relatives, make new contacts, obtain endorsements in your areas of expertise, dig up information on companies and positions you're interested in, learn about the people who'll be reading your cover letter and résumé or interviewing you for the job, find the inside track to certain positions, and much more.

In fact, data shows that LinkedIn is especially helpful when it comes to landing higher-paying jobs. It's the place where hiring managers go to scan the horizon for potential candidates, particularly to fill positions in the management and professional categories.

In this chapter, I show you how to open a free LinkedIn account, create a professional profile to make you a more attractive candidate, and tap the power of LinkedIn's most useful features. Along the way, I offer guidance and tips specifically for job seekers over 50.

Keep in mind that LinkedIn is continually changing. When it rolls out new features or formats, it does so progressively to the overall network. So what you're seeing on your screen may not be what someone else is seeing. And because these features change frequently, what you're reading here may differ from what you see when you log in to your LinkedIn account, so remain flexible. You may need to poke around a little or consult the LinkedIn help system to find a certain feature.

Knowing How LinkedIn Can Help You in Your Job Search

Studies show that employers and recruiters are more likely to use LinkedIn in their recruitment and hiring efforts than job seekers are to use it for securing employment (see the nearby sidebar "Just how helpful is LinkedIn?"). As I see it, that fact is reason enough to be on LinkedIn, because it gives you an edge over others competing for the same job. If you're not convinced yet, here are some ways you can use LinkedIn to land your next job:

- ✔ **Create a multi-faceted tech-savvy résumé.** Unlike your one-dimensional print résumé, your LinkedIn profile highlights all your skills and interests in a far richer fashion, even featuring videos, slideshows, work samples, and more.

- ✔ **Build a professional network.** Your LinkedIn profile makes you a member of the largest online professional network in the world, and networking is the number-one way to find a job.

- ✔ **Spread the word.** When you find yourself out of work, your first impulse may be to hide, but the best thing you can do is let everyone know you're looking for a job. LinkedIn helps you do just that.

- ✔ **Catch the eye of recruiters.** Recruiters prowl LinkedIn to find the most qualified candidates. Just being a LinkedIn member increases your chances of being discovered.

- ✔ **Research organizations and people.** When you need to know more about organizations that require your skills or about a person who'll be interviewing you, turn to your connections on LinkedIn. You can also use LinkedIn to reach out to others in your field who may be able to offer valuable advice or assistance with your job hunt.

- ✔ **Help hiring agents perform their due diligence:** Prior to hiring a candidate for a job, a hiring agent must perform due diligence to weed out any candidates who may not be suited for the position. Take away any reason they may have to reject you by putting relevant details in your profile. If they can find the information they need on LinkedIn, they may not dig any deeper.

Just how helpful is LinkedIn?

Study results are fuzzy regarding just how helpful LinkedIn is in landing a job, and they seem to vary depending on whether you talk to job seekers or employers/recruiters:

✔ According to a recent survey by JobVite, 94 percent of employers use LinkedIn to research, vet, and recruit employees, but only about 36 percent of job seekers use the social media platform.

✔ A study by the Society for Human Resource Management found that 77 percent of employers use social networks to recruit, a sharp increase from the 56 percent who reported doing so in 2011. Among recruiters using social tools, 94 percent said they use LinkedIn.

✔ "The Long Road Back: Struggling to Find Work after Unemployment," AARP's recent survey sponsored by the AARP Public Policy Institute's Future of Work@50 initiative, found that for those who had been unemployed in the last five years, the most effective way to find a new job was reaching out to a network of contacts, followed by asking relatives and friends about jobs, contacting employers directly, using a headhunter, and consulting professional associations. Interestingly, "used online social networks" didn't make the top five list of most effective means of finding a job. Only 20 percent used online social networks. Of those, just 45 percent of the reemployed said doing so was very or somewhat effective.

You can draw different conclusions from this data. Perhaps online networking is more useful for employers and recruiters than it is for job seekers. Maybe job seekers are slow to adapt to new technologies, and tapping these resources will give you an edge. Or perhaps sites such as LinkedIn are more helpful for certain jobs and less helpful for others. Even though the data is a little fuzzy, I strongly recommend using these online tools in your job search efforts. For many people I know, LinkedIn has made the difference between getting the job and getting a ding letter.

Putting Yourself on LinkedIn

Getting a LinkedIn account is a snap. Head to www.linkedin.com, complete the Get Started form, click the Join Now button, follow the on-screen prompts, confirm your email address, and you're on LinkedIn. Your LinkedIn account is free and takes less than two minutes to create.

However, making yourself an attractive target for employers and recruiters requires additional time and effort. In this section, I offer guidance on how to create an attractive professional profile that serves as your LinkedIn résumé and raise your profile's impact on LinkedIn to get yourself noticed. I also offer guidance on tweaking your privacy settings to limit access to certain people and, more importantly, avoid annoying your connections with unsolicited notifications from your account.

Building an irresistible LinkedIn profile

Your profile is your personal representative on LinkedIn, reflecting the person you are and the employee you will be. It's where recruiters and prospective employers go when they want to find out more about you. When a hiring manager looks at it, you want that person to see a clear portrait of your background, skills, and experience and to learn a bit about how you spend your time outside the workplace.

Equally important, a comprehensive online profile subliminally helps ease concerns about your age: It sends the message that you've successfully transitioned to 21st-century culture and technology. A well-crafted LinkedIn profile can give you a substantial advantage when you're on a job hunt, so it's worth taking the time to launch one or give your existing LinkedIn profile a makeover.

In the sections that follow, I guide you through the process of creating an irresistible profile.

 Be very open about the fact that you're looking for new opportunities and very clear about the opportunities you're looking for. Having a definite idea of what you want shows employers that you're not going to waste their time trying to "find yourself" as so many younger candidates are apt to do. In addition, it lets headhunters and employers know that you're not someone they have to persuade to switch jobs or companies.

Conducting preliminary research

Before you start to flesh out your profile, do some preliminary research to find out more about your industry and the people in it and to get some ideas for how to create an attractive profile:

- ✔ **Check out the competition.** Use the Search box at the top of any LinkedIn page to search for people in your field, and then check out their LinkedIn profiles. Collect key words to include in your summary and note ways to clarify the work you do in a clever, non-jargon way. With a little sleuthing, you can come away with some great models to use as a springboard to help your profile stand out.

- ✔ **Read postings for jobs you may be interested in.** Click Jobs, near the top of any LinkedIn page, and search for jobs you're interested in. Read the job descriptions, and note the knowledge and skills required for those jobs, so you know which skills to highlight in your profile and which skills you need to develop. See the later section "Finding Job Postings on LinkedIn" for details on how to search for jobs.

Editing your profile

To edit your profile, mouse over Profile in the menu near the top of any LinkedIn page and click Edit Profile. Once there, you can do the following:

✔ **Edit your contact info.** In the bottom-right corner of your basic information section, click Contact Info. Click the entry you want to change, enter the desired change, and click Save.

✔ **Edit sections.** Your profile is modular, consisting of sections you can edit, add, delete, and rearrange. To edit a section, mouse over it and click the entry you want to edit, enter the desired changes, and click Save. To remove an item from a section (for example, a position in your Experience section), mouse over it, click any entry in the item, and click the Remove option near the bottom of the item.

✔ **Add and rearrange sections.** Just below the section that contains your basic information is a prompt to add a section to your profile. Click View More just beneath this prompt to view additional sections you can add. Click a section to add it to your

profile. To rearrange sections, mouse over the section you want to move, mouse over the double-headed arrow that appears in the upper-right corner of the section, drag it up or down, and drop it in place.

✔ **View your profile from different perspectives.** Click the View Profile As button, and you can choose to view your profile as people in your LinkedIn network will see it or as the public sees it. To choose which people see what, mouse over your profile icon in the upper-right corner of any LinkedIn page, click Privacy & Settings, and use the resulting options to enter your preferences.

Prior to making numerous changes to your profile, turn off the option to have people in your network notified of any changes. This option appears on the right side of your Edit Profile page. Drag the slider button, so the Notify Your Network? option is set to No. Otherwise, your contacts will receive a barrage of notifications as you make changes to your profile, which is very annoying.

Starting with an attractive photo

According to the experts at LinkedIn, a profile that contains a photo is seven times more likely to be viewed by a recruiter or hiring manager than a profile without a photo. And nobody really knows how many job candidates are passed over by a prospective employer simply because the employer can't access a photo of the person.

Look at it this way, if you leave a networking event with a handful of business cards, intending to follow up on LinkedIn, it's much harder for you to remember who's who without pictures. A missing photo can easily lead to missed connections.

Get a professional head shot. By "professional," I mean one that makes you look professional and looks as if it were taken by a professional photographer. Your profile photo should be of you and you alone, not of you and your significant other. It should have a muted background. Groom yourself, dress the part, strike a pose, and have your photographer snap the photo and send the digital image to you in the form of a JPEG file. Unless you're the Annie Leibovitz of selfies, don't go there.

Log in to your LinkedIn account and pull up the page to edit your profile. Click Add a Photo or Change Photo, and use the resulting dialog box to upload your photo.

To personalize your profile, consider adding an attractive background image. Click Add a Background Photo atop your profile page and use the resulting dialog box to select a photo to upload. Don't choose anything that's too busy and might distract from your personal photo.

Claiming and using your branded URL

A *branded URL* (often called a *vanity URL*) is your portfolio's web address that contains your name instead of a generic entry. For example, you can find me at www.linkedin.com/in/kerryhannon. On your Edit Profile page, you can see your LinkedIn URL below your profile photo. If your name appears at the end of that link in the form you want it to appear, you're good to go. If it doesn't match the name you want to use to establish yourself as a brand, then take the following steps to change it.

1. **Click the URL link under your profile photo.**

   Your Public Profile page appears.

2. **Under the Your Public Profile URL section on the right, click the Edit icon next to your URL.**

3. **Type your name in the form you want to use for building your personal brand.**

   (Your name can be 5 to 30 letters or numbers but can't contain spaces, symbols, or special characters. I advise sticking with letters — no numbers. See Chapter 9 for more about personal branding.)

   Custom URLs are available on a first-come, first-served basis, so if the name you want to use is already taken, you must use a slightly different version of your name, perhaps by adding a middle initial.

4. **Click Save.**

Make the most of your branded URL by including it in all correspondence, including in the heading of your résumé, below your signature on your cover letter, and near the bottom of all email messages you send.

Consider creating a Quick Response (QR) code that links directly to your profile. A QR code works like a bar code. Anyone with a smartphone and a QR reader (app) can scan your QR code and instantly access your LinkedIn profile. You can use a free service, such as Kaywa (qrcode.kaywa.com), to generate your QR code. Add your LinkedIn QR code to your business cards and résumé.

Creating a captivating headline

Your *headline* is the text that appears near the top of your profile, just below your name. When employers run a LinkedIn search, the search results display names, photos, and headlines. Your headline can be up to 120 characters long, and I suggest you make the most of those 120 characters.

To edit your headline, mouse over that area of your profile and click the pen icon that appears next to your headline. A pop-up appears, prompting you to enter your professional headline. Click in the box and type a headline that's likely to catch a viewer's interest and that describes exactly what you do or want to do professionally. For instance, mine reads, Expert/Author/Speaker. If you aren't sure what to enter, click Show Examples for suggestions. Make sure your professional headline highlights any key words you want to use to promote yourself.

If you're job hunting, I recommend including some indication that you're actively looking for employment, something along the lines of "Actively pursuing new opportunities X, Y and Z." This signals to recruiters and hiring managers that you're on the market and saves them the time of trying to woo someone away from an existing employer. Another option is to place your desired job title in your headline and then use your summary to mention that you're looking for a particular position. (See the later section "Writing your summary: Your career story" for details.)

Editing your contact information

The Contact Information section of the LinkedIn profile is perhaps the most overlooked section of all. In this section, you can add links to your other online properties, including your personal website/blog, Twitter account, and portfolio (if you have one). Of course, you can also add your branded email address (see Chapter 9 for more about that), an instant messaging (IM) address, and your phone number and mailing address to make it easy for recruiters and employers to contact you. Fill in as many links as you can to give recruiters a wide range of ways to get in touch with you and to provide a well-rounded look at what type of person you are.

Having other websites, including LinkedIn, link out to your personal website/blog raises your website/blog's search engine ranking, so when someone uses a search engine to search for you or for someone who does what you do, your site appears higher in the search results.

To edit your contact information, click the Contact Info button in the lower-right corner of the basic information section at the top of your profile, mouse over the entry you want to edit, and click the pen icon next to the entry. Follow the on-screen cues to enter and save your change.

Writing your summary: Your career story

The Summary section is where you tell your story in your own voice. It becomes your mini-bio, your sizzle reel. Take this opportunity to hook anyone who pulls up your profile and persuade them to dig deeper to find out more about you. Here are some guidelines to follow when composing your summary:

- **Write one or two short, snappy paragraphs.** Highlight your key skills and examples of accomplishments. Approach your summary as though you're writing a short cover letter.

- **Write in the first or third person.** Use the first person — *I, me,* and *my* — to add a personal touch, or describe yourself in the third person — *he, she, him,* or *her,* — to make your summary sound more objective. Neither option is better or worse, but choose one and stick to it; don't have one paragraph in third person and another in first person.

- **Focus more on skills and less on experience.** By focusing on experience, you may pigeonhole yourself into certain positions and limit your opportunities. By focusing on skills, you expand your horizons, because skills developed in one area of expertise may transfer to another. This is especially important on LinkedIn, where you can have only one summary; you can't customize it for different positions you're interested in as you can with a résumé and cover letter.

- **Tell what you're looking for.** Conclude with a sentence that starts with something like, "I am currently looking for new opportunities . . ." followed by a description of the work and situation you're looking for. For example, "I am currently looking for an opportunity to use my skills in writing and analysis in the field of green energy."

Although you can add a separate section to your profile for volunteer gigs, consider mentioning any volunteer work that you're particularly passionate about. This gives you an opportunity to write about what motivates you, the type of work that excites you (the work you choose to do even when you're not getting paid for it), and the skills you've developed in that capacity. You may conclude your summary with something like, "I am passionate about the work I did with [nonprofit organization], where I [description of skills or accomplishments]."

Detailing your job experience

When you get to the Experience section of your LinkedIn profile, you may want to pull up or print out a copy of your résumé, which should contain most of the information you need to flesh out this section. Then, go at it. Enter your entire work history. For each position you held, mouse over the Experience section, click +Add Position, enter your information in the resulting form, and click Save. As you enter details about the positions you've held, follow these guidelines:

- ✔ **Include all positions you held for six months or longer.** Don't try to obscure your age by including only the last two or three positions. As a mature employee, your experience and longevity in the workplace is what differentiates you from younger job seekers.

- ✔ **Use your formal job titles.** Don't try to be creative by using a job title such as Money Guru or Sales Slam-Dunker. You may want to tweak your title to make it more descriptive of what you did or want to do; for example, if your previous job title was Investment Specialist, and you want to specialize in mutual funds, you may change your title to "Mutual Funds Specialist."

- ✔ **Keep it punchy.** When describing job responsibilities, skills, and accomplishments in the Description box, lead with verbs and keep them short; for example, "Led strategy," "Developed budget," "Managed . . . ," "Devised . . . ," "Created . . . ," and so on.

- ✔ **Include accomplishments.** In the Description area, be sure to mention quantifiable accomplishments; for example, "Completed key project two months ahead of schedule," or "Outperformed projections by 40 percent," or "Increased sales by 20 percent."

- ✔ **Rearrange positions strategically.** Arrange your positions in reverse chronological order with your most recent position first, unless you have good reason to do otherwise. For example, if you're looking for a particular position, you may want to list previous positions in which you excelled in skills required by the position you're seeking.

You can get creative in the Description box by creating and formatting your job description in your word processing application and then copying and pasting it into the Description box. You may need to experiment with formatting to see what works best. For example, short bullet list items (that don't wrap) look good, but long bullets don't. Also, bullets tend to look better if you create them manually with tabs and wingding characters, such as ✓, than if you use the word processor's bullet style.

Including volunteer positions

Scroll down to see whether your profile has a Volunteer section. If it doesn't and you've served as a volunteer, add the Volunteer section and add any volunteer positions you've held. (The option to add sections is just below your profile photo.)

Highlighting your passion and commitment to philanthropic organizations shows employers that you don't spend your time away from the workplace sitting on the couch but rather out doing something and making a difference, giving back. According to LinkedIn, 42 percent of hiring managers surveyed said they view volunteer experience as equivalent to formal work experience. It can set you apart from other candidates.

Volunteer work can be a great icebreaker. One woman I know who was hiring is a dog lover and saw two candidates on LinkedIn who were qualified. One of them volunteered at ASPCA. Guess who got the job.

LinkedIn also has a section you can add to your profile called Volunteering Opportunities, which prompts you to specify whether you'd like to join a nonprofit board or contribute your skills pro bono (for free). Nonprofits can then contact you to offer positions or seek your assistance. These aren't paid positions, but volunteering usually offers excellent networking opportunities, skill updates (and proof of updated skills), and a chance to feel good about yourself. You can sign up to follow the nonprofits on LinkedIn, which can help you learn more about the group and any paid positions that open up down the road.

Adding your educational achievements

Letting LinkedIn know the diplomas and degrees you've earned does more than just pad your profile for the benefit of recruiters and employers. It also helps you get connected with people who attended the same schools. Based on the information you enter about the schools you attended, LinkedIn can recommend people you know who may be on LinkedIn and get you connected.

To add a school, scroll down to the Education section, mouse over it, click +Add Education, fill out the resulting form, and click Save.

A perpetual question I get is whether 50-plus job seekers should include graduation dates, which are a nod to their age. In my opinion, this is a personal choice. Ultimately, omitting graduation dates doesn't mask your age, but I don't put mine on my profile. Other experts think it offers a point of connection with possible hiring managers who might be peers.

Listing your skills

LinkedIn allows you to list up to 50 skills or areas of expertise. Your connections on LinkedIn can then choose to endorse you. (See the later section "Giving and getting recommendations and endorsements" for details.) To add skills, scroll down to the Skills & Endorsements section of your profile and click +Add a Skill. Click in the What Are Your Areas of Expertise? Box, type a skill or area of expertise, and click Add. You can drag and drop skills to arrange them in their order of importance.

Carefully decide which words to use to describe your skills and areas of expertise. Use words that recruiters and employers are likely to enter when searching for someone with your experience and skills. If you're targeting a specific job or job title in your search, you may want to choose words that match those used in job descriptions for positions you'd like to apply for.

When you're listing your skills, be sure to check the Skills and Endorsement Settings. Make sure the I Want to be Endorsed option is set to Yes and that all the checkboxes below that option are checked. One of the best ways to get endorsements is to give them.

Adding other important sections to your profile

The more details you include in your profile, the bigger the target you become for recruiters and the more reasons you give prospective employers to give you the thumbs up. Just below your profile picture is the Add a Section to Your Profile area. Click View More at the bottom of this area to check out other sections you can add to your profile. Here are a few of the available sections you should consider adding if you have anything relevant to put in these sections:

- **Causes You Care About:** Adding a Causes You Care About section shows that you're more than just the work you do. You're sensitive to the needs of others.

- **Certifications:** In certain industries, certifications are essential in demonstrating that you have the knowledge and skills to perform the job. A certification in some cases may be the equivalent to holding a college degree, and more important.

- **Courses:** Include seminars, classes, workshops, and other educational achievements to show that you're a lifelong learner and dedicated to self-improvement.

- **Honors & Awards:** Include any honors or awards you achieved, such as Employee of the Year, competitions you've won, or other notable and relevant achievements.

✔ **Languages:** If you have proficiency in any languages other than English, add the Languages section to your profile and indicate the languages you know and your proficiency in each. In the global economy, knowing another language may be key in landing certain jobs.

✔ **Organizations:** List organizations you're involved with and any leadership and service positions you hold now or have held in the recent past.

✔ **Patents:** If you hold or have held patents for innovative products or designs, list them here.

✔ **Projects:** Highlight any projects you've been involved with to demonstrate that you have the experience and skills relevant to any positions you're pursuing. This is also a great section for adding side gigs you've had, say, as a consultant, speaker, or home-based business, even one that's a hobby.

✔ **Publications:** If you've published anything at all, you're a step ahead of most people on the planet. If you published on a topic related to an industry in which you're trying to find work, that publication shows that you're an expert in some aspect of the industry.

Adding media samples to your profile

If you're in a creative profession in which employers or clients review work samples as part of their evaluation process, add media samples to your profile. You can add documents, presentations, videos, and so on to the Summary, Education, and Experience sections of your profile.

For best results, use compatible file types or content providers. Visit www. embed.ly/providers to check out a list of compatible content providers.

To add media samples to your profile, here's what you do:

1. **Mouse over Profile at the top of any LinkedIn page and click Edit Profile.**

2. **Mouse over the section you want to add a media sample to and click the Add Media icon (the blue box) in the upper-right corner of the section.**

   If you don't see the Add Media icon, you can add samples by clicking the file type next to Add Media at the bottom of each profile section.

3. **Type a website address of the media file if it's stored somewhere online or click Upload a File, and choose the media file stored on your computer.**

4. **Follow the on-screen cues to complete the operation.**

Knowing what to omit

The more you include in your profile, the more likely you'll be discovered by a recruiter or employer. Likewise, if an employer is considering you for a position, the more the person is able to find out about you on LinkedIn, the more likely they'll choose you over other candidates. Of course, that depends on whether they like what they find. Here are a few suggestions on what to omit from your profile:

- **Anything you don't have time to do properly:** Spend some time crafting everything you post. Anything that's slapped together in a hurry will look that way. A little high-quality detail is better than a lot of junk.

- **Mentions of political or religious affiliations:** Unless you're looking for a job with certain political or religious organizations, you probably don't know the affiliations of the person who's going to make the hiring decision, so don't mention which way you lean. Choose other "Causes You Care About" with care; choosing "Environment" may seem harmless, for example, but it could get misinterpreted in industries that often come into conflict with environmentalists.

- **Personal details:** The Personal Details section, containing your birthday and marital status is optional, and I see no reason to include it.

- **Current position:** If you're currently unemployed, be sure to remove the check mark from the I Currently Work Here box for any position you listed under Experience. Don't be concerned that your job shows an end date. It's okay to be in between jobs.

Knowing when you're finished

In the upper-right portion of your Edit Profile page is a Profile Strength meter. When the meter indicates "All-Star," your profile is acceptable. However, there's always room for improvement. Check out below the Profile Strength meter for additional information and guidance on how you may be able to improve your profile. For example, LinkedIn may recommend additional courses or programs in your field. Here, you can also see how many people have viewed your profile in the past 90 days and how your profile has performed over the past 30 days.

When you're done fleshing out your profile and carefully editing it and correcting any errors, turn on the Notify Your Network option below the Profile Strength area. Simply drag the button from No to Yes. By doing so, you give LinkedIn permission to notify your LinkedIn connections whenever you update your profile.

Keeping it current

Completing your LinkedIn profile doesn't mean you're done. Whenever you achieve a new milestone — you land a new position, earn a relevant certification, complete a major project, whatever — log back onto LinkedIn and update your profile. Every achievement demonstrates that you're progressing and growing as a person and a professional, that you're not stuck in the past. One of the biggest mistakes people make on LinkedIn is letting their profile stagnate.

Controlling what you share in your public profile

By default, your entire profile is online for all to share. It's likely to appear in search results whenever someone searches for you by name (or for someone who has a similar name), and unless you specify otherwise, everybody can see everything in your profile. Making your profile accessible to all is what you usually want, particularly if you're actively job hunting. You want recruiters and employers to have full access to your public profile.

If you want to be more selective or simply want to check how much of your profile LinkedIn is set up to share, click Profile, near the top of any LinkedIn page, mouse over the down arrow next to the View Profile As button and click Manage Public Profile Settings. This displays your profile as it will appear in public along with a bar on the right that contains your public profile settings. You can choose Make My Public Profile Visible to No One, so that only those you choose to connect with on LinkedIn can view it, or choose Make My Public Profile Visible to Everyone. If you choose the second option, which I strongly recommend, you can then click the box next to any item you want to hide from the public to remove the check mark next to it (something I don't recommend).

Below your public profile settings is a link called Create a Public Profile Badge. Click the link to get a code you can copy and paste on your website to display a link that visitors to your website can click to access your LinkedIn profile.

Checking and adjusting your privacy settings

Before you become very active on or invested in LinkedIn, I encourage you to check your privacy settings. These settings are important not only for protecting yourself but also for preventing any of your contacts from being inundated with notifications of activities you've engaged in on LinkedIn and becoming annoyed with you because of them.

To check your privacy settings, mouse over your profile photo, in the upper-right corner of any LinkedIn page, and click Privacy & Settings. Click on the links below Privacy Controls to find out what your options are and make adjustments. Until you get a feel for LinkedIn, I recommend keeping your profile public (as explained in the previous section) but adjusting the two following Privacy Controls to maintain a lower profile on LinkedIn:

- ✔ **Turn on/off your activity broadcasts:** I suggest turning this off if it isn't already until you gain experience on LinkedIn, especially if you're the type of person who likes to experiment with a new technology. You don't want to inundate your connections with notifications of everything you're doing until you know what you're doing and can be more deliberate in what you share and the activities you engage in. You can turn this setting on before updating your profile, so your connections are informed of the change.

- ✔ **Select what others see when you've viewed their profile:** If you want to be able to check out other people's LinkedIn profiles without them knowing it was you, change to one of the anonymous settings.

If you're currently employed, consider removing the check mark next to the I Currently Work Here box for your current position under Experience. Otherwise, LinkedIn broadcasts anniversary notices to all your LinkedIn contacts every year on the starting date you entered, which some people find annoying.

Getting Connected on LinkedIn

The whole point of putting yourself on LinkedIn is to get connected. Networking opens the door to employment opportunities by converting cold calls into warm calls. Ideally, people get to know you *before* you need a job, so you have an inside track when you do need a job. Less ideally, LinkedIn enables you to find the jobs you're interested in and leverage your existing connections with current and former coworkers, people you've gone to school with, friends, and relatives to find that all-important inside track to the job you want.

Getting connected on LinkedIn involves more than simply reaching out to people you know on LinkedIn, although that's a key first step. It also involves giving and getting endorsements, engaging in relevant group discussions, and following the right companies and individuals. In this section, I introduce you to the various ways to get connected on LinkedIn.

Connecting with people you know

The first, easiest, and most effective method to connect with people you know on LinkedIn is to reach out to your current contacts and invite them to connect with you.

When possible, write your own personal notes instead of sending a generic e-vite that LinkedIn sends when you click the Connect button. It may sound old-fashioned, but etiquette never goes out of style. Remind the person of how you know them, when you met, or someone you know in common, and then say you'd like to connect with him or her. Instead of clicking the Connect button to send your invitation, mouse over the down arrow in the top section of the person's profile and click Personalize Invitation. If this option doesn't exist, then you can click the Connect button in the top section of the person's profile, and a prompt that contains a text box appears that allows you to personalize your invitation. (The prompt appears only if you *don't* have Personalize Invitation in the drop-down menu.)

Before you can connect with someone on LinkedIn, however, you have to find the person. Fortunately LinkedIn provides several tools to help you do just that:

- Search for people you know by entering their full name in the search box atop any LinkedIn page and clicking the Search button. If LinkedIn displays any matches, click the match that looks most promising to pull up the person's profile and verify that this is the person you want to connect with. If it is, click the person's name or profile photo (not the Connect button) and follow the instructions given earlier to send the person a personalized invitation.

  Flip through business cards you've collected from colleagues and clients and search for them on LinkedIn. Send them an invitation to connect.

- Mouse over Connections near the top of any LinkedIn page, click Add Connections, and use the resulting options to import your email contacts from Gmail, Outlook, Yahoo! Mail, Hotmail, AOL, or other email programs or services. LinkedIn uses your email address book to track down any of your email contacts who happen to be on LinkedIn. You can then choose which ones you'd like to connect with.

- Mouse over Connections near the top of any LinkedIn page, click Find Alumni, and use the resulting options to track down people who attended one of the schools you listed in your Education section whom you may know. Click the person's name or profile photo to access the person's profile, where you can choose to connect with them.

✔ Click Home to access your LinkedIn feed. Scroll down to the icon that shows a silhouette of a person with a plus sign next to it. The box has "See anyone you know?" at the top. In the bottom right corner of the box, click Find More People You May Know. LinkedIn provides links to other people you may know based on where you worked and went to school and the people you've already connected with on LinkedIn.

✔ Engage with others on LinkedIn, as explained later in this section. When you meet someone you'd like to connect with, send the person an invitation to connect.

Don't send an invitation to people you don't know or barely know until you've done your homework. Research the person carefully and invite the person only if you sincerely believe that you can establish a mutually beneficial relationship with the person. The people who can help you most are generally the most successful in their field and hence the busiest. Have a compelling reason the person should accept your invitation before sending it. They know the connection will help you. You need to show them how connecting with you will help them.

Giving and getting recommendations and endorsements

When you're trying to impress employers, what you say about yourself isn't half as important as what others who've worked alongside you say about you. LinkedIn provides two ways for colleagues, bosses, clients, and others on LinkedIn to vouch for you:

✔ **Recommendations:** A recommendation is a written statement by a LinkedIn member vouching for the quality of your work or the services or products you offer. They may come from former teachers, mentors, managers, colleagues, coworkers, or clients. Positive recommendations give recruiters and employers more reason to trust one candidate over another who doesn't come as highly recommended.

✔ **Endorsements:** An endorsement is an acknowledgement by a LinkedIn member that you have a skill you claim to have. Your LinkedIn connections can endorse your skills with a click of the mouse, making them much easier to give.

One of the most subtle ways to encourage your connections to give recommendations and endorsements is to write positive recommendations for them and endorse their skills. To give a recommendation to one of your LinkedIn connections, click Connections, near the top of any LinkedIn page, click the connection you want to endorse or recommend, scroll down to the

Endorsements or Recommendations section and follow the on-screen cues to endorse a skill or recommend your connection. When you do, your connection is notified and is likely to reciprocate by endorsing your skills or recommending you.

Requesting a recommendation

To ask for a recommendation, head to your profile page, scroll down to the Recommendations section, and at the bottom of that section, click Ask To Be Recommended. Follow the on-screen cues to complete your request; you need to specify what you want the person to recommend you for and choose up to three connections to ask.

When you're ready to request a recommendation, consider the following suggestions:

- ✔ Make it easy for someone to write your recommendation, by giving them some idea of what to write, as in this example:

  > Hi, Kerry. Hope all is well with you. I'm writing to ask you to write a brief recommendation related to the AARP book promotion that we worked on together that I can include on my LinkedIn profile, perhaps highlighting the time sensitivity of the project and how my project management and problem-solving skills helped to expedite our efforts. I'm currently trying to secure a position that requires strong project management and problem-solving skills and could really use your recommendation in those two areas. Thanks for your consideration. If I can return the favor in any way, please let me know.

- ✔ If you feel comfortable doing so, request that the person write a recommendation that upends older-worker stereotypes that a hiring manager might have by highlighting the fact that you're a source of timely and creative ideas or have up-to-date technical skills.

- ✔ Request recommendations from coworkers or managers in several different age brackets. Having a younger colleague go to bat for you sends a subtle message that you work well with those younger than you.

- ✔ Send requests to your LinkedIn connections who are most likely to write a recommendation that's relevant to the type of employment you're currently seeking. For example, if you worked in sales and marketing in the past and are currently looking for a marketing position, ask the people you worked with in marketing for recommendations.

- ✔ Request recommendations from connections who can offer different perspectives, such as a supervisor, a coworker, and a client.

Managing endorsements

LinkedIn has no system in place for you to request endorsements, although you're certainly free to contact your LinkedIn connections by sending them a message on LinkedIn or emailing them outside of LinkedIn to request that they visit your profile and endorse your skills. Otherwise, you generally receive endorsements organically as your connections check out your profile and as LinkedIn prompts your connections to endorse your skills (especially if you endorse theirs).

Rearrange your skills in the Skills section of your profile to list the skills most relevant to the job you're seeking first. You can rearrange skills by dragging and dropping them with your mouse and then clicking the Save button. For example, if one of your skills is public speaking, or that's the area you want a recruiter or employer to see first, you can slide that public speaking category within your skills list to the top of the chart. Otherwise, LinkedIn lists your skills in the order in which they're most highly endorsed.

Getting involved in LinkedIn Groups

A great way to show recruiters and employers what you're interested in, to demonstrate your expertise and ability to communicate in writing, and to expand your LinkedIn network is to join groups and actively engage with other members in those groups. You can find LinkedIn groups related to specific organization and industries, certain professions, schools you attended, past employers, and a wide range of other interests. You can even create your own group.

To find groups you may be interested in, mouse over Interests, near the top of any LinkedIn page, and click Groups. Click the Find a Group button, enter a topic or keyword(s) that describes your interest, and click the Search button. LinkedIn displays a list of groups that match your search entry. Click the group's name to find out more about it and, if you're interested in joining the group, click the Join button. If you choose to join a private group, the group manager needs to approve your request before you can engage with the group; this may take a few minutes to hours or even days.

After you join a group, you can and should engage with others, but before you post anything, I suggest that you hang out for a while and read some of the discussions to get a feel for the group's culture. For instance, Life Reimagined's LinkedIn group promotes lively discussions on job hunting and other career topics that may be of interest to you.

To check out other discussions, go to your Groups page by mousing over Interests and clicking Groups. Icons near the top of your Groups page indicate the groups you belong to; you can click a group icon to go directly to that group. Below the group icons is a feed from all the groups you belong to along with an area where you can enter a discussion topic and open the discussion in one of your groups.

Whenever you or other members of a group post a discussion topic, it appears in the group and in the discussions feed on your Groups page. Below every discussion is a link you can click to like the post, comment on it, or follow the discussion.

In addition to helping you grow your LinkedIn network and engage with other professionals in your field, groups offer the following perks:

- ✓ Let you keep up with the latest trends and technologies in your field.
- ✓ Give you an opportunity to establish yourself as an expert in your field. The group page lists the top contributors, which is instantly recognized by any recruiters or employers who visit the group.
- ✓ Allow you to connect with professionals in your field in a less formal forum. You never know where that spark of something you have in common make come into play.
- ✓ Demonstrate that you're willing to learn new things.
- ✓ Provide you with another opportunity to post fresh content. According to LinkedIn, if you share once a week, you increase your chances of having your profile viewed by a recruiter tenfold.

To blog or not on LinkedIn

Many LinkedIn users try to build credibility by publishing long-form blog posts on the site. To be honest, these really don't have much impact. Getting distribution on LinkedIn is difficult unless you write something that captures the fancy of your connections, who then share it, and, perhaps, it goes viral, or LinkedIn's Pulse aggregator takes notice. But the site now has thousands of these long-form posts to sort through, so don't hold your breath.

If you have an interest in writing a blog, I recommend you publish on your own blog, if you have one. Then you can also post it on LinkedIn in an attempt to drive LinkedIn traffic to your blog.

Following companies and individuals

LinkedIn allows you to follow companies and certain high-profile individuals on LinkedIn without necessarily establishing a LinkedIn connection. Following a company offers the following benefits:

- Keeps you in the loop about anything new that's going on at the company or in the industry. This information can come in handy as you compose a cover letter and résumé or prepare for an interview.

- Lets you know who you know. When you visit the company's page, a box on the right shows your connections at that company. If you're seeking employment with that company, these connections can be very helpful in getting the inside scoop about a job or what the company is like.

- Lets you keep an eye on who's being hired and who's departing. If someone's leaving the position you want, this could be the perfect opportunity to get in touch with the company's HR department.

To find a company you want to follow, search for the company by name or mouse over Interests and click Companies to browse a list of companies that LinkedIn deems relevant based on your experience and connections. When you find a company you want to follow, click its +Follow button.

You can also follow *thought leaders* — high-profile individuals who publish popular articles regularly. This is a relatively new feature that lets LinkedIn members follow people they want to learn from and may want to connect with in the future without establishing a formal connection, and to keep thought leaders from being inundated with invitations to connect. Mouse over Interests and click Pulse to view a list of thought leaders you may want to follow.

Requesting a LinkedIn introduction

The most effective approach for connecting to someone you don't know and who doesn't know you is often to go through an intermediary who knows you both, and LinkedIn has a feature that enables you to do just that. If one of your first-degree connections has a first-degree connection with the person you want to connect with, you can ask your connection to introduce you to the person. Here's how:

1. **Find the LinkedIn profile of the person you want to be introduced to.**

2. **Click Get Introduced on the right side of that profile.**

3. **Look through the shared connections that LinkedIn indicates could introduce you to that person. (There may not be any.)**

4. **Click one of those connections and enter a subject for your message.**

5. **Write a message to the person who you hope will make the introduction.**

6. **Click the Send Request box.**

Carefully craft your request message. This sounds like a no-brainer, but it all comes down to doing the dance. And any time you're asking someone to introduce you to someone you don't know, especially in the work arena, it's not as simple as a "Sally meet Bob," and "Bob meet Sally" interaction. Who you are and what you're seeking from the person you want to meet reflects on the person making the introduction, so tread lightly. You're asking them to vouch for you. That's a big deal.

Write two messages — one for the person you want to meet via LinkedIn and another for your connection, the person you're asking to make the introduction:

✔ **To your connection:** Tell your connection precisely what you're looking to gain from meeting her connection. Do you want to ask her advice on what the culture is like at the company she works for? Do you want to find out more about the industry? Even if your ultimate goal is something big, such as asking a new contact for a job interview, start with baby steps. And that's probably simply that you want to learn more about the company or the industry.

Acknowledge that the favor you're asking is huge and let your contact know that there's no deadline and you won't harbor any resentment if she can't or won't act as your intermediary. She may have reasons you aren't privy to.

✔ **To the person you want to connect to:** In the note you send to your target person, be clear right from the start what you'd like to ask that person. You're asking someone for his or her valuable time or guidance, so get to it. Introduce yourself in a short sentence or two. Then say precisely why you're contacting the recipient.

Be selective . . . or not

I connect only with friends or people I've met in person or worked with professionally. That LinkedIn "connection" is part of my brand and reflects on me, my online identity, so I want to be linked publically only to people I know and respect.

But not everyone shares my philosophy about accepting invitations. Many people figure the more connections, the better. So follow your own counsel on this one.

Finding Job Postings on LinkedIn

Any company can pay to post a job on LinkedIn, making it now one of the leading job boards. To check job postings, click Jobs near the top of any LinkedIn page. Scroll down the page to view job postings that LinkedIn recommends based on information you entered in your profile, your LinkedIn connections, and on your job-search preferences. You can change your job search preferences for location, company size, and industries:

1. **Under What Location(s) Would You Like to Work In, enter your preferred locations (city and state) and click Next.**

2. **Drag the Company Size sliders to specify the size of company you want to work for and click Next.**

3. **Select the industries you're interested in and click Finish.**

4. **Click Close. LinkedIn displays job postings that match your job search preferences.**

You can also use the Search box atop every LinkedIn page to conduct your job search or click Home and check your LinkedIn feed, where you can usually find what LinkedIn deems are the top three jobs openings for you. Visit any groups you belong to and click the Jobs tab near the top of the group's page to view additional job listings.

Your job activity is private, so if you have a job right now, you needn't concern yourself about your current employer finding out that you're looking for something else . . . unless, of course, you're using the company computer to conduct your job search or you posted on your (public) profile that you're looking for a new job.

Although you may have a pretty good idea of the basic job you're looking for, I advise beginning with a broad search and then gradually narrowing your criteria until you get to a reasonable number of results. CBS, for example, may have 400 job listings on LinkedIn, but they're nationwide and in a range of the company's divisions. So whittle down to the town and type of work you're after.

When you find a job that catches your eye, click it. The job page that appears typically has a button you can click to apply on LinkedIn or go directly to the organization's website to apply. It also shows how many people have applied for the job so far, and whether any of your first-degree LinkedIn connections work for the company.

It's always a good idea to network yourself into companies through your connections before applying directly. Here's how:

- ✔ If you have any first-degree contacts who work at the company, consider contacting them to find out more about the company and the opening.

- ✔ If you don't have a first-degree contact at the company, you can click the company's link, near the top of the job's page, to open the company's page and check to see whether you have any second-degree contacts who may be able to provide the connections you need.

- ✔ If you find a connection who may be able to help you, click the person's name or profile photo to access his profile and click the Message button to send the person a message.

- ✔ If the job listing contains a photo of an individual who posted the job, possibly a recruiter, click the photo to find out more about the person. If you're lucky, the person is a first-degree connection, and you can contact her directly. If the person is a second-degree connection, consider asking one of your first-degree connections who's connected to the person for an introduction.

For additional guidance on tapping the power of LinkedIn, check out *LinkedIn For Dummies*, by Joel Elad (Wiley).

Chapter 11

Clearing the Application Hurdle

The first hurdle standing between you and the job you want is the application, and that hurdle is likely to be higher than it was the last time you were pounding the pavement for a job. Now, many larger organizations and even some smaller ones use high-tech analytics to automate the process of dinging all but the most promising candidates long before human eyes ever rest on an application.

Fortunately, by the time you finish reading this chapter, you'll have a competitive edge. You'll know how to target your application to the right organization, the right job, and the right person. You'll know how to fill out an application in a way that gets it past any automated screening systems and in the hands of the decision maker. And you'll know how to add a personal touch, which is increasingly important as the world becomes more and more impersonal.

In this chapter, I show you how to take a focused approach to maximize impact and navigate the application process when you find the right organization and position to pursue.

Before you start applying for job openings, rehab your résumé and cover letter, as explained in Chapter 8. These two documents come in very handy, whether you're applying for openings online, via email, or in person, because they have most of the information you need to complete a job application and may be required as part of the application. I recommend that you have two versions of your résumé:

> ✔ **Print version for traditional mail:** This can be in the form of a Word document or PDF. It can also be attached as a file to your email, faxed, or delivered in person. This layout can include bulleted points, italics, bold type, and other formatting.

✔ **Plain text or text-only versions:** This plain vanilla version is what you use for copying and pasting directly into online applications. Some applications also require applicants to upload plain-text versions of their résumés.

Taking a Selective Approach

Prospective employers are highly selective. After all, they stand to invest considerably in the person they decide to hire. They want an employee who not only has the skills and knowledge to do the job but also has a personality that clicks with the organization's culture. In fact, according to CareerBuilder, one in four employers dismiss candidates who aren't a good fit for their company culture.

But you're putting a lot on the line as well. You're going to invest hours of your precious life along with your skills and knowledge to improve your employer's success. You want to work for an organization where you feel at home and enjoy the company of your coworkers. You want to be happy and successful, and, as you're serving your employer's needs, you want an employer that's as committed to addressing your needs. So you, too, should be highly selective.

To avoid all the angst of elimination and the disappointment of a future breakup, narrow your search to the organizations that are most likely to be the best match for you right from the start. In this section, I give you tips on where and how to search to find the organization that fits you.

Avoid the temptation to apply to every job opening that looks halfway promising. This scattershot approach not only lacks impact, but it also saps your energy and enthusiasm. You'll soon get disappointed by all the ding letters or no responses to applications you submitted for jobs you probably wouldn't like. Besides, such an approach makes you appear and feel desperate instead of feeling like the confident person someone wants to hire.

One of the best ways to focus your application efforts is to search for jobs that fit your niche. In Chapter 1, I explain how to discover your *niche* — the sweet spot where your interests, knowledge, skills, and personality converge. In Chapter 5, I show you how to tap into niche job boards. When you begin to consider where you want to work, target organizations and positions that match your sweet spot — organizations that offer what you need and need what you offer. Here are a few additional suggestions on how to narrow your focus:

✔ **Choose a location.** Choose a city or town or a geographical location. Some job seekers focus on college towns.

✔ **Choose an industry.** Find an industry that interests you, such as consumer electronics, toys, hotels, restaurants, travel and tourism, finance, real estate, law, healthcare, manufacturing, nutrition, or green energy, and focus your efforts in that direction.

✔ **Pick a position.** Rank your most desirable positions from one to ten, and target your search to the top few on your list. (You can always broaden your search later if opportunities are limited.)

✔ **Choose an organization size.** Do you see yourself fitting in better at a large corporation, a company with a few hundred people, or a small business where everybody knows one another?

✔ **Target organizations for over-50 workers.** Check out AARP Employer Pledge: Experience Valued, a national initiative to help employers solve their current and future staffing challenges and direct job seekers to employers that value and are hiring experienced workers. There you can view openings at the more than 285 organizations that have signed the pledge to level the playing field for experienced workers. Learn more at `www.aarp.org/work`.

After finding your niche, keep in mind that a big part of your job-search success is your positive, "I belong" expert attitude. It's key to persuading employers that your skills and experience make you stand out among your peers.

Submitting Applications Online and Off

Applications can be tricky and picky, particularly if you're someone whose big selling points are your integrity and charisma and you're required to submit the application online. Applications provide little, if any, opportunity to showcase such strengths. But as impersonal and restrictive as they may be, formal applications are required for most jobs, and nearly all company websites now require you to apply online through their job portals.

In this section, I help you navigate the process of completing and submitting applications online, via email or traditional mail, in person, and at application kiosks. I explain how to avoid common pitfalls that may lead to automated rejections, and how to apply for federal government jobs online.

Reading and following directions

Although this bit of advice may seem too obvious to mention, when completing applications, you must read and follow the directions precisely, paying particular attention to any "required" fields. A required field is a good indication that the information is important.

If you're applying online, copy and paste as much information as you can from your résumé instead of typing it in manually. This method not only saves you time and effort, but it also ensures that the information you supply is consistent and from a source that you've already painstakingly edited. Although some web browsers now feature spell-checking, copying and pasting the information is more foolproof.

Pay special attention to the following areas:

- ✔ **Past employment:** Give a comprehensive employment history in months and years, including any jobs you may have omitted from your résumé due to lack of space. Be precise when entering dates of employment and salaries. Enter as much detail about former employers and supervisors as possible and requested on the form.

- ✔ **Disabilities:** List any disabilities at your own disclosure. Employers can't specifically ask on an application or in an interview if you have a disability that would interfere with your ability to perform the job. Only after a job offer is made can the employer question about disabilities.

- ✔ **Criminal history:** If you have a criminal record, consider whether it can be expunged. In some instances, however, even if your criminal conviction was sealed, dismissed, or expunged, you may still have a duty to disclose your record. Consult a lawyer to advise you so that you can make truthful and appropriate disclosures.

- ✔ **Unemployment benefits:** Be straightforward about having collected unemployment benefits.

- ✔ **Veteran status:** Some employers give special consideration to applicants who served their country in the military, so take advantage of this benefit by indicating your military service.

- ✔ **Race, gender, and other such details:** Most employers ask you to reply to questions about race, gender, and so forth as a way of gathering data for the Equal Employment Opportunity Commission (EEOC). You aren't obligated to include this information to be considered for employment. However, if you're a woman or a minority, I strongly suggest you do it.

Be honest. Most applications include a box at the end that you must mark or click to verify that all the information you provided is accurate and complete to the best of your knowledge. If you're honest, you can check this box with confidence, knowing that the employer won't be able to dig up information that's inconsistent with the information you supplied.

Handling salary boxes

Many applications request or require a salary history and perhaps even a minimum salary requirement. On a paper application, you may be able to wiggle out of this by leaving the fields blank or writing "Negotiable" as your minimum salary requirement. If you're applying online, however, you may need to enter numbers in these fields to have your application accepted.

If the application asks for salary history, it usually requires a starting and ending salary for each position. Enter your starting and ending salaries as requested to the best of your knowledge. You may have to look back in your files for old pay stubs or tax returns. If you can't recall your starting or ending salary at prior positions and your employers are still in business, they may be able to look up the information for you.

If your total income might price you out of the competition, give your base salary (or add commissions and bonuses, if applicable), omitting benefits. If you get in the door for an interview and the salary discussion is raised, you can explain that you specified your base salary, not including additional benefits and perks. (More on salary negotiation in Chapter 14.)

If you must enter a minimum salary requirement, you have a few options:

✔ Enter your must-have minimum salary or whatever salary you'd be comfortable accepting.

If the application has a box for entering additional details, consider qualifying your minimum salary amount by adding something like, "The minimum salary requirement specified is based on anticipated job responsibilities and workload and does not account for other forms of compensation."

✔ If the job description specifies a salary range, make sure the salary you enter is within that range.

✔ Specify a figure that's generally accepted for that position, based on job location and your experience. Use tools such as Glassdoor.com (www. glassdoor.com), PayScale.com (www.payscale.com), or Salary. com (www.salary.com) to see what others earn in similar positions. That should at least give you a ballpark number to keep you from being screened out from the get-go.

✔ Enter a wide salary range, if possible, such as $55,000 to $85,000. Be honest with yourself, though, that the low salary amount is something you can live with and would consider accepting. If you have the chance to talk to a real person in human resources before filling out the form, ask what the salary range for the position is. Some postings list a range, which you can use as a guide.

You don't want to specify a minimum salary requirement so low that it compromises your ability to negotiate a fair and satisfactory compensation package, but keep in mind that you can negotiate for more later. During the interview, you may say that the minimum salary you specified didn't account for certain benefits or that the minimum covered certain basic job responsibilities, but you now see that the job will require much more from you than you had anticipated. For more about negotiating, see Chapter 14.

Sneaking your application past screening technologies

When applying online, consider the fact that recruiters and employers often use automated systems to pre-screen applicants. Every application submitted for a position is screened and scored for relevance based on key words and numerical values the applicant entered. For example, if a job requires experience in marketing and sales, and the applicant didn't happen to mention "marketing" or "sales" experience, the application is likely to be ignored. To give your résumé a better chance of clearing this first hurdle, do the following:

- ✔ **Scatter throughout your application and résumé key words and phrases that appear in the descriptions of the jobs for which you're applying.** For example, if the job description requires someone with experience in WordPress, HTML, and CSS, mention all those terms by name somewhere in your application and résumé (if included).

- ✔ **Unless otherwise instructed, list the names of employers first, followed by the dates you worked there.** Some screening systems may reject an application simply because the attached résumé specifies starting and ending dates before naming the employer.

- ✔ **When attaching or uploading documents, such as a résumé or cover letter, use an acceptable file format.** If the application doesn't specify, stick with a standard format, such as .doc or .txt. Text documents are easier for automated systems to properly index.

- ✔ **Avoid uploading charts, images, or PDFs, unless otherwise instructed.** Most automated screening technologies can't index non-text files.

Acing federal job applications

Applications and résumés for federal government jobs are generally funneled through USAJobs (www.usajobs.gov). Before you can apply, you must create an account; click the Create an Account link, in the upper-right corner of the opening page, and follow directions. After you create an account, log on, click Profile, and enter the details requested. Tabs at the top of the Profile area enable you to enter Contact Information, Hiring Eligibility, Other (your preferences, such as willingness to travel and whether you want full- or part-time work), and Demographic.

After completing your profile, click Resumes, and use the options on the resulting page to build a new résumé or upload a résumé. You can build or upload up to five résumés and tailor them to specific positions. Scroll to the bottom of the page and click Sample Resume or What to Include for additional details. I suggest using the site's résumé builder to add your résumé instead of uploading it, so you're sure to enter all the details recruiters and employers will need and enter the information in a format that's acceptable to the automated screening system.

After you log on for the first time, build a generic résumé. As you find positions to apply for, create new résumés tailored to those positions:

1. **Conduct a job search using the Keyword and Location boxes at the top of any page.**

2. **Click the link for a job that catches your eye.**

3. **Read the overview to decide whether you're interested in applying for the position.**

4. **If you're interested, click the other tabs to read more about the job and take notes to help you tailor your résumé to the position.**

   Most job descriptions have several tabs, including Overview, Duties, Qualifications & Evaluations, Benefits & Other Info, and How to Apply.

   Note key words in the job description, so you can use them in your custom résumé. You'll find most of the key words you need via the Overview, Duties, and Qualifications & Evaluations tabs.

5. **Click the Save Job button, so you can quickly return to it later.**

6. **Mouse over My Account and click Resumes to return to the Resumes page.**

7. **Below the link for the generic résumé you created, click Duplicate.**

   A duplicate résumé appears in your list of résumés.

8. **Below the link for the new résumé, click Edit.**

   You can then tailor this new résumé to the position. (Use the Saved Jobs tab on your opening page to return to the job you saved and apply for it.)

Click Resource Center at the top of any page to find out more about federal jobs and how to apply for them. The Resource Center even contains tutorials to bring you up to speed on the basics. GovLoop offers a free résumé toolkit that may also help: `www.govloop.com/groups/rockyourresume`. For additional help with applications and revamping résumés, check out Go Government (`www.gogovernment.org`) and Job-Hunt.org's Guide to Federal Government Job Search at `www.job-hunt.org/federal-government-job-search/federal-job-search.shtml`.

While you're at it, head to the Home page (click the Home link in the upper-left corner of any page) and check out the links below the Search tool: Individuals with Disabilities, Veterans, Students and Recent Graduates, and Senior Executives. If you qualify for inclusion into any of these groups, you may have additional options to explore that aren't available to other applicants.

Networking is just as important for government jobs as it is for jobs in the private sector. Don't forget to check your LinkedIn connections to see whether you know anyone who works for the department you're interested in (see Chapter 10).

Mastering alternative ways to apply

Although applying online is commonplace these days, it's not the only game in town. You have at least three other options:

- ✔ **Email:** If you know who will make the hiring decision and have the person's email address, consider emailing your résumé. Write your email message in a similar style to your cover letter. Introduce yourself, remind the person where you met or how you came in contact with the company, pitch yourself as the perfect candidate for the job, and wrap up by telling the person that you look forward to discussing the position in greater detail.

- ✔ **Snail mail:** Mail a cover letter and a copy of your résumé to the person who will make the hiring decision or to the organization's human resources department.

- ✔ **In person:** You can deliver your cover letter and résumé in person or even fill out an application on-site. Just be sure you have all the information you need to complete the application, including employment history, addresses of places you worked, and contact information for your references. And be prepared for an on-the-spot interview (see Chapter 14 for details).

Snail mail still works

Believe it or not, plenty of employers still want you to send a printed résumé to their office. In general, these are smaller businesses, local or small trade associations, and nonprofits that haven't spent the funds to install an online job application system.

If you mail a résumé, send it with a cover letter, as explained in Chapter 8. The good news is that you don't have to deal with a robo-screener. A human resources employee will appraise your résumé. In such cases, the appearance of your résumé may carry more weight.

Before emailing your résumé, send your email message and résumé to a friend to look over. If you've already had others review your résumé, you can ask your friend to review only your email message.

Always follow the suggested method for submitting applications and résumés as stated in the job posting. Some employers never open attachments from people they don't know, and others may get annoyed if you try to side-step the organization's screening process. I also discourage submitting unsolicited résumés for employers to consider you for future openings. Someone in human resources may file your résumé, but nobody is likely to look at it ever again. I think these blind submissions are just a waste of time and other resources.

Applying at hiring kiosks

Kiosks are cropping up at certain businesses as a means to apply for a job. Some retailers, for instance, use kiosks instead of having you fill out a paper application on the spot. Most kiosks use a touchscreen; others have a keyboard with a mouse. If the kiosk has a phone, it's generally to hook you up with the help desk for any problems you have completing the application. When applying at hiring kiosks, follow this advice:

- Bring your résumé, addresses, and phone numbers of places you worked, and contact information for your references.

- Take your time. Don't sit down at a kiosk to apply for a job when you have to be somewhere else in 15 minutes. Give yourself an hour. You'll probably finish early, but that's better than doing a rush job.

Some employers may tack on a more detailed personality assessment with additional questions beyond your work experience.

Following Up after Submitting Your Application

Following up with an employer after submitting your résumé shows your level of interest and commitment to the job. Making a follow-up call may be one of the shrewdest tactics in your job search, for these reasons:

- A call to the hiring manager can instantly shine the spotlight on your name and application by encouraging the person to pull your application out of the stack.

- You may actually get someone on the phone. It happens. If you call on a day when the hiring manager picks up the phone and the planets are all aligned, you can make an impression.

- Tenacity is admired. Some employers are looking for the hungriest candidate to interview and will judge you favorably on your persistence.

- Taking initiative makes you feel empowered. When you're being proactive, your attitude shifts. You don't feel as helpless and frustrated and down on yourself because no one has called you to set up an interview. You know you're doing everything you can do.

Thinking before you speak

If the job ad or post says "no phone calls," call once anyway. Nothing ventured, nothing gained, in my opinion. Not all job experts agree with me on this, but I believe if you aren't a pest and annoying, one call can't hurt. And if it does, you probably wouldn't want to work for such a prickly person anyway. You may get a few hang-ups, but so be it. You never know when you'll get a positive response.

Ideally, contact the employer by phone, but time your phone call appropriately. Check the job posting for a *close date,* the deadline for accepting applications. If no close date is mentioned, wait five workdays after applying to follow up. If a close date is mentioned, wait five workdays after the deadline has passed. Your patience gives the hiring manager time to review the résumés. If a phone call is not an option, you can try emailing the person.

Before you place the call, have specific questions to ask, so you sound competent. After the usual pleasantries, you may want to say something like, "I'm calling because I recently applied for the _____ position and would like to check on the status of my application. Whom would I need to contact about that?" After you ask your question, be prepared for any number of responses.

The person on the other end of the line may be the hiring manager or may give you the name of the hiring manager or transfer your call to that person. You may be told that the position has been filled or that no decision has been made. Be prepared for various scenarios and be ready to improvise.

If you're nervous, practice your pitch a few times before you dial. Maybe you can find a pal to run your lines with via a mock follow-up phone call between the two of you.

If you're given a generic response, consider following up with one or more of these questions:

✔ Have any decisions been made yet?

✔ May I follow up in another week if I haven't heard anything from you?

✔ What's the time frame for the hiring process for this position?

✔ Are there any other materials I can provide you with at this time?

Making the call

If you find out the name of the hiring manager, try to contact that manager, because that's who is running the show. Have a script prepared in advance, so you sound intelligible when you finally have the chance to speak with the person. Here's a sample script for an applicant who has an inside connection at the company who referred him for the job:

> Hi Mr./Ms. [Last Name]. My name is Jason Jones, and I'm calling you because Susan Smith in marketing recommended that I send you my résumé. Susan told me that you're looking to hire a creative designer as soon as possible for a project that has a quick turnaround. I've been able to design a marketing strategy that was quickly approved by the City of Pittsburgh for a last-minute image campaign that they needed to kick off with the upcoming Steelers football season. I'm about to leave on a scheduled vacation for two weeks, and I didn't want to miss the opportunity to speak with you in person. I'm wondering if you would be interested in setting up a time to talk with me before I leave.

Your task is to concoct a striking, brief opening — a sound bite — designed to thaw a hiring manager's no-cold-calls defense. You get it, but you're exceptional, and she'll welcome what you have to offer!

After you deliver your pitch, the rest of the conversation is all up to you and the hiring manager.

I suggest you call early morning or early evening when the hiring manager's gatekeepers are less likely to be on guard duty.

Composing a follow-up email

If you can't get through via phone, you can certainly send an email message. Email is a fairly good way to make sure the organization received your application, but it pales in comparison to the effectiveness of a phone call in establishing rapport with the person in charge of making the hiring decision.

When composing an email message, pay particular attention to tone. You want to convey the sense that you're approachable, graceful, sociable, and persistent. Make it conversational in tone while getting down to business, as in the following example:

> My proven background in graphic design looks like a good fit for your advertised requirements and my qualifications for the marketing manager position. I know you have received my résumé and application. I'm uncertain whether you're at the interview stage yet, but I would be pleased to answer any preliminary questions you may have. May I call you tomorrow morning at 10 a.m.? If that's not a good time, please let me know a day and time that works better for you.

Don't take delays personally. Lots of companies are slow to make hiring decisions, and with vacations and holidays, the progress can drag on for months. If you take delays personally, you may become frustrated and come across as being angry or aggressive, which will definitely work against you.

Part IV

Taking the Stage: The Interview and Its Aftermath

Interview Prep Checklist

- ☐ Research the company.
- ☐ Check your LinkedIn network for any inside connections.
- ☐ Find out who's going to interview you and learn more about them.
- ☐ Jot down your top three selling points.
- ☐ Rehearse your CAR (challenge, action, result) story.
- ☐ Pack a copy of your résumé and the job description.
- ☐ Bring a list of questions to ask.
- ☐ Be impeccably groomed and professionally dressed.
- ☐ Look beyond your age.
- ☐ Allow plenty of time to get to your interview — don't be late.
- ☐ Pump yourself up with self-affirmations prior to the interview.

Visit www.dummies.com/extras/gettingthejobyouwantafter50 for a bonus article on the latest interviewing techniques to use and pitfalls to avoid.

In this part . . .

✔ Prepare for your job interview by researching the company, knowing what you're going to say before you're asked, and working out your pre-interview jitters.

✔ Ready yourself for your next job interview, make a positive first impression, navigate different interview formats, avoid the most serious mistakes, and follow up after the interview.

✔ Negotiate for more of what you want, including money, time, flexibility, and benefits, and negotiate a starting date that works for you.

Chapter 12

Prepping for a Job Interview

Few events in life are more nerve-wracking than job interviews. You're on stage, alone, in the spotlight, with one or more people grilling you to determine whether you're the best candidate for the job — whether you can perform the job and are a good fit for the organization. The interviewers already have a job, so they have nothing to be nervous about. You, on the other hand, are expected to deliver an award-winning performance. Although job interviews can be nerve-wracking, you need to remain calm and cool. If you get flustered, you're likely to come across as lacking confidence, and your performance may fall short.

The key to retaining your composure throughout the interview comes before the interview begins, through preparation. The better prepared you are, the less you have to worry about, and the less nervous you'll be. Consider this chapter your training session prior to stepping in the ring with an interviewer.

Knowing What Interviewers Are Looking For

One way to ace an interview is to give the interviewers what they want, which may be difficult to determine based solely on the questions they ask. Even when you're answering irrelevant questions, interviewers can pick up on the traits they like to see in a job candidate. Depending on what type of job you're seeking, employers are looking for different characteristics, which include the following:

- ✔ **Curiosity:** An enthusiasm to learn new things and find solutions conveys an eagerness to learn. Ask questions about the company and its services, products, customers, competition, and so on to demonstrate your natural curiosity.

  Don't ask a potential employer questions you already know the answers to, because you'll come across as being clueless. After all, you should have done some research about the company prior to the interview. Let your natural curiosity prevail. (See the later section "Preparing to Answer and Ask Questions" for details.)

- ✔ **Insight:** An understanding of the company, what it does, how it functions, and what its challenges are helps you demonstrate your ability to gain insight into an organization. Research, as explained in the next section, helps you develop the type of insight you need to demonstrate.

- ✔ **Engagement:** Your ability to carry on an intelligent conversation with the interviewers demonstrates engagement. Listen carefully to what they say and respond thoughtfully to show that you heard, understood, and are able to formulate a relevant response. If you're introduced to others in the organization, greet them respectfully, ask how they're doing, and listen to what they say. Engagement is all about showing that you care.

- ✔ **Intellect:** Brainpower never goes out of style, and again, doing your homework prior to the interview can provide the framework of understanding about the organization to answer and ask questions in an intelligent manner. Maintaining eye contact, speaking clearly, and using proper English also convey a certain level of intelligence and sophistication.

- ✔ **Creativity:** The aptitude for being inventive and original in your thinking is a magic ingredient. You may be able to demonstrate creativity as you respond to questions or if given an opportunity to talk about a way you creatively solved a problem or met a challenge for a previous employer. Don't try to force creativity into the conversation, but take advantage of any sensible opportunity to do so.

- ✔ **Drive and determination:** Grit and purpose are core attributes for a successful employee. Interviewers want to see a whatever-it-takes attitude. Be prepared to discuss situations at work or in your personal life when you faced adversity or experienced a setback and managed to overcome it.

✔ **Efficiency:** How productive are you? A key attribute employers seek is someone who is effective in his or her work with good organization skills.

✔ **Open-mindedness:** A willingness to try new ways of doing things and a tolerance for taking risks are valuable attributes in team members and leaders. When answering questions that call on you to consider a certain option, think about your answer carefully. Unless the option requires you to do something criminal or unethical, give it careful consideration.

As Professor Walter Kotschnig, who taught comparative education at Smith and Mount Holyoke Colleges in Massachusetts before he became a Foreign Service officer who was present at the formation of the United Nations and who went on to represent the United States at conferences worldwide for nearly three decades once advised his students, keep your mind open, "but not so open that your brains fall out." Show that you're open to new ideas, but ask questions to find out more about those ideas, so you can judge their validity and feasibility.

✔ **Passion for the organization:** Interviewers want to see that you love the company and what it does as much as they do and that you're committed to its success. You can demonstrate your passion for the organization by researching it carefully; following it on LinkedIn, Facebook, and Twitter; and mentioning specifically what you like most about the organization during the interview. Be prepared to explain why you want to work for the organization and what you can do to help it further its mission.

✔ **Passion for the role:** Being an engaged employee comes down to loving your work and your job. No employer wants to hire someone who's resentful of taking on a role they feel is beneath them or they're overqualified for, nor do they want to hire someone who treats the position as a stepping stone to what they really want. Talk passionately about the work you do and the work you'd like to do for the organization. Discuss how you want to immerse yourself in the job and really make a career out of it. Engaging with professional organizations, such as professional groups and relevant LinkedIn discussion groups also demonstrates passion for what you do.

✔ **Punctuality:** Employers look for people who are reliable and they can count on.

✔ **Team Player:** In the end, whether or not you get tapped for a job often comes down to a hiring manager's gut sense of how well you will play with the other kids. Someone who is willing and happy to chip in and works easily and collaboratively with others is highly valued.

Being overqualified is a major issue for many older workers. For more on this important topic, see Chapter 13.

What are you looking for?

In addition to thinking about what interviewers are looking for in a job candidate, consider what you're looking for in the job. By considering your needs along with your prospective employer's needs, you focus your attention on the goal of making a good match instead of just getting a job. To engage in this soul-searching exercise, try your best to answer the following questions:

✔ What do I really want in this job?

✔ What truly matters to me when it comes to a job? The people I will work with? The company's mission? Having flexible hours? Opportunities to travel or to learn new things on a regular basis?

✔ Is it the money that truly motivates me or is it the chance to make a difference or feel valued?

✔ What are my vital strengths and skills that make me someone that an employer would want on the team?

Depending on your answers, you may really hype yourself up for the job or convince yourself that this particular opportunity isn't right for you. Whatever the outcome, it helps you make the best decision for you and the organization and bring your best self to the interview.

Doing Your Homework Before the Interview

Prior to your interview, do your homework. Research the company, the department and position you're applying for, and the people you'll be working for and with. Rehearse your story, so you're well aware of your key selling points. Get in character, so you're thinking and acting like someone who already has the job. Be able to look past your age and highlight any mentoring you've done, so you're able to demonstrate your ability to work with younger colleagues. In the following section, I provide specifics on how to tackle each part of this homework assignment.

Researching the company

A big first step in preparing for an interview is finding out as much as possible about the company, the department and position you're interviewing for, the people you'll be working with, and the company leadership. Here are a few ideas on how to gather the information you need:

✔ **Visit the organization's website, if it has one.** Look for a link to the site's About page, which is usually at the bottom if you can't find it anywhere else. The About page typically has information or links to other pages that have information about the company's history, mission, and people. Look for the following:

- Blog, News, or Press Releases page, where you can read about the latest happenings at the company.

- Mission statement, which typically indicates the organization's philosophy and goals.

- Who We Are page, which often contains photographs and bios of the company's leadership. Get to know everyone's name, and try your best to match names with faces.

- Employee directory, which provides names, bios, and possibly even contact information for employees. If you can find an employee directory, you've hit pay dirt, because you can find out who works in the department you're applying for and perhaps contact the person to find out more about the department and the position you're applying for.

Interviewers really want to know what interests and intrigues you about their company. During the interview, be forthright and clear about what the organization does that motivates you and about the challenges of the position you're interviewing for. Let them know why you think you're a good fit.

✓ **Visit the company's LinkedIn and Facebook pages and follow it on Twitter.** Read any discussions to get up to speed about what people within and connected to the company are talking about. For more about LinkedIn, Facebook, and Twitter, check out Chapters 9 and 10.

✓ **Search for the organization on the web and via Google News.** You never know what a general search may turn up about an organization. You may find out about unresolved issues with customers or vendors that you're uniquely qualified to address or a problem you're able to solve that would save the organization money.

Try to identify the biggest problem that someone in the position you're applying for needs to solve. If you have some ideas of what you can do to address that problem, you have a distinct advantage over other candidates for the position.

✓ **Request printed content about the organization.** The organization may have a press or investor's packet that contains additional details you won't find on the website.

✓ **Check your LinkedIn network for an inside connection.** If someone in your network works for the organization, contact that person to find out more about the organization and possibly obtain the name and contact info for someone in the department you're applying for. (If someone in your network worked for the organization in the past, he or she may be able to help, too.)

✔ **Contact someone in the department you want to work in.** You may be able to find someone in the department by checking an employee directory on the site, tracking down someone you know who works for the organization, or calling the organization and asking for someone in the department to contact you. Ask to meet over lunch or for coffee. Discuss the department and the current opening. Ask about the department's mission within the organization, its goals, and any challenges it faces. Try to find out who will be conducting the interview.

✔ **Find out as much about your interviewers as you can.** Checking them out via their LinkedIn pages and a Google search should provide some background. Sure, employers want to hire you for your skills, but they also want to have a connection with you. To help make this connection, find out where the person you'll be meeting went to school and worked, and anything else you can dig up. You don't want to sound like you're a stalker, but if there's a connection you can hit on, use it.

The interview is a two-way street. Yes, you're there to sell yourself, but the interviewers need to sell you the job. Approach the interview as you would any courtship prior to committing to a long-term relationship. Both parties should have a genuine interest in ensuring that they're a good match before making the commitment.

During the conversation, subtly let the interviewers know that you've researched the organization by referencing facts you gleaned through your research and asking intelligent questions you'd be able to formulate only after having done some research. This insider knowledge shows that you're on top of the business and the industry in which it operates. Knowing some background information also makes responding to questions much easier. You're better equipped to frame your answers in the context of the organization and its needs instead of delivering generic responses.

Preparing and rehearsing your story

The big question interviewers have and often never ask is "Why should we hire you instead of the other candidates we're considering?" If you're doing it right, throughout the interview, you'll be answering that question indirectly by what you say, how you say it, how you look, how you move, and the questions you ask. But you need to answer that question even more directly by telling your story and highlighting your main selling points in the process.

In this section, I offer guidance in preparing your selling points and working them into the interview.

Preparing your CAR descriptions

Résumé writing pros advise their clients to tell their CAR story. CAR stands for challenge, action, and result. It's a good outline for a plot. You describe a challenge that you or the organization you worked for faced, the action you took to solve the problem or address the issue, and the result. Here's an example:

> Sales at the XYZ Realty had plateaued. I created a process that made selling houses an assembly line. Real estate agents showed properties and reviewed the paperwork, but we hired and trained additional personnel to complete the paperwork. Our agents were able to sell 40 percent more properties, far more than required to cover the costs of the additional personnel.

Write several of these CAR stories. Don't be too formal in your writing. This is where you can show a little personality and let reviewers hear your voice and the pride you take in your accomplishments. Importantly, make sure the CAR stories are relevant to the position.

Preparing your elevator pitch

Another approach to presenting your selling points is to use an *elevator pitch* — a persuasive, prepared speech that you can deliver in 20 seconds or so, the duration of a short ride in an elevator. The goal of your elevator pitch is to answer the question, "Why should we hire you?" Although you may not be able to deliver your elevator pitch in its entirety, if at all, having an elevator pitch ready ensures that you know the answer to the question.

Your pitch should cover who you are, what you do, and why you're uniquely qualified for the position. It should finish with a question that sparks further conversation about how you're able to meet the organization's needs. Here's an example:

> I'm Rhonda Newcomer, a marketing professional who specializes in building brand identity via social media and networking. I noticed that several dissatisfied customers have posted negative reviews of your products and services on Facebook, and I know how to address that issue. During my six-month contract term at XYZ Corp., the organization's following grew 75 percent on Facebook and Twitter with positive comments outnumbering negative comments by 20 to 1. We also followed up with dissatisfied customers and convinced them to remove their negative reviews. What do you see as your biggest PR challenge?

Try to point out a problem that the organization didn't even realize it had. If you can assign a dollar amount to that problem, all the better. Just be sure to have a solution for solving it that requires the organization to hire you.

Like CAR stories, your elevator pitch should focus on a problem, the action you took, and the result. If you're having trouble with your action statement, try starting with one of the following phrases:

"As manager of _____, I developed a plan that. . . ."

"While working at _____, I created a process that. . . ."

"While working in _____, I directed a team that. . . ."

Weaving your selling points into the interview

During the interview, stick to your main selling points. It's easy to veer off topic. To help you stay focused, write down and practice at home your three main selling points. Have specific examples that highlight your strengths to share with the interviewer.

Toward the end of the interview, click through your mental checklist to make sure you've covered each of your selling points. Don't leave until you have. If you sense that the interviewer is moving toward wrapping up the interview, politely interject that you want to make sure you mention X, Y, or Z, and why.

Although touching on past accomplishments is essential, balance past achievements with forward thinking conversation. For instance, don't forget to mention how your skills can help the organization with its current and possibly future issues. You also need to talk about how you can contribute to the organization's goals both now and in the future.

Getting in character: Thinking like an expert or consultant

Approach the interview as if you're a highly paid consultant. State clearly what you think needs to be done and why based on your experience. Think like an expert. If you're desperate and thinking, "I just need a job to pay the bills for the next ten years," employers are on to you. They're going to pick the best, most interested, most innovative candidate, not the person who's just looking for a paycheck and planning their exit strategy.

Careful research and strategic thinking puts you on the path toward thinking and acting like a highly paid consultant. It enables you to identify problems and other issues the company is facing or will be facing in the future and provides the information you need to formulate a strategy that prepares the organization to meet the challenge. Then, all you need to do is fit yourself into that picture, so the prospective employer sees you as essential for the organization's success.

Forgetting about your age

Job seekers over 50 often ask me whether they should dye their hair or get Botox treatments before launching their job search. What I tell them is that they don't need a *facelift;* they need a *faith-lift.* You're only as old as your attitude. I've met 23-year-olds who are jaded, faded, bitter souls who I wouldn't hire to mow my lawn. I've also met 90-year-olds I can't keep up with — they wake up eager and curious and move through their days with a sense of wonder and gratitude. Those are the people that other people are attracted to and that employers want working for them.

Yes, you should be properly groomed and well dressed, and you should ditch the out-of-style clothes and glasses frames and don more current ones, but other than that, I recommend that you work more on lifting your spirit than your skin. Skip the negativity about your age and appearance. After you've been out of work for a while, you forget your value. You take for granted your achievements and contributions. Take time and center on your best moments, the circumstances you shine in, and be clear in interviews that if they put you in those situations, you'll be a star. Have some swagger.

If you have trouble tooting your own horn and find that you're getting down on yourself, ask people you trust who know you well to help you develop your highlight reel and remind you of all those talents and skills you've honed throughout the years. Ask them to list two or three things you're really good at. After reading the positive comments, you'll have the swagger you need.

Mentioning any mentoring you've done

Reverse mentoring, in which you accept guidance from someone who's younger, shows that you can work well with and take direction from colleagues and supervisors who are younger than you. But any mentoring you've been involved with can help by showing that you can get along with, learn from, and teach others. It also demonstrates that you're a lifelong learner. You didn't stop after receiving your diploma, and you're humble enough to admit that you have more to learn.

If you can slip it into the conversation, explain how mentoring has always been a part of your work and management style. Show your interviewer that it's a process that you have benefited from over the years as a mentee and a mentor and hope you can continue to reap its benefits and return the favor.

Preparing to Answer and Ask Questions

Interviews are extended Q&A sessions, which makes them difficult to prepare for, because you never really know what questions will be asked or which direction the interview will turn. By preparing answers to questions in several different categories, however, you place your brain in Q&A mode and dredge up information buried deep in your memory banks that enables you to more nimbly field a wide variety of questions.

In this section, I lead you through the Q&A preparation process, so you're prepared to answer some of the most common and uncommon questions and have a few questions of your own.

Engage in a few mock interviews, as explained later in "Getting Comfortable in Your Own Skin." Although you can't anticipate every question an interviewer may ask, you can improve your speed and responsiveness. Think of it as playing shortstop in baseball. You never know how fast or at what angle the ball is coming at you, but if you field enough balls, you develop the instinct required to catch anything hit in your direction.

Answering general questions

In this section, I reveal common questions interviewers may ask, and even if they don't, these are good questions to ask yourself and answer prior to the interview.

Keep your answers short, especially when talking about yourself and your experiences. An interview is all about the company. Interviewers don't want to know your life story, just that you have one and are eager, smart, open to learning, and skilled in ways that will advance the organization.

What are your hobbies and interests?

This is a great time to show your passion for something you love. Talk enthusiastically about your hobbies, interests, and causes. Passion is appealing and youthful, regardless of your age. When prospective employers notice a twinkle in your eye as you describe your outside interests, they're drawn to you as a candidate and more likely to offer you the job.

If possible, research your interviewers prior to the interview to find out about their interests, hobbies, and causes. (See the earlier section, "Researching the company.") You may even find a common connection or an interest you share that gives you an opportunity to connect with an interviewer on a personal level.

How do you learn best?

This is your chance to pull back the curtains on what makes you tick, the kind of work scenario that will help you shine and, in turn, help the organization succeed. Identifying your learning style is important, because whether you learn best independently or collaboratively, it helps your future employer determine where you fit best in the organization. A good fit is mutually beneficial.

How would you solve the following problem . . . ?

You can't possibly anticipate the specific problem the interviewer will describe, so try to think up a few work-related problems you solved in the past. Remember your CAR stories — challenge, action, and result. Think of problems the industry is facing right now and how you would go about solving those problems. When answering the question, you don't actually need to come up with a solution. All you need is a strategy for solving the problem; for example, you may gather information, assemble a team, brainstorm solutions, and so on.

Pause. Don't make rapid-off-the-top-of-your-head answers. This isn't *Jeopardy*. There's no race to push the buzzer. Rattling off the first answer that pops into your head may come off as flippant. Give yourself a little time to mull it over before giving your answer.

Identify inefficiencies in a process the company uses.

Be careful here. Interviewers want to know that you're not wearing rose-colored glasses and can offer a critical analysis. They aren't paying you yet, so point out operations that could be streamlined without offering a specific solution. Show that you have some ideas, but hold them close to your vest. It's okay to be a little coy here.

Have you ever been in a situation where you had to persuade other people who were not your direct reports to do something?

"Absolutely," should be your answer. And then give a quick and to-the-point example. You should have this one prepared ahead of time to illustrate your ability to communicate with people and get results even when someone doesn't have to listen to you. Be prepared to answer these two follow-up questions:

> How did you do it?

> What were the consequences?

How have you managed or worked with difficult personalities in the past?

A good answer to this question is that you've found that it's not so much that people are difficult as it is that situations are challenging. By using certain communication strategies, you can often diffuse tension and turn the focus from anger and blame to collaborating on how to resolve the underlying issues or problems. Point out that sometimes what seems to be a difficult personality in the workplace can be caused by a problem outside the workplace that needs to be resolved. Be prepared to give an example.

Of course, this is only one possible answer to this question, but whatever answer you give, you want to show that you recognize the challenges of group dynamics and the complexities that underlie interpersonal conflict — that you're not prone to making snap judgements.

Give me a tour of your life.

Start at the beginning and narrate your highlight reel. Touch on key events in your life. The challenge here is keeping it short. Be prepared with an elevator pitch, as described in the earlier section "Preparing your elevator pitch."

Tell me three things about how you define yourself.

This is a good opportunity to focus on your skills. Spin your answer to explain how your skills, strengths, experience, and goals relate to the company and the position you're interviewing for.

When you're not at work, what two things do you do better than anybody else?

Without boasting, explain what you're really good at. Maybe you're the idea person, the efficiency expert, the go-to gal or guy when something needs done, or the person who calms everyone down when tensions rise.

What am I not going to like about you in 90 days?

One answer to this question is this: "If I thought there was something you weren't going to like about me in 90 days, I wouldn't waste your time by being here. I really think we're a good match." Other options include humor or pointing out a strength as though it's a weakness; for example, if you're being hired to cut costs, you could say something like "My husband seems to think I'm overly frugal."

What do you think you're not going to like about me?

Boy, talk about a loaded question. Humor can come in handy here with an answer such as, "Maybe that you ask too many difficult questions." You could also answer, "If I thought there was something I wouldn't like about you, this interview would be a whole lot shorter. I really think we're a good match." Whatever you do, keep your response positive.

If this interview were reversed and you were interviewing me, what would you be looking for from me?

This is all you. Think about your ideal supervisor. What qualities in that person would you value most? Perhaps you're looking for a supervisor who values your opinion, doesn't micromanage, and provides you with the resources to do your job properly. Or maybe you prefer a supervisor you can work with in close collaboration to improve the department's strategic success.

What percentage of your life do you control?

Your answer to this question depends on how much control you need to have in the position you're applying for. If you're being hired in to crack the whip and improve productivity, your answer should show that you have a great deal of control over your life. If the position requires close collaboration with others, you may want to point out that you don't see yourself as controlling any aspect of your life but as working with others to achieve the best outcome for everyone involved.

Responding to tough questions for people over 50

As a 50-plus job seeker, expect at least a few questions about your age, even if they don't directly reference your age. While potential employers are concerned about your age and how it may affect your job performance, they probably won't come right out and say it because they fear an age-discrimination lawsuit. Here are a few common, age-related questions interviewers may ask.

Are you up-to-date with the latest technology?

Your research about the company and the position should reveal the technology you need to know to do the job. Check the job description if you're unsure. Mention your knowledge and experience of those technologies along with any other technologies you know that could be beneficial in that position.

Aren't you overqualified for the job?

Interviewers ask this question because they're afraid you'll be bored with the job, dissatisfied with the pay, or difficult to manage because you know or think you know more than your supervisors. Develop an answer that allays these fears. You may say something like the following:

> At this point in my career, I'm looking for a position I feel overqualified to do, so I can do the job to the best of my abilities and perhaps bring additional skills to the table that may be of use. I know the risks of hiring overqualified candidates running roughshod over a department, and I can assure you that's not going to happen with me. I'm very willing to let someone else take the reins and make the big decisions, so I can focus on doing what I'm most passionate about.

Why have you been out of work for so long?

Be candid when answering this question. Perhaps you took a leave of absence from the workforce to raise your kids or care for an elderly parent and then had a tough time getting back into the workforce. If you worked as a contractor during your absence or you acquired additional training and skills, be sure to mention these.

What is your greatest strength?

When answering this question, think in the context of the position and job responsibilities. Find a strength, perhaps not your greatest strength, that will best serve the organization's needs. This may be your ability to solve problems, manage a team, or identify areas of inefficiency.

Would you be comfortable working for a lower salary than you had in your last job? Why?

Nobody wants to work for *less* money, and you can admit this freely, but as an older worker, you have the perfect answer to this question (assuming the answer is relevant to your situation) — at this point in your career, you're looking for more than just a paycheck. You're looking for _____. Fill in the blank. Perhaps you've always wanted to work in the industry, you're looking forward to learning new skills, you love the company and its mission and want to contribute in some way, and so on. Don't say you don't care about the money. Say you care more about something else.

Have you ever worked for a younger boss? How did you make it work?

Even if you've never been supervised by someone younger than you, you need to have an answer to this one. Scour your past for times when you worked for or alongside younger people. You may point out that everyone has different knowledge and skills that aren't dependent on age. Focus on what young people have taught you or are capable of teaching you. Don't get into how much you can offer younger people, because that's probably what the interviewer fears — you trying to take the leadership role with a younger supervisor.

Thinking over career and industry questions

Certain questions may focus on the industry in general and on your career goals. This section covers a few common questions to get you thinking about these areas.

What led you to move from one job to the next?

Have some fun with this question as you spin your own career path tale of how you've been challenged and excited and energized with each move. Focus on how the transitions challenged you intellectually and how with each change you were energized and ramped up your skills, growing and stretching and contributing to your employer's bottom line.

What are your thoughts on where the industry is heading?

No one can predict the future, but employers want someone who's thinking about it every day. Be prepared to discuss the major players in the industry and the challenges they face. Information is readily available on the Internet via general web and Google News searches, which is one reason researching the company and the industry prior to your interview is so important.

Try to identify challenges and problems in the industry and think of creative approaches that may help solve them. For example, an oil and gas company could hire a certain firm to clean up and digitize its land records to boost revenue.

Where do you see yourself in ten years?

Employers are looking to hire people who are eager to advance in their careers in some way. They want someone who's motivated and has career goals and a strategy for achieving them. Studies show that if you fall into this category, you'll be more motivated, engaged, and productive. There's really no correct response, but it's not going to do you any good to say, "I haven't given it much thought." Also avoid saying anything about retirement. Think in terms of future career goals or challenges you'd like to take on.

Answering the salary question

When asked about salary in an interview, the best response is to say that although the position is not precisely the same as your last job, you would need to understand your duties and responsibilities in order to establish a fair salary for the job. If pressed to be more specific, ask what the salary range is and factor that in your response. So if the salary range is $50,000 to $60,000 and you want to make at least $55,000, you're probably best off asking for something between, say, $55,000 and $60,000.

Sometimes, if you're working with a recruiter hired by the company, you can be more frank about salary than if you're dealing directly with the hiring manager. Recruiters know what the market demands and may be able to go back to the employer and say that your salary figure is reasonable.

And finally, think beyond salary. If you're hitting up against a salary deal breaker, take a breath and think creatively. Try asking for salary review in six months, tuition reimbursement, parking allowance, transportation passes, or extra vacation days.

Don't take lower-than-expected pay personally. Employers base a salary on the requirements of the job, the availability of qualified job candidates, and their budget, not on what you were paid in the past. Knowing what you're willing to accept is important; if it's outside the range the employer is willing to pay, then say so and move on.

Preparing a few questions of your own

Much of what makes a great job interview is intuitive. It's chemistry between you and your interviewer(s). When asked whether you have any questions, you have an opportunity to reveal more about yourself and what you're looking for and to demonstrate that you can ask intelligent, challenging questions.

Be respectful, but ask tough questions. Obvious, safe questions make you seem ho-hum compared to other candidates and reveal that you haven't done your research. Challenging questions indicate that you know what you want, you're committed to finding the right fit (not just any old job), and you're smart. In addition, interviewers will remember you for challenging them when other candidates chose to play it safe

In this section, I offer ten questions to consider asking and several questions you should never ask.

Ten questions to consider asking

Here are ten questions to consider asking and to spark your own imagination to come up with additional questions.

- **Why did *you* choose this company?** The answer to this question helps you size up the company from the perspective of someone who works there. Variations of this question include "What challenges make you excited to come to work each day?" and "What do you like the most about working here?" These questions let somebody see that you're genuinely attracted to the job and decide whether the company is a good fit for you.

- **How would I exceed your expectations on a short-term basis, say in the first 30 to 60 days on the job?** This is a great question, because it conveys your eagerness to start and your commitment to serving the organization's needs while providing you with insight into the tasks and challenges you'll be facing if you get the job.

✔ **What qualities do your very best employees have in common?** Again, this question expresses your desire to take the position only if it's in the best interest of the organization, while the answer gives you a clear idea of what you'll need to do to succeed as an employee.

✔ **Is there anything about me, my skills, or my background that you would like me to clarify?** This question shows that you want the company to make a well-informed hiring decision, plus it gives you the opportunity to talk about your skills and other qualities you bring to the table that may not have been mentioned yet.

✔ **Does the company encourage entrepreneurship?** An increasing number of companies large and small are offering workers the freedom, flexibility, and resources to work as an entrepreneur within the organization. The buzzword for it: *intrapreneurship.* An employer or manager who creates a work environment that encourages and supports entrepreneurial culture and opportunities for work on projects outside your direct responsibility can make a huge difference in your happiness at work.

✔ **What types of mentoring programs do you offer?** You may go a step further and add that you enjoy mentoring younger workers, and you've also benefited from pairing up with a younger worker who reverse-mentors you — offering help with technology, social media, and so on. This shows you're hip to the underlying perception of intergenerational tension in the workplace. It also demonstrates your willingness to work with younger coworkers. And it shows that you're comfortable reporting to a boss who may be younger than you.

✔ **What's the salary range for this position?** Preface this question by saying that your interest in the position doesn't revolve around money, but you would be interested in knowing what the range is.

Expect a pause and then a ballpark figure. Try not to show delight or disappointment. This isn't a time to negotiate or even to indicate whether the range is acceptable. Save that for the negotiating table, after you get a formal offer.

If the interviewer deflects or struggles to answer, reply smoothly, without missing a beat, that you're looking forward to learning more details when the interviewer is free to share them in your next discussion.

✔ **Is full-time the only option, or would you consider a contract or consulting arrangement?** Ask this question only if you're open to such an arrangement; otherwise, you may be giving a prospective employer a reason not to hire you for a permanent position. A contracting or consulting arrangement enables you to pursue your passion while perhaps avoiding some of the less attractive responsibilities of the position.

Questions you should never ask

While you're keenly focused on putting your best foot forward and asking smart and sometimes tough questions, it's oh-so-easy to say something that could knock you out of the running. When an awkward question slips through your lips, even the smoothest of interviews can go south. Here are some examples of questions you should steer clear of in interviews.

- **Does my age concern you?** When you're interviewing for a job and you're over 50, you're painfully aware that ageism is alive and well in many workplaces, but this question is likely to make your interviewers uncomfortable. Instead, ask if they have any concerns about your skills or experience.

- **Will I be working for someone younger than me?** This question is a red flag indicating that you may have trouble working with or for someone who's younger than you. The best option is to accept the fact that you'll probably have a younger boss. If that's a deal breaker, then, as you get closer to getting the job offer, ask to meet with your potential boss and the team you'll be working with. This approach enables you to subtly obtain the information you need without making an issue out of it.

- **Can you tell me about your company's benefits?** Don't put the horse before the cart, at least not during your initial interview. Save this question for when you're negotiating the offer.

- **What training is provided?** Most employers want to hire people who can hit the ground running, not people they have to train and carefully supervise.

- **Can I telecommute? Do you offer any flextime options?** Such questions wave red flags, implying that you're not really committed to the position. These questions also suggest that you're uber-independent and may not work cheerfully with direct supervision or that you have other demands that could interfere with giving the job your undivided attention. Again, you can ask these questions later, when you have offer in hand.

- **How long will it take to get promoted?** The employer is looking to fill a current need, so focus on getting the position first. If you feel compelled to ask about promotions, talk in terms of career paths within the organization, and keep the focus on meeting the organization's needs.

- **Can I bring my dog to work?** Sure, there are pet-friendly workplaces, but it's probably not worth bringing up unless you see other pooches roaming the hallways.

Getting Comfortable in Your Own Skin

Confidence is crucial to acing an interview. To project confidence, you need to be comfortable in your own skin. Research and preparation help, but you can do more to hone your presentation skills. In this section, I show you how.

Practicing toward perfection

You can make all the great impressions in the world on paper, but where the rubber meets the road is when you meet someone face-to-face. When you get the nod for an interview, it's show time, and no accomplished actor ever takes the stage without a rehearsal or two or three.

Practice your patter with one or more mock interviews. Here are a few ways to engage in mock interviews:

- Have a friend, partner, mentor, or teacher act as an interviewer and run through a dress rehearsal in your living room.
- Use Skype to conduct a remote interview, which is a great way to practice online interviews. You can also use Google Hangouts.
- Use a smartphone with videoconferencing.
- Use an online job interview simulator. You may be able to access simulators through your alma mater's career center, a professional organization you belong to, or a job-search site. A simulator enables you to practice answering interview questions at home, using a computer with Internet access, a webcam or built-in camera in your computer, and a microphone. You may also be able to engage in mock interviews by using a smartphone app. Check out the following sites and apps:
  - Interview Simulation (www.thiswaytocpa.com/career-tools/interview-simulation)
  - Interview4 (www.interview4.com/job-candidates)
  - InterviewStream Prep (www.interviewstream.com/interviewstream-prep)
  - Monster.com Interviews (available at www.itunes.apple.com)
  - My Interview Simulator (www.myinterviewsimulator.com)

Record your interview, if possible. If you're doing your mock interviews in person, use your smartphone and a tripod with the camera pointing at you, so you record your answers, facial expressions, and body language. (For more about body language, check out Chapter 13.) If you're conducting your interviews online or using an app, see if the site or software you're using has an option to record. After each interview, watch and critique your performance, so you can work on improving areas of weakness.

Exploring other ways to hone your interview skills

Although some people are naturals, most require training and practice to master the art of the job interview. To get the training and practice you need, consider the following options:

- ✔ **Join Toastmasters.** Since 1924, Toastmasters International has helped people from all walks of life improve their speaking skills and self-confidence in front of an audience. Most meetings consist of about 20 people who meet weekly for an hour or two. Participants practice and learn skills of effective speech: focus, organization, language, vocal variety, and body language. You learn how to focus your attention away from your own anxieties and concentrate on your message and your audience, which goes a long way toward acing an interview.

  I encourage you to join Toastmasters both to help you develop effective public speaking skills and to extend your network.

- ✔ **Take a public speaking course.** You can find public speaking courses at your local community college. Most courses cover techniques for managing communication anxiety, speaking clearly, tuning into your body language, and much more.

- ✔ **Sign up for an improvisational comedy workshop.** If you have a secret yearning to be a *Saturday Night Live* cast member and develop interviewing skills at the same time, sign up for an improv comedy workshop. These workshops help you build your confidence and stage presence.

- ✔ **Work with a coach.** A good career coach can give you feedback and offer advice to sharpen your presentation. See Chapter 3 for how to find a coach.

Practice until you feel totally confident and comfortable delivering your CAR and elevator pitches and fielding questions.

Chapter 13

Acing Your Job Interview

*Y*ou researched the organization and perhaps the people who'll be interviewing you, prepared responses to common questions, practiced answering questions, and prepared a few questions of your own. Now, it's show time, your opportunity to deliver the performance of your life and win the hearts and minds of the small audience that's about to decide whether you have a future with the organization.

Before you take the stage, read through this chapter for additional coaching and stage direction. In this chapter, I explain how to make a good first impression and carry it through the duration of the interview, avoid serious blunders that could very well sink your chances of landing the job or getting a second interview, deliver your best performance in phone and video interviews, and follow up with a thank-you note that's likely to result in a curtain call.

Making a Positive Impression

Every career coach will tell you the importance of making a positive first impression, and I lend my voice to that chorus, but I say go further; make a positive impression from the time you show up to several days after you step out the door. You want to dazzle the interviewers with your grace and sophistication throughout the interview while you present yourself as the best candidate for the job in terms of knowledge, skills, and experience. By the time the interview wraps up, your interviewers should be looking forward enthusiastically to your future with the organization.

In this section, I offer guidance on making a good first impression and building on that throughout the interview.

Feeling your best

A one-hour interview can feel like a marathon, so have something to eat and drink prior to the interview. Here's what I recommend:

- ✔ **Eat a high-protein breakfast.** Avoid sugary or starchy foods, such as doughnuts or even bread, that tend to give you a quick sugar high and then make you feel exhausted during the interview.

- ✔ **Drink water to stay hydrated but not too much.** You don't want to have to use the bathroom 15 minutes into the interview. Limit caffeine the day of and even the night before the interview. One cup of coffee or tea in the morning is fine.

- ✔ **If you feel better after exercise, perform your normal exercise routine before showering and getting dressed for your interview.** Exercise can help you work out some anxiety and make you feel more vibrant and relaxed at the same time.

Getting groomed and dressed

Maybe it's been awhile since you've been on a first date, but you no doubt recall the preparation process — the trimming and primping, the showering and shaving, and carefully choosing an outfit to wear, including the right shoes. Although you want to look more professional than alluring as you prepare for a job interview, practice the same attention to detail as you did or do when preparing for a first date. You want to look your very best.

If it's been awhile since you had to look your best, you may have gotten yourself into a style rut. You don't want to step into an interview as though you just stepped out of a time machine from the '80s or '90s. Make sure you have a fashionable new suit, shoes, hairstyle, and glasses (if you wear them). You don't have to dress like a millennial, but do dress in style of the times.

Here are a few additional tips:

- ✔ **Lean toward more formal garb.** Even if the office dress code is "business casual" or you're told that everyone wears jeans and sneakers, dress more formally.

- ✔ **Shine your shoes.** If your shoes are scuffed, buy new shoes or pay for a professional's elbow grease. Skip the super-high heels and open-toe shoes. You do want polished footwear, though.

> ✔ **Take the time to really look in the mirror before you head out.** A quick pit stop in the office building's restroom, or the Starbucks next door, before you enter the firm's actual domain is a good idea. Check for rogue dog or cat hairs, missed buttons, undone zippers, and bits of bagel in your teeth.

True story: I once interviewed for a job with aluminum foil from the cleaners wrapped around all the brass buttons on my red blazer. I had pulled it straight from the cleaner's bag without checking. Yikes! The interviewer never mentioned it. I still laugh sheepishly about it today. I got the job, but ahem, attention to details, please.

Arriving early

Don't be late. Your interview starts long before you shake hands. Arrive 10 to 15 minutes early. It's more than a case of punctuality. When you arrive early, you have a chance to center yourself. It removes one layer of stress. If you're skating in under the bell, it's probably evident in your startled eyes, hurried appearance, and damp handshake.

Pumping yourself up just prior to the interview

As you're sitting in the lobby waiting to be called in for your interview, take some slow, deep breaths and say to yourself, "I will do the very best I can." Give yourself a pep talk. Run through your selling points and why you're the best candidate for the position. Remind yourself that you're here to team up with the interviewers to find out whether you're a good fit for the organization and it's a good fit for you; it's not just about selling yourself to the organization. Relax. Smile.

I encourage you to approach this meeting as you would a conversation with someone you want to know better and you want to know more about you. Look forward to the interview, not with a sense of dread, but with enthusiasm. This is an opportunity to meet and get to know a new colleague, someone who shares your goals and is committed, as you are, to the organization's success. You're teaming up with your interviewers to find out whether you and your prospective employer are a good match. You're allies, not adversaries.

Beginning the interview at the door

Begin your interview at the door. Greet the receptionist with the same respect as the person who will be interviewing you. You're on stage from the instant you state your name at the front desk. Most one-on-one job interviews last between 25 and 30 minutes, so your total on-site performance time is precious. Because it's short and sweet, milk every minute of it, from your time in the waiting room onward.

Don't spend your time in the on-deck area gabbing on your cell, for example, or responding to emails or even tweeting. Focus on why you're there. It's okay to review a list of questions you want to ask. Soak up the office atmosphere. Look around. It will give you clues as to whether this is a place you want to hang your hat.

Fine-tuning your delivery

If you haven't engaged in a job interview for some time, you may feel awkward, not knowing how to greet your interviewers, what to say, or even how to behave. You don't want to be overly self-conscience and stiff, nor do you want to be too chummy. Here are a few suggestions on how to handle various stages and aspects of the interview process:

- ✔ **Start with a relaxed meet and greet.** Step up with a firm one-handed handshake. Two hands can be a little forthright and maybe even too familiar.

- ✔ **Kick off the first few minutes of your interview as you would a conversation with someone you just met at a reception.** Keep it relaxed and conversational but not too personal. My standard advice: Commenting on wall décor or a desk accessory is acceptable, but saying you like someone's tie or shoes may be stepping over the line.

I personally like to scan wall and desk photographs to see whether I can find a common bond. A framed image of a Labrador retriever or a horse always sets an instant connection for me. These initial moments are where the chemistry between the interviewer and you can spark. Think speed dating.

- ✔ **Offer a copy of your résumé before you sit down.** Presenting your résumé to an interviewer is akin to bringing a gift to a host or hostess. You're passing along something of value in exchange for the invitation to meet and for the person's time. By handing over your résumé in the opening moments of the interview, you make it an interactive asset, a conversation piece. If you want to emphasize or explain certain areas or responsibilities, the interview is your chance to draw attention to them.

People often think if something is on their résumé, the significance is clear to the interviewer, but those bullet points don't always speak for themselves. You may need to call them out and draw the lines that connect your qualifications to the requirements for the position.

✔ **Follow the leader.** Synch up with the interviewer's rhythm. It's important to go at her tempo. Don't try too hard or talk too fast. Answer concisely and in a confident, calm manner. Pause before you respond — even repeat the question if need be — to buy yourself some moments to gather a measured response.

✔ **Listen and formulate relevant responses.** Keep focused on your interviewers and the reality that you're sitting in that chair to sell solutions to their problems or challenges. Don't be thinking ahead to what you want to say next about yourself. The interview is about them and their needs and how you can help serve those needs. It's not about you. Listen closely to what they're saying.

✔ **Keep answers terse and to the point.** Crisp, relevant answers allow interviewers to ask all their questions and gather as much knowledge about you as possible. Aim toward answering each question in two minutes or less.

As discussed in Chapter 12, keep your message focused on your three key selling points — why you're the best person for the position. Three key points are generally easy to remember and stick to.

Shaping up with posture and body language

What you say and how you say it are important, but you also need to focus on what your body is doing and saying while your ears are listening and your mouth is talking. Follow these suggestions:

✔ **Sit up straight.** No slouching. Breathe in and out slowly and deeply, and relax.

✔ **Maintain eye contact.** A clear, direct gaze portrays candor and sincerity, but don't stare, because that can be creepy. Glance up or over every so often as you carefully consider a point, or shift your focus from one eye to the other to the person's mouth and then back to the eyes every five to ten seconds.

✔ **Lean forward to show interest.** When the interviewer begins to answer a question you asked, lean slightly forward to show interest.

✔ **Keep hand gestures to a minimum in both frequency and amplitude.** If you've got a point you want to play up, a hand gesture is fine. For most of the interview, though, keep your hands laced together with your thumbs on top, resting calmly in your lap or propped lightly on the arms of the chair or the table in front of you. Pressing your fingertips together in a steeple formation is also a simple sign of self-assurance, but don't overdo it.

✔ **Avoid stroking your neck or throat, which can make you look nervous.** A confident, loose (unclenched) fist lightly tucked under your chin is okay in small doses.

✔ **Don't cross your arms over your chest.** You may think this makes you look serious, but it can come off as a defensive stance.

✔ **Avoid twisting and spinning your pen, rings, necklace, or bracelets.** You may do this unconsciously, so be mindful of what your hands are up to. For an interviewer, it sends off a signal of nerves or even anxiety.

Interviewing with a younger hiring manager

When interviewing with a younger hiring manager, treat the person as a colleague and not as a mentee:

✔ **Focus on the organization's current and future needs.** You may be the deal of the century for the organization based on your past accomplishments, but focus less on those and more on how your experience and skills meet the organization's current and future needs.

✔ **Don't cop an attitude.** For example, don't try to tell them why the job description is faulty or unrealistic in some way. If you feel more qualified than the interviewer, hide that fact. Try not to be condescending or professorial.

✔ **Let go of any resentment at being in this position.** Having to prove yourself to someone less experienced or skilled than yourself bruises the ego. You can't fix that, and if you try to bury your resentment, it'll bubble up to the surface, so let it go.

✔ **Don't be a fuddy-duddy.** Avoid reminiscing about the good old days or complaining about anything, especially the current state of the industry or culture. Don't suggest that something a hiring manager says is like something your children would say, don't chat about details that date you, such as the grandkids' birthdays, and don't start a sentence with "When I was your age. . . ."

✔ **Find common ground.** Even if you and your interviewers are literally generations apart, you can find common ground by focusing on the needs of the organization.

 Prep yourself for the interview by including plenty of people in your professional network who are younger than you, so you can tune into the needs, interests, and qualities of the so-called millennials you may be working for. Reverse-mentoring is another useful approach. You'll have more success interviewing with people younger than you if you network with younger people and treat them as your peers on a regular basis.

Stats on career changers

Interestingly, a recent study published by the American Institute for Economic Research, a nonprofit group based in Great Barrington, Massachusetts, called "New Careers for Older Workers," shows that 82 percent of those who attempted a transition to a new career after age 45 were successful in doing so. Some respondents reported that they initially took pay cuts but successful career changers reported that after a period of hard work and persistence, they worked their way up the income ladder.

Avoiding the Most Serious Missteps

When you're looking for a job, you have a lot on your mind and may be more prone to making mistakes that undermine your efforts. Here are the top mistakes to avoid:

- ✔ **Showing up late:** Punctuality is a soft job skill that employers rank high on their list of deal killers. Showing up late is a big hurdle to overcome unless you have a great reason.

- ✔ **Failing to prepare:** Unless your prospective employer has actively recruited you, you need to show up having done your research about the company and the industry. See Chapter 12 for details.

- ✔ **Acting arrogant:** Humility rules the day. Employers want people on their team who work well with others and don't hold themselves above anyone else. You should be confident and have swagger as I like to urge older workers but never go egotistic. If you believe in yourself, you don't need this haughty crutch.

- ✔ **Dropping names:** It's okay to name names of people you may know in common or those big players in your industry whom you've worked with recently, but, in general, this technique is a turnoff and reeks of insecurity.

- ✔ **Bringing up compensation too early:** Wait for signs that the organization wants you before thinking about how much they're willing to pay to get you. Besides, if you bring up the topic too soon, you may end up low-balling yourself.

- ✔ **Focusing too much on yourself:** Focus not on what your employer can do for you. Focus on what you can do for your employer. After your prospective employer decides that you're the best candidate for the job, you can shift your focus to getting what *you* want.

- ✔ **Not being engaging enough:** Although you don't want to chatter away about yourself for any extended amount of time, being stiff and standoffish is just as bad. This is a two-way street. Take the time to dance.

✔ **Giving long-winded answers:** Crisp, relevant answers demonstrate efficiency in thought and language. You want to show a potential employer that you're decisive, organized, and clear-thinking.

✔ **Misrepresenting the facts:** You have nothing to gain from embellishing or massaging the truth, whether it pertains to past jobs and responsibilities, graduation dates, experience, or simply your age. Honesty is nothing to play around with. After being caught in a lie, you may not be able to restore your credibility or regain your composure.

✔ **Not following up:** This is like not calling after a first date. When employers don't hear back from you, they assume that you're not all that interested.

✔ **Backing out of an accepted offer:** This is unprofessional and can come back to haunt you if another employer gets wind of it. Moreover, it portrays you as someone who's fickle and somewhat dishonest.

Managing Alternative Interview Formats

The world of interviewing has changed quite a bit probably since you were last out pounding the pavement. For employers, telephone and video interviews can cut the amount of time and travel expenses spent recruiting. But for you, the new ballgame may add tensions to an already nerve-wracking process. Without that in-person connection, communicating your enthusiasm and other less tangible qualities can be quite challenging.

The key to performing well in less traditional interview formats is to know what to expect and to practice, so you're comfortable with these formats. In this section, I explain what to expect and how to successfully navigate these different interview formats.

Regardless of interview setting, preparation is essential to optimizing your performance. You need to do your homework, prepare questions of your own, and rehearse. See Chapter 12 for details.

Acing the telephone interview

To improve your performance on a telephone interview, follow these suggestions:

✔ **Use a landline phone, if possible.** Avoid spotty cellphone and VoIP (Voice over Internet Protocol) connections. A landline removes the technical difficulties that may unnerve you during the interview.

✔ **Pick a quiet location.** Find a comfortable place without distractions from people, pets, music, and street noise. Inform everyone in the household that you're going to be on a very important phone call and are not to be disturbed.

✔ **Turn off other phones and mute the speakers on your computer.** You don't want anything ringing or dinging in the background.

✔ **Lay out a copy of your résumé and the job description.** You may need to refer to details from these documents during the call, but don't read off of them, because reading can sound stiff.

✔ **Have paper and pen handy.** Jot down notes during the conversation, if that helps you follow the conversation and keep track of what's been said. However, if note-taking interferes with your ability to listen and respond, then keep your note-taking to a minimum. You should still have paper and pen handy, just in case.

✔ **Have a drink nearby.** A glass of water is best or a cup of coffee or tea if you're looking for a little caffeine bump. Keeping your whistle wet helps you steer clear of throat clearing, which is awkward and ruins the flow of conversation. And if you haven't said anything in a while, warm up your voice before the phone rings.

✔ **Smile.** Interviewers can hear a smile over the phone. You'll sound upbeat and convey a sense that you're happy to have the opportunity to discuss the opening. Smile especially when you answer the phone and greet the caller, when you talk about your work and what you're passionate about, and when you ask questions about the company.

Put a mirror in front of yourself, so you can make sure you're smiling.

✔ **Pay attention to your posture.** Stand or sit up straight, during the call. I prefer standing. I think it makes my voice sound stronger and more energetic. I even walk while the interviewer is talking.

✔ **Be ready to go ten minutes ahead of time.** You don't want to sound hurried.

✔ **Answer professionally.** When the phone rings, smile, and greet the caller with something like, "Hi, this is [name]." If you know who's calling (from Caller ID), consider following up with "Is this [name]?" Don't try to pretend that you don't know who's calling, because that can make you sound phony.

✔ **Listen carefully before you speak.** Pause before you answer to gather your thoughts. Then talk. Try to answer each question in two minutes or less. Otherwise, your interviewer may tune out. Because you can't see the person, it's tempting to fill in any pauses in the conversation, but rein it in.

- **Enunciate your words and don't speak too fast.** Projecting your voice distinctly and enthusiastically is fundamental.

- **Avoid fillers such as "like," "you know," and "um."** Use precise language to communicate your thoughts. Remind yourself that short pauses are acceptable and much preferred over fillers that can make you sound less sophisticated.

- **End on an up note.** If you really want the job, finish your conversation by saying, "Thanks for the call. I'm very interested in what we've discussed today and would appreciate the opportunity to meet you in person. What's the next step?" Think of this as your call to action.

Exceling in Skype or video interviews

Virtual interviews are rapidly becoming more commonplace, according to a survey by OfficeTeam, a temporary staffing services firm. Six in ten of the 500 human resource managers interviewed said their company often conducts employment interviews via video, up from 14 percent in 2011. Video interviews involve talking live with an interviewer via Skype or other video-conferencing technology or video-recording responses to questions from a recorded interviewer.

These tips can help you become comfortable with these interview formats and ace your interview:

- **Check your equipment.** You'll need a dependable Internet connection, a webcam, and a microphone. If possible, use an Ethernet cable to connect to the Internet and turn off Wi-Fi, so your connection is faster and more reliable.

- **Perform a background check.** Look at what will appear behind you. If it's a clutter-fest with file folders and paper piles, or even personal items such as pictures from your vacation, do a clean sweep. Having a painting, bookcase, or attractive plant in the background is best, but make sure the painting and books are tasteful.

- **Adjust the lighting.** You want soft light illuminating your face. Think of those klieg lights that shine on television anchors' faces. If your room has a window, face it, or put a lamp on the desk in front of you. Avoid backlit scenarios that put you in a shadow and glaring front-lighting that makes you squint.

- **Experiment with the interview platform.** If it's a live video interview, you may need to download the application software and set up an account. If it's a pre-recorded interviewer, you'll receive instructions ahead of time about what's needed to participate.

✔ **Reboot your computer.** Rebooting ensures that you're not running applications that may interrupt the interview. If you have applications set up to automatically run whenever you start your computer, exit those applications.

✔ **Adjust your webcam and chair.** Adjust your camera and chair so you're in the middle (horizontally) and the top of your head is near the top of the screen. You should be looking up slightly at the camera, a position that helps define your chin and subtly conveys a message of strength and confidence.

✔ **Do a dry run.** Practice with a friend or family member on the platform you'll be using or something similar. With Skype, you can record it to review. This also helps with figuring out just how loud you need to talk and how to position your webcam.

✔ **Dress for an in-person interview.** Solid colors are best. Avoid white. Don't forget some makeup, even if you're a guy. It takes the shine off your skin.

✔ **Have a cheat sheet.** Sticky notes on your screen can remind you of talking points you want to be sure to highlight about your experience and why you're a good fit for the job as well as questions about the firm and the position. Have your résumé and the job description handy, too.

✔ **Try your best to look into the camera when talking.** You'll be tempted to look at yourself or the interviewers on the screen, instead, but doing so breaks eye contact with the interviewers. Remember, their eyes are the camera.

✔ **Smile when appropriate.** Smiling provides a big boost for your video presence and energizes the interview. Try warming up ahead of time by thinking of something funny to make you laugh, or grinning at yourself in a mirror to loosen up your facial muscles. Smile especially during the meet and greet.

✔ **Moderate your body language.** Breathe deeply and slowly and relax. Keep your shoulders back and your hands quiet. No hair spinning around your pinky, lip chewing, squinting your eyes, or overblinking.

✔ **Raise technical issues, if necessary.** If something goes awry — say, your Internet connection blips out, or you're having trouble with your computer's camera or microphone — speak up. If it happens during a taped interview, just abort and contact the recruiter to explain and reschedule.

✔ **Say thanks.** End your interview by saying, "Thank you for considering me for the job. I look forward to hearing from you." Smile, and continue eyeing the camera until the recording or interview stops.

Shining in automated interviews

Automated interviews are those in which a recorded interviewer asks questions, and you're given a set amount of time to record each answer. Video recruiting firms, such as WePow and HireVue, call it "modern recruiting" and have signed on clients including Geico, Hilton Worldwide, Nike, and Walmart to develop digital interviews with candidates.

Many candidates, especially older candidates, who tend to be more accustomed to interacting with people than performing in front of a webcam, may have a tough time with automated interviews. Establishing rapport with interviewers when you have to answer in two minutes or less can be quite a challenge. And you can't look around someone's office for impromptu conversation starters.

It really is more like acting than interviewing, so rehearse. Sit yourself in front of your webcam, set it up to record, and practice answering questions until you're comfortable with the format. Watch and critique your recorded responses to improve your delivery. All the suggestions in the previous section for video interviews apply to automated interviews as well.

Go to YouTube.com and search for "job interview examples," to watch good and bad techniques.

Feeling violated by a robo-recruiter

A couple of days after a 55-year-old woman I interviewed zapped her résumé and online job application to a large healthcare provider, she received this email:

> Good afternoon,
>
> We are so happy that you are interested in the position of Organizational Development Specialist.
>
> Good news! We are interested in learning more about you. To do that, we would like for you to participate in a digital interview via WePow.

But that's where things went south fast. The videoconferencing firm emailed her directions on how to set up her computer and record a test video to get familiar with the process. And she followed the electronic instructions to a tee. One tip did amuse her: "Smile! Smiling makes a huge difference in how you are perceived."

She was given 20 seconds after the videotaped interviewer (not a live person in real time) posed a question and then two minutes to respond. "It was tough because I have quite a bit of experience, and it was very difficult for me to answer in two minutes," she says.

Here was the real trouble, she explains. She never once talked with a human being. The entire exchange with the potential employer was all completely computer generated.

"I felt violated in a way," she says. "It takes away your ability to be a person. It puts you into a process that they're in control of (the software actually takes over your computer and activates the camera, microphone, and so forth) and clearly looking for something, but you don't even get a chance to understand what it is."

The last question the robo-recruiter asked: "Is there anything else you would like to tell me?"

Her response: "I get my energy from being around people. I'm having a tough time trying to tell you who I am when I am talking to my computer. And I would really like the opportunity to sit down and have a conversation with you."

"It was just incredibly awkward. At the end of the 20-minute interview, I felt completely humiliated." She never heard back from the employer.

Following Up Post Interview

After the interview, follow up with your interviewers. Always send a thank-you note, and if you haven't heard back from the organization within a few days, check in to keep your name in the running and find out whether there's anything you can do to help them make a hiring decision. In this section, I cover additional details about following up after the interview.

Sending a thank-you note

Write a thank-you note to everyone you interviewed with that day and send it within 24 hours of the interview. I personally like a handwritten note, but email is acceptable if that's the only option. Even better, send an email message, which arrives immediately and a handwritten note, which takes a day or two to arrive. When sending email, wait until later in the day to send it; don't send it immediately after the interview. You don't want to seem desperate. Reiterate your interest in the company, your qualifications for doing the job, and your desire to take things to the next level or, if you're not interested, say something along the lines of "During the interview, I realized that the position is not what I am looking for at this time." Use your correspondence to wrap up and leave a positive impression.

Your thank-you note provides an opportunity to mention anything you may not have been able to work smoothly into the interview. You can also clarify responses to questions you stumbled on or feel as though you answered poorly.

Checking in when you haven't heard a thing

If you haven't heard back from the organization within a few days, be patient. They may be evaluating other candidates. Wait approximately five business days and then follow up with a note asking whether they've made a decision. If you still haven't heard back, consider sending another follow-up note. Then, stop, at least for the time being. It's up to them to contact you if they're interested.

Interviewers not responding after a job interview, as rude as that is, is fairly common practice these days. If they're not interested, they may feel uncomfortable contacting you to relay the bad news or their response could expose them to legal action, so they go silent, torturing you with uncertainty.

If you really want to work for a particular organization, even after they've given you the cold shoulder, keep your contact at the organization posted on any changes in your résumé, new skills added, consulting assignments, and so forth. Periodically remind them that you're still enthusiastic about one day working for them, are passionate about the organization's mission, and believe you have a lot to offer and then say specifically what you have to offer.

Regardless of how antsy you get to hear back from an organization, never do any of the following:

- ✔ Don't call or contact a hiring manager two or three days in a row.

- ✔ Don't give deadlines or ultimatums. Unless you have good reason, such as a pending job offer or promotion you need to decide on soon, don't tell the organization that you need to hear back by a certain date.

- ✔ Don't contact a hiring manager through his personal email, home address, personal cellphone, or home telephone.

- ✔ Don't disparage the potential employer on social media if she doesn't respond to your emails.

- ✔ Don't write snarky emails asking for a status update on the position.

- ✔ Don't be a pest. Trust me. They may have somehow not received your first phone message or email, but not the subsequent ones.

- ✔ Don't send gifts or humorous notes in hopes of getting noticed.

Rejected? Conducting a Postmortem

Rejection stings, but don't take it personally. Hiring is always about them, not about you. This is business, and you have no way of knowing all the ins and outs of why a job is filled with someone other than you, so let it go. For all you know, the job description may have changed, or it was filled by someone in-house. Sometimes rejection really is protection from finding yourself heading down a path or working in a job that isn't right for you.

Either way, you can learn from the experience. Maybe you did make some mistakes. Perhaps you stumbled during the interview. Maybe the interview revealed that you need to develop knowledge and skills required for the position you're pursuing. Or maybe you weren't comfortable with a particular interview format, and you need to work on that. Use an unsuccessful interview to address weaknesses and strengthen your chances of acing the next interview. The interview also taught you that whatever you did to land the interview worked, so you're probably on track with that aspect of your job search.

If an actual person informs you that you weren't chosen for the position, take the opportunity to ask why. Find out what you may have said during the interview that turned the employer off or what skills you may be lacking. That way, you can make adjustments for the next time.

To further sharpen your job interview skills, check out *Job Interviews For Dummies* by Joyce Lain Kennedy (Wiley) and the tips at www.aarp.org/work.

Chapter 14

Negotiating for What You Want

F ew people in the United States like to haggle, especially when a potential job opportunity is on the line, but if you're not prepared to negotiate, you could end up being paid less than you're worth and falling short of your employment goals. The resulting bitterness or resentment from accepting less than what you had hoped for can negatively affect your job performance and satisfaction, which is bad for you and your employer. Yet you need to come to peace with the fact that you may not get everything you want.

Your goal should be to achieve a mutually beneficial employer-employee relationship, and you may need to make trade-offs to achieve that goal. Perhaps you accept less pay for fewer hours, a more flexible schedule, or a longer vacation. Maybe you agree to provide your own health insurance for a bump in pay, or you accept less pay for the opportunity to earn bonuses tied to your performance. With a flexible attitude and some creative thinking, you can often negotiate a package that meets your needs as well as those of your employer. In this chapter, I describe your options, so you have the information you need to think more creatively about monetary compensation and other perks.

Evaluating Monetary Compensation: Salary and Benefits

If you're like many people, working in your 50s and beyond often comes down to having a decent salary that reflects your experience, solid benefits, *and* a flexible work schedule. As part of your research when job hunting, consider what compensation packages are feasible for someone in your field with your level of experience and in the location where you plan to work. Prior to interviewing for a specific position, dig deeper to find out more about employer-specific scenarios and benefits.

In addition to health coverage and vacation time, benefits could include sick time, health insurance, short- and long-term disability insurance, life insurance, survivor income, stock options, retirement plans, contributions to retirement, educational and training opportunities, and parking or public transportation. In this section, I focus on the various forms of monetary compensation. In the next section, I turn your attention to the benefits of flexible work arrangements.

Don't focus solely on salary. Consider the entire package, including salary, flexible work options, and time off. Do the math. What's your salary requirement? Are you willing to trade less pay for fewer hours? If you can afford to, consider your ideal work-life balance. What benefits will you need, and which ones can you forgo? If your spouse has health benefits through his or her employer, for example, you may not need them, and that can be a bargaining chip to trade for something else you want, such as more vacation days.

Every dollar the company pays for health insurance, time off, parking or public transportation (if applicable), contributions to retirement, and so on, is more than a dollar in your pocket, because you're not getting taxed on those amounts.

Researching salaries

Many employers specify a salary range for the positions they advertise, which takes some of the guesswork (and anxiety) out of salary negotiations. To get a clearer idea of what's generally accepted for a specific position based on job location and your experience, use the following resources as points of reference:

✔ The Economic Research Institute's Salary Assessor (www.erieri.com/salaryassessor) to find out what a particular position pays where you live.

- Foundation Center's 990 Finder (990finder.foundationcenter.org) to find IRS Form 990 tax filings for nonprofit organizations, which show how much their executives and other key employees are paid.

- Glassdoor (www.glassdoor.com) is an expanding database of 6 million company reviews, CEO approval ratings, salary reports, interview reviews and questions, benefits reviews, office photos, and more. This information is entirely shared by the employees.

- PayScale (www.payscale.com) uses crowdsourcing and big data technologies to compile its database of 40 million individual salary profiles.

- Salary.com (www.salary.com) provides salary information for more than 4,000 job titles. Salary.com is an IBM company, founded in 1999.

- U.S. Office of Personnel Management (www.opm.gov/policy-data-oversight/pay-leave/salaries-wages) for salary ranges for federal jobs.

The salary info you dig up on these sites should give you at least a ballpark number to keep you from being screened out from the get-go and enable you to negotiate from a well-informed position.

When applying for a position, tap into your network to find out about typical pay for the job.

Paying special attention to starting pay

Starting pay is crucial, because after you're on the payroll, ramping up your salary can be painstakingly slow, and you may never catch up to where you would have been had you negotiated a higher starting salary. For example, imagine two people receive a job offer of $45,000. One negotiates for $5,000 more, and both receive 3 percent raises every year. After 20 years, the difference in their lifetime earnings is a stunning $134,351.87! Consider how much more that would represent if it were invested in an IRA over those 20 years.

Negotiating a higher starting salary takes spunk and mettle, but you can do it with the proper preparation. See the later section "Honing Your Negotiating Skills and Strategies" for details.

Ignore all the lip service you'll probably hear about raises that will likely come your way after your first glowing performance review. Go for the proverbial bird in the hand over the two or three in the bushes.

If you're offered a salary lower than what you've targeted and the hiring manager won't budge, consider negotiating for an earlier salary review. Most employers review salaries once a year, so ask for a six-month evaluation. Three months is too soon. Nine months is your fallback suggestion. But don't count on this tactic landing you a big bump or even getting one at all. Just be sure that you're confident your performance will support the reconsideration of your base salary.

Assessing health insurance coverage

Health insurance is often non-negotiable. Either the employer offers health insurance or it doesn't. Health insurance is more likely to play into your decision and your ability to negotiate in these two scenarios:

- **When you're choosing between a smaller and a larger employer:** A larger employer is more likely to offer health insurance. Employers with 100 or more workers are required by the Affordable Care Act to offer 70 percent of their full-time workers (those working 30 or more hours a week) coverage. In 2016, employers with 50 or more full-time workers are required to offer coverage.

- **When you're already covered:** If you're covered under a spouse's plan, you may be able to decline the insurance plan at work in exchange for a higher salary or other perk. Hiring managers at small businesses, in particular, may be open to this tactic because the cost of offering insurance to workers can be a big ticket item. The average for annual family coverage paid by employers per employee was $20,011 in 2014, according to the Henry J. Kaiser Family Foundation.

The truth about raises

According to a survey of nearly 1,100 U.S. companies by compensation consultant Towers Watson (www.towerswatson.com), U.S. employers plan to give pay raises averaging 3 percent in 2015, about par with the 2.9 percent average raise in 2014 and 2013, but averages can be misleading. A broad gap may separate pay raises for top-rated workers and those for employees with average or below-average ratings. Office stars may receive well above the typical pay hike granted to workers. And managers dole out bigger bonuses to valued employees as an incentive to stay put.

Average hourly earnings in the United States rose a tiny 2.1 percent from 2013 to 2014, according to the Bureau of Labor Statistics. Yet top executives who changed jobs in 2013 averaged a 17 percent pay increase, according to the executive search firm Salveson Stetson Group (www.ssgsearch.com), far above the 11 percent increase in 2008 and 2009. These figures include base salary, bonus, and any signing bonus.

To me, this says that at many companies the funds are available, if you can prove your value.

That said, you do want to find out what kind of healthcare benefits are available (HMO, PPO, high-deductible HSA). If having super healthcare benefits (dental, vision, prescription coverage, and so on) is important and the company doesn't have them, that could be a deal breaker for you.

Comparing retirement plans

Unless you're a top executive, you may not be able to negotiate retirement plans, but if you have two or more job offers on the table, you definitely want to compare plans. The best place to get complete information about retirement plans and other benefits is from the human resources (HR) person. Ask how long before you can contribute to the 401(k) or other retirement plan. Does the company match contributions, and, if it does, what's the cap? When are you fully vested?

Counting vacation and sick days

Time is money. In fact, as you age and your financial responsibilities shrink while your nest egg grows, time may become more valuable than money and can be a valuable trade-off commodity. Many older workers are happy to exchange more time off for less pay, and employers generally have greater leeway exchanging time for money than coming up with more money.

When considering an offer, carefully weigh starting salary and time off in the form of vacation days, sick days, personal days, and holidays. If you've become accustomed to four weeks or more of paid vacation days and the employer is offering only two weeks and only after you've worked for the organization for a year, you have some room for negotiation:

- **Request more vacation days from the get-go.** For example, request three or four weeks instead of the standard two.

- **Ask that your allotted vacation days accumulate more rapidly.** For example, instead of receiving one day per month, request a day and a quarter or a day and a half per month.

- **Ask to be eligible to take vacation time prior to your one-year anniversary.** Waiting an entire year before you can take a vacation may be unrealistic for an older worker who's accustomed to annual vacations, but if the employer needs you to be there, this may be non-negotiable.

- **Request a certain amount of unpaid vacation time.** If time really is more valuable to you than money, find out how flexible the organization is when it comes to taking unpaid leave.

What's average?

When negotiating vacation and sick days, it helps to know what's normal. In the United States, 13 vacation days per year is average. Thirty-eight percent of employees who've worked a year with their employer and have access to a paid vacation plan received between five and nine paid vacation days per year. Thirty-five percent received 10 to 14 paid vacation days. Businesses that offer this benefit observe an average of nine paid days a year for full- and part-time staff, according to a survey by the Society for Human Resource Management (SHRM).

Consider negotiating to have paid traditional holidays such as Independence Day, Thanksgiving, and Christmas be counted as part of your total number of paid leave days. That way you're free to choose which ones you want to take.

Paid sick leave is rarely a negotiable point. Employers are understandably reluctant to hire an employee who's planning to be out for extended periods of time due to illness. Can you say red flag? Generally speaking, though, the average number of sick days is currently around eight days for one year of service to ten days after 20 years of service.

Considering bonuses

Employers may be more willing to negotiate performance-based pay, such as bonuses, than base pay. Ask about the possibility of earning a future bonus for an outstanding performance in a certain time frame, or for reaching a certain target goal, say a certain sales figure. To avoid future disagreement, make sure the bonus is tied to a verifiable goal or milestone and get the details in writing. Granted, salary increases are generally based on current salary, not including bonuses.

If employers in your industry are having difficulty filling a position you're applying for, consider holding out for a signing bonus. These vary among industries and companies from no signing bonus to very generous offers. The amount of a sign-on bonus can range from 20 to 200 percent of the base salary (more for executive-level positions or positions that are hard to fill, such as nurses or skill-based healthcare jobs). If you negotiate for a signing bonus, you may be required to sign a contract committing to work for the organization for a certain number of years. Breach the contract, and you're required to pay back all or part of the signing bonus.

The timing of the signing bonus can also differ from company to company. Some employers pay the entire bonus up front. Others divvy it up, so you get a portion when you start and the remainder in three to six months.

Exploring the signing bonus upside for employers

Why are employers willing to play ball with a signing bonus? Other than the obvious reason of signing high-demand professionals to a contract, a signing bonus tends to boost productivity and loyalty, according to a recent survey from *The Accounting Review*. The study looks at the effects of signing bonuses on employer-employee relationships. The study finds that particularly when a market has an excess number of workers, a signing bonus can engender more trust and loyalty between the employer and new employees. This may translate into a new hire feeling more committed and working harder.

But a signing bonus can also lead to higher expectations, which can result in strained employer-employee relations if the new employee doesn't live up to them, the study found. "When there is an excess of supply of labor, employers who offer a signing bonus expect greater effort from their workers than they do when either no signing bonus is offered or when there is an excess demand for labor," said Jungwoon "Willie" Choi, the study's author.

Surveys from global human resources association WorldatWork (www.world atwork.org) and other human resources organizations found that signing bonuses have made a comeback since the Great Recession as the employment market has improved, but bonuses are still not as commonly offered as they were during the dot-com boom of the late 1990s.

Prospecting for other perks

You can find plenty of other financial perks around the edges. Here are a few to consider:

- ✔ **State-of-the art equipment and software:** If it will make you excel at your job, this is a no-brainer. Ask what kind of office equipment is customary, what operating systems the devices run on, what programs are commonly installed and how that equipment is supported. Availability to certain equipment and software, for instance, can be essential for your mobility, productivity, and future raises.

  Don't push it. Requesting a company cellphone when you'll be on call is fine, but asking for an iPhone with an unlimited data plan is going too far.

- ✔ **Share options:** If you're negotiating with a publicly traded company, particularly if it's an executive-level position, ask about share options. Do some research into what's customary with the particular employer. Also be sure the company is in good financial shape before you go out on the limb. You can do this by setting up a Google Alert, reading information under the About Us link on the corporate website, and using corporate research sites such as Hoovers (www.hoovers.com).

✔ **Free education and training:** This is one of my personal favorites. Check to see whether your future employer includes reimbursement for certain tuition expenses. Some employers pay 90 percent of all costs of obtaining a bachelor's degree in any field as well as the same percentage of expenses for earning a master's degree related to the employee's field. Job-related certifications are also covered by the employer.

Some companies require a high GPA to receive the full benefit. Others provide reimbursement on a sliding scale, offering the full benefit only to those with a top grade average. Others require that employees remain employed with that particular company for a certain number of years after completing the course. Five years is a typical restricted period.

✔ **Professional development:** Professional development includes courses, conferences, credentialing programs, and other facilitated learn- ing opportunities designed to improve a person's ability to do a job. Showing an interest in this benefit should win you some points, because professional development benefits your employer as well, and it shows a long-term commitment to your profession.

✔ **Tuition reimbursement:** This is different from taking a training course or two. Let your employer pay for your schooling. Around half of employers offer education assistance, and you may not even need to study something directly related to your job to take advantage of this perk. Employers are allowed to provide up to $5,250 in educational expenses as a tax-free fringe benefit to their employees. This includes undergraduate and graduate level courses. Anything above $5,250 is gen- erally considered taxable income. However, there are some exemptions. Any assistance over $5,250 is excluded from your income if the educa- tion is a qualified, working-condition, fringe benefit.

You probably won't be able to convince a company that doesn't offer tuition reimbursement to offer it to you. But it's something to keep in mind when choosing an employer.

Exploring Flexible Work Options

While a 40-hour-plus workweek remains the norm, many workers, including the over-50 set, are looking for more flexibility; as a result, employers have adapted to these demands. With a little smooth talking and determination on your part, you may find a good job in which you set the hours and maybe even work out of your home for a portion of the time. You may not be able to negotiate such an arrangement right out of the gate, but your employer may allow you to move in that direction over time if you demonstrate a strong work ethic and self-discipline.

To land a position with an alternative schedule or negotiate a flexible arrangement, you need a clear concept of the type of work and schedule you can manage, as I explain in this section.

Chances are good that you won't surprise a hiring manager by asking for a non-traditional work schedule or workspace — not in an era when work-life balance is in and the need for face time is out. But the likelihood of negotiating a flextime and/or telecommuting arrangement is still up for debate. Someone at the executive level has a greater chance of receiving this type of benefit, because they're not as easy to replace, and their skills are at a premium. Entry-level employees have a more difficult time negotiating such arrangements.

Checking out flexible-friendly companies and industries

FlexJobs (www.flexjobs.com) analyzed recent work-from-home job listings to determine the companies that posted the most jobs with remote work options (telecommute, work-from-home, virtual opportunities) in 2015. Based on data from more than 30,000 companies, these were the top 25 employers with the most available at-home positions:

1. Teletech
2. Convergys
3. Sutherland Global Services
4. Amazon
5. Kelly Services
6. Kaplan
7. First Data
8. IBM
9. SAP
10. Westat
11. UnitedHealth Group
12. Dell
13. Working Solutions
14. Intuit
15. US-Reports
16. Xerox
17. PAREXEL
18. Aetna
19. Humana
20. VMware
21. Salesforce
22. American Express
23. HD Supply
24. Forest Laboratories
25. ADP

"The demand for telecommuting is growing, as is the acknowledgment by employers that remote job options can help attract and retain the best candidates," Sara Sutton Fell, founder and CEO of FlexJobs, stated. "These 25 companies are at the forefront of this trend, and the list provides great insight into the variety and the quality of the employers that offer telecommuting options."

Top industries offering remote work opportunities include healthcare, information technology, education, nonprofit and philanthropy, and sales and marketing. Job titles include sales representative, senior analyst, nurse case manager, account executive, web or software developer, accountant, and virtual teacher.

Taking a look at telecommuting

The appeal of *telecommuting* (working from home or some other remote location), partially or entirely, is easy to understand. It gives you a sense of autonomy and control of your time and can save you gobs of time and money commuting to work. When it comes to what makes people love their jobs, this is a biggie. Telecommuting employees are happier and more loyal, and they have fewer unscheduled absences, according to a survey by outplacement firm Challenger, Gray & Christmas. My research and interviews with hundreds of workers, in part for my book *Love Your Job: The New Rules for Career Happiness,* clearly show that more flexibility in scheduling day-to-day activities leads to greater happiness on the job. That's especially true as you get older.

Obviously, not all jobs are conducive to telecommuting. If you're a teacher at a local school, for example, telecommuting isn't an option. With today's wired world, however, telecommuting is becoming more popular in many professions and is simple to execute. All you need are a reliable computer, high-speed Internet access, and the self-discipline to do your job essentially unsupervised.

When considering telecommuting, envision the desired arrangement and account for the following factors in terms of meeting your employer's needs:

✔ **Days/hours:** Would you telecommute entirely, only a few days a week, or a few hours a day? Do you need to be onsite to perform certain job duties on certain days?

✔ **A workplace:** Do you have a suitable place to work? You need a quiet place with few, if any, distractions, along with enough space to lay out whatever you need to do your job. A spare room with a door is best, so you can separate work from the rest of your life.

✔ **Equipment:** Are you equipped to telecommute? Are your computer and Internet connection up to snuff? Do you have reliable phone and cell-phone service?

A variation on telecommuting is *hoteling,* sharing offices and desks. The impetus: Cutting the soaring cost of office space in some cities. You may be able to negotiate an arrangement in which you work part of the time at home and part of the time in a shared office setting, where you have access to additional resources and perhaps colleagues.

✔ **Work ethic:** Gut check time. Do you have the self-discipline to perform your job duties essentially unsupervised and without coworkers nearby? As an older worker, you're probably more capable of working unsupervised than are younger workers, but you may perform better with others nearby to hold you accountable.

✔ **Workplace camaraderie:** One valuable asset that's often lost through telecommuting is the workplace camaraderie that ties colleagues together and gives them the sense that they're working toward a common goal. You may be able to achieve camaraderie through email, Skype, traditional phone calls, and occasional business lunches, during which you talk shop.

If you're a people person, don't underestimate how much you may miss the chit-chat in the hallways, talks at the water-cooler, birthday celebrations, and other forms of human contact. Find a way to connect with coworkers, either by working in the office a few times a month or meeting outside of work.

Focusing on flextime

Flextime is an arrangement in which you commit to work a set number of hours per day or per week with your arrival and exit times negotiated with your employer. You still work a standard 40-hour week, just not the typical 9 to 5 five days a week. You can come in late and leave late, or come early and leave early. Employers are generally much more open to negotiating flextime arrangements than allowing employees to telecommute.

Talk to other workers using flex hours at your company and try to get a sense of their experience and feedback from supervisors. If you have the chance to use flextime, it might be best to move your schedule early in the day rather than later. But if you really do work best later in the day, make that case to your supervisor and then show her the results.

Penalized for working later in the day

Employees who started work earlier in the day were rated by their supervisors as more conscientious and thus received higher performance ratings, according to a study, "Morning Employees Are Perceived as Better Employees," by Kai Chi Yam, Ryan Fehr, and Christopher M. Barnes of the Department of Management and Organization at the Michael G. Foster School of Business, University of Washington, published in the *Journal of Applied Psychology* (June 2014).

Research participants gave higher ratings of conscientiousness and performance to the 7 a.m. to 3 p.m. employees than to the 11 a.m. to 7 p.m. employees. "Compared to people who choose to work earlier in the day, people who choose to work later in the day are implicitly assumed to be less conscientious and less effective in their jobs," the researchers found.

Considering a compressed schedule

A *compressed schedule* condenses your workweek into fewer days, so you have more days off. A popular option is the 4/10 schedule, in which you work ten hours a day four days a week instead of the standard eight hours five days a week. The draw for employees is that they have three days off every week.

Jumping into job sharing

Job sharing allows two employees to split one full-time position. You alternate doing the same job by day, week, or whatever arrangement you agree upon. In essence, you divvy up responsibilities, accountability, and compensation. The hitch is you have to make sure that you and your colleague can efficiently coordinate and communicate in a way that doesn't cause your manager any unwanted stress, gets the job done professionally, and avoids interpersonal conflict over who's working harder or doing more. This may be an arrangement you work out after you're on the job for a while and have the chance to find the right person to job share with. That said, if an employer has a situation in mind, it might be worth tossing this in the hopper as something you would be interested in pursuing.

Seeking more flexible jobs

Some industries and professions are more conducive to flexible work arrangements. Here are a few areas you may want to explore:

- **Government work:** If you're interested in the public sector, the federal government is known for strong employee benefits, including flexible work schedules and telecommuting options. The federal government offers locality pay, so your salary reflects your area's cost of living. Visit USAJobs (www.usajobs.gov) to search and apply for jobs with various federal government agencies. State and local government jobs may be flex-friendly, too. In many school districts, the day ends when school lets out, and many other school districts are transitioning to virtual classrooms where teachers provide instruction remotely via computer.

- **Small companies:** Small-business owners can't always lure top-level talent with sweet benefits such as stock options, 401(k) plans, and generous health insurance, but often they can offer more flexibility than their larger competitors do. Flexible scheduling is a fairly low-cost benefit that enables them to hire and hang on to good workers. One place to start your search is the Great Place to Work Institute (www.greatplacetowork.com), which ranks small- and medium-sized companies according to the level of trust between employees and management and the percentage of employees who say they're happy at their jobs.

✔ **High-demand professions:** Look where the jobs are. There's a shortage of workers in both the healthcare and education fields right now, for instance. Nurses, physical therapists, and elementary and secondary schoolteachers are in demand. These are fields where flexible scheduling is more common than in the corporate world. You may not need to return to school; within these areas are opportunities for skilled workers who have backgrounds in everything from accounting to marketing and more. Consulting firms such as Flexible Resources (www.flexibleresources.com) specialize in matching corporations with workers looking for flexible work options.

Investigate the company culture. Even if you don't line up an alternative schedule right away, you still want to shop for a company where flex arrangements are allowed, after you've proven yourself and the employer gets to know you. When interviewing, ask questions about parent-friendly policies, if you still have children at home or are caring for an aging relative. If possible, chat informally with a few people who have flexible setups to get a feel for how it's working and any pitfalls to watch out for. Don't assume that a policy is normal practice just because it's on the company website or in the employee handbook.

Negotiating a flexible arrangement

The key to negotiating an alternate work arrangement when discussing the employee benefits package is to make it clear how this type of perk would benefit the firm, not just you. Coming into work an hour later than the rest of the team, for instance, may save you half an hour on your commute, which is good for you, but it may also enable you to be more productive, which is good for convincing your employer to go along with it.

Many bosses fear losing control if their employees aren't under their thumb. Your mission is not only to ease that fear but also to show how much better and more efficiently you can do your job if they offer you flexibility.

To improve your chances of convincing your new or future employer of a flexible work arrangement, follow these suggestions:

✔ **Get real.** Can you realistically manage telecommuting seven or eight hours a day? Are there only certain hours you're able to work each day or each week? Estimate accurately in advance, because if you propose a schedule that you end up being unable to fulfill, you'll lose credibility.

✔ **Run it past your supervisor first.** You might not want to propose this initially. Many employers will want you to learn the ropes and company culture before heading out of the office for any period of time. Even if flextime is a company policy, if your manager isn't onboard, the arrangement will never work out.

✔ **Put it in writing.** Draft a proposal that plainly describes your work schedule, the total number of hours you would work, how unplanned overtime would be handled, how often you would visit the office, and how often you would talk with your boss. You may agree to work in the office when projects are being launched or problems arise that the company needs to solve. For some help, visit WorkOptions (www.workoptions.com), where you'll find downloadable proposal templates for telecommuting, compressed workweeks, job sharing, and part-time schedules as well as other resources.

To seal the deal, ask for a trial period of three to six months so both you and your boss can see how the arrangement works out and fine-tune it if needed.

✔ **Explain what's in it for your company.** This is not about you, really. If the employer doesn't get something out of it, it'll never work. So make a case for what the company has to gain. Maybe it's paying less in salary for an experienced worker willing to work fewer hours, or better productivity, thanks to a telecommuting deal that eliminates wasted rush-hour time. With fewer interruptions by coworkers, maybe you'll get more done in less time. Point out that if you work from home or have a part-time job-sharing deal with a coworker, you'd be saving the company office space and reducing costly overhead.

Improved efficiency should be at the top of your "why you should let me telecommute or give me a flexible work schedule" list. Increased productivity was, in fact, one of the leading reasons for allowing employees to work from home, according to both the Challenger and Korn/Ferry surveys.

✔ **Be willing to compromise.** Stay open to your employer's suggestions, and remember that your boss really doesn't care about *your* cost of commuting. He does care that you perform well and are reliable.

Avoiding common drawbacks

Steering clear of the office and making your own hours sounds like the American Dream come true, but it does have some potential pitfalls, including these:

✔ **A bigger workload than expected:** A flexible work schedule — whether it's a work-at-home agreement, a job-sharing setup with a coworker, or a four-day workweek — doesn't always mean a reduced

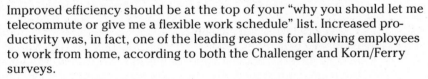

workload. Whatever your schedule, your employer will still expect you to perform at the level you would if you were in the office full-time, under the boss's watchful eye. This means you could find yourself logging more hours than you agreed to — good for your employer but unfair to you.

✔ **Flimsy boundaries:** Try to set clear boundaries so that your work doesn't take over your life.

✔ **Supervisor distrust:** If your manager senses any sort of work slow-down from your end, she's more likely to assume that you're slacking off than if she were able to observe you hard at work in a traditional work setting.

✔ **Coworker envy:** Even when the full chain of command has approved your flexible hours, don't be surprised by underlying resentment from those working a standard, full-time week. Coworker envy, too, can be palpable, making you feel alienated and out of the loop.

✔ **Missed opportunities:** It's not quite out of sight, out of mind, but being out of the office means you may miss out on promotions, plum assignments, and certain perks. Without promotions or key opportunities, your salary could stagnate, resulting in lower real income and retirement savings. It's not necessarily a conscious snub, but some bosses and coworkers may interpret your schedule as a sign of a low dedication to your job. Do your best to convince them otherwise.

Looking at Special Considerations for Women

If you're a woman, and you feel as though the job offer is sub-par for your profession and what you're bringing to the table, consider pushing a little outside your comfort zone to get a fair shake. I say "consider," because being a tough negotiator is riskier for a woman than a man. Push too hard and you may just shove yourself out of a good opportunity. Perform your risk-reward analysis, and if you feel that the risk is worth it, hang tough.

Many people in the equal-pay debate argue that second-rate negotiating skills are at the root of the gender pay gap. Teaching women to be better negotiators — or getting them to negotiate at all — would fix the problem. But the causes are more complex than that. Negotiation is a man's game with men's rules.

At the negotiating table, a woman's biggest difficulty isn't that she can't learn to be "more like a man." The real problem is the behaviors that both men and women associate with good negotiators are tied up with ideas of masculinity — such as level-headedness, confidence, and assertiveness — rather than more feminine qualities, such as accommodation and consensus.

Recognizing the gender-based retirement gap

A well-publicized fact is that men generally earn more than women. Less publicized is that lower earnings and other factors hurt a woman's retirement more than a man's. Factors that contribute to this gender-based retirement gap include the following:

✔ Many women don't go to bat for themselves when negotiating for starting salaries. They've accepted low-ball offers as far back as their first job, and that has hurt them for decades, because raises are usually based on a percentage of pay. Some women in their 50s or 60s settle for low pay just because they're happy to get hired at their age.

✔ Men are four times more likely than women to ask for a salary bump, according to economist Linda Babcock of Carnegie Mellon University. A LinkedIn survey of more than 2,000 professionals found men more likely to say they feel confident in career negotiations (from asking for a raise to closing a business deal) than women — 37 percent versus 26 percent.

✔ Women usually earn less than men. Their median wage is 78 percent of men's, according to a 2014 Census data report. An analysis by The Institute for Women's Policy Research found that the wage gap is common in occupations virtually across the board. The group's research shows that women have lower median earnings than men in all but one of the 20 most common occupations. The exception: bookkeeping, accounting, and auditing clerks. In this sector, women and men have the same median earnings — about $656 a week.

✔ Women CEOs earn only 69 percent of what their male counterparts make.

✔ Women live five years longer than men, on average. This means they need to set aside more money than do men to avoid outliving their income.

✔ Many women take time off to raise a family or care for an aging relative. That causes them to miss out on raises, slashes the amount they'll receive from Social Security in retirement, and gives them fewer years to finance a retirement plan at work and get their contributions matched by their employers.

✔ Women are more likely than men to work part-time or for smaller firms and nonprofits. This often translates to not having access to an employer-sponsored, tax-deferred retirement plan.

✔ From the age of 65 to the end of life, most women in the United States are single. That means they don't have someone to share the cost of daily living expenses or to help with retirement savings. What's more, study after study shows that after losing a partner due to death or divorce, a woman's standard of living generally drops.

The moral of the story is that if you're a woman, it's even more important for you to negotiate a higher starting salary if the compensation package you're offered is less than the industry standard for your profession.

I don't advise women to "man up," because when we do, we still can lose. Researchers repeatedly have documented that people react more unfavorably to women who ask for more money, compared with men who do. A woman who negotiates is often seen as especially demanding and consequently a less-than-ideal person to have on a team. It isn't fair, but as a woman it is a reality you need to be aware of when considering your options and planning your strategies.

See the later section "Honing Your Negotiating Skills and Strategies" for more details.

Settling on a Starting Date

For starters, don't provide a starting date until you have an offer. The starting date is usually a negotiable item, typically two weeks from when you accept a job offer. But depending on the job and your potential employer, it could be as much as a month.

If you're currently employed, my advice is to get out of your old job as soon as reasonable, and two weeks is generally best. If possible, give yourself a breather of around two weeks between jobs, so you're at the starting gate rested and with the energy and enthusiasm a new beginning deserves.

If asked about a starting date, it's okay to give a broad answer. You can say something like, "It depends on when precisely you'd be making me an offer, but in general, I would be available to start three weeks after we've established that." This approach gives you the opportunity to negotiate your exact starting date, after you receive a formal offer.

If the employer wants you to start earlier than suits you, be prepared to give a solid justification why you can't. For example, your current employer requires a specific period of notification or you're committed to finishing a project, or you have a vacation already planned and paid for, or you have a medical procedure scheduled. Most employers will respect your commitment to your current employer, because it demonstrates loyalty and consideration. Be diplomatic. Instead of saying "no" outright, see if you can negotiate a starting date that works for both of you.

Here are a few additional considerations that may impinge on your choice of starting date:

- ✔ If you're currently employed, you may need to smooth your exit by staying through an appropriate time to train your successor or finish a project.

✔ If some upfront training is involved for the new job, look for a way to work that into your schedule, so a later starting date is less of an inconvenience for your new employer.

✔ If your new employer wants to set an even later starting date, try your best to accommodate this need. Additional time may be needed to run a background check or drug screen or to wrap up a project before the department has time to bring you on board. Perhaps the employee you're replacing gave a longer-than-standard notice, and the firm doesn't have the budget for you both to be on the payroll at the same time. Whatever the reason, try to take it in stride.

Honing Your Negotiating Skills and Strategies

Although the parties engaged in negotiation often assume adversarial relationships, the best approach for both parties is to work together to meet one another's needs. Negotiation doesn't need to be a zero-sum game proposition in which a win for one side is a loss for the other. In fact, when played as a zero-sum game, negotiation often results in a loss for both sides because neither side gets what it wants and walks away bitter about giving up too much. Here are some suggestions for needs-based negotiating:

✔ **Know your value.** The more you learn, the more you earn. Research salaries for the position you're applying for in that area of the country (see the earlier section "Researching salaries" for details). Tap into your network to get additional opinions on what your contacts deem fair. If you're a woman and you have a male friend who holds the same position, ask what he thinks. (I've used this technique every time I switched jobs or taken a new assignment.)

Don't use your salary knowledge to argue. For example, don't say something like, "The average salary for this position in this city is $65,000." They probably know that, and calling it to their attention may come across as confrontational. Be more diplomatic; for example, say something like, "I was expecting something more in the $_____ to $_____ range based on the position and my experience and skills."

✔ **Be prepared to tell them what you want.** Of course, you don't want to tell them too early in the process, because you could end up low-balling yourself. But if the offer they make is too low for your liking, simply say something along the lines of, "I was expecting an offer more in the $_____ to $_____ range. How did you arrive at the offer?"

Let the hiring manager offer you an amount, and then take a day or two to consider. You may be able to renegotiate for more if you don't think the first offer was fair, but you will need to have your reasons down pat.

✔ **Speak in "I" statements.** "I" statements are very difficult to argue against, because all you're saying is what you think and feel. Without getting inside your head, nobody can deny that you don't really think or feel what you're telling them you do. "I" statements open up the conversation to explore options.

✔ **Ask questions.** It's okay to ask the interviewers how they came up with a specific dollar amount. Maybe they're including something in their calculations that you hadn't considered. Probe to find out more, to make them think more deeply about what they're offering, and to give them room to save face and present a better offer.

✔ **Don't refuse an offer outright.** Don't fall for the trap of thinking you need to answer yes or no. As soon as you say no, the conversation is over. Put the hiring manager in that uncomfortable position by pausing a few seconds to contemplate the offer and then asking additional questions or explaining what you need to feel fairly compensated for the skills and experience you bring to the table. Explain how much you're looking forward to meeting the needs of the organization, but that you need the organization to meet your needs as well.

✔ **Speak in terms of value.** You may say something like, "If I were an average employee, I would be happy with your first offer, but I don't think you're looking for someone who's just average." And then go on to describe in detail the job duties and responsibilities as they've been explained to you and how you will excel at delivering on your end of the bargain.

✔ **Don't back down.** Give the conversation more time to percolate instead of reluctantly accepting an offer. Ask additional questions about the responsibilities of the job and the employer's expectations, so he starts to realize that you know what he's getting is worth more than he's offering. A few seconds of silence and a delayed decision are powerful tools for getting them to loosen the purse strings.

✔ **Don't issue an ultimatum.** An ultimatum traps you and the interviewer, providing neither of you with a graceful, face-saving exit. Keep the conversation going until you've succeeded in meeting the needs of both sides.

✔ **Be sensitive to the employer's needs and current circumstances.** If the company is laying people off and reducing costs, you may have to cool your jets until things improve. Of course, if the organization is in financial trouble, you may want to think twice about working there, but if this is the job you want, have a plan B. If the salary you want is out of the question right now, your boss may have an easier time offering you a one-time bonus or stock options to show her appreciation for your signing on. Or she may give you a few extra personal or vacation days or comp time.

Practice your negotiating skills. Knowing how to negotiate well is vital in the interviewing stage and during performance review sessions. And, of course, there's an app for that. One worth checking out: Close the Wage Gap (www.closethewagegap.com) from a Carnegie Mellon team. It includes a practice interview video and negotiating tips.

Negotiate all financial aspects of employment, such as your sign-on bonus, in person or over the phone. Be sure all details of your employee benefits package — including any special adjustments you've been granted — are clearly stated in in your contract or offer letter.

Part V
The Part of Tens

For the latest information on personal branding, visit www.dummies.com/extras/gettingthejobyouwantafter50.

In this part . . .

✔ Discover ten great jobs for workers over the age of 50 — high-demand jobs that you're probably already qualified to do.

✔ Brush up on ten common interview questions so you can prepare your answers well in advance and deliver them with panache.

✔ Find out whether you really want a career change or something else entirely, and if it's a career change you're hankering for, take the steps necessary to mitigate the risks and smooth the transition.

Chapter 15

Ten Great Jobs for Workers Over 50

In This Chapter
▶ Checking into jobs for older workers
▶ Sparking your imagination for more job ideas
▶ Checking websites for additional thoughts

*E*ven people over 50 wonder what they want to do when they grow up. You're probably qualified to do a wide variety of jobs, but you want to do something you love, something that makes you look forward to waking up each morning. Perhaps you even want to do something that makes the world a better place or helps other people get through the day.

In this chapter, I present ten jobs for workers over 50. I selected these jobs for two reasons: (1) Demand for these services is growing, so you're likely to find openings, and (2) you're probably qualified right now to do any of them, although you may need to get a certification to prove it.

Don't consider this list the beginning and end of your journey to find meaningful, rewarding work that pays the bills. This is just a starter list. Use it as a springboard for stimulating your own imagination. For additional job ideas and career guidance, I recommend you visit www.aarp.org/work as well as www.lifereimagined.org, which offers a suite of programs developed to help lead you to a healthier, more fulfilling life in terms of wellness, work, relationships. Life Reimagined's LifeMap offers tools, online coaches, and personalized content to help you navigate your future. Learning Advisor, powered by Kaplan in partnership with Life Reimagined, can advance your skills and transform your career through learning.

Three books worth reading: For inspiration, pick up a copy of AARP's *Life Reimagined: Discovering Your New Life Possibilities,* by Richard Leider and Alan Webber. For practical tips, see my books AARP's *Great Jobs for Everyone 50+* and *What's Next? Finding Your Passion and Your Dream Job in Your Forties, Fifties, and Beyond* (Berkley Trade/AARP).

Patient Advocate

As the population ages, the demand for *patient advocates* — individuals who help patients work with others who will have an effect on their health, from medical specialists to insurance companies — is likely to surge. You can work full- or part-time, on your own, or as part of a hospital, nursing home, rehab center, or even insurance company. No licenses are required, but several credentialing programs are offered at community colleges and some nonprofits. Learn more from the Master List of Health and Patient Advocacy Educational Courses (www.healthadvocateprograms.com/masterlist.htm) and the nonprofit Patient Advocate Foundation (www.patientadvocate.org).

Translator/Interpreter

The global economy has resulted in an increasing demand for translators and interpreters, so if you're fluent in English and another language, you can probably find plenty of work in this field. (*Interpreters* deal with spoken words; *translators* deal with written words.) Job opportunities for interpreters and translators are projected to grow 46 percent from 2012 to 2022, according to the Department of Labor.

Spanish is the most in-demand language, but the need for Arabic and Chinese speakers is growing. Specializing as a judicial-system or healthcare interpreter increases your opportunities, but you need to know the vocabulary in those fields. No certifications are required, although several are offered through trade organizations such as the American Translators Association (ATA; www.atanet.org). The ATA works with the Red Cross to provide volunteer interpreters in crisis situations. Working with a mentor and networking with native speakers will keep your skills fresh. The ATA also offers formal mentoring programs and has chapters in many states.

You're usually better off translating/interpreting from the language you know less well *to* the language you're more fluent in. For example, native Spanish speakers are better at translating from English to Spanish, and native English speakers tend to be better at translating from Spanish to English. The reason is that the words and expressions come to you more readily in your native tongue — you have more options (including colloquial phrases) in your native tongue to paraphrase or explain the meaning of a foreign word or expression.

Certified Financial Planner

If you have financial expertise, you can help the growing demographic of older Americans with their investments and estate planning, and handle tax matters for them. This doesn't have to be a full-time job — you can take on as many or as few clients as you like. Not surprisingly, as retirees fear outliving their money, personal financial advisers are expected to be one of the faster-growing occupations over the next decade, with a projected growth rate of 27 percent by 2022, according to the Bureau of Labor and Statistics (BLS).

No minimum experience or education is required by law, but it's a good idea to get the Certified Financial Planner designation awarded by the nonprofit Certified Financial Planner Board of Standards (www.cfp.net). You must complete substantial coursework and pass a comprehensive, 10-hour exam required to attain this title.

Home Modification Pro

As the population ages, more homes will need to be retrofitted to accommodate older people's special needs: better lighting, special ramps, grab bars in the shower, and more, all to prevent accidents. If you have a background in construction or are an architect or interior designer, you already know the basics. Though such a job is likely to be demanding, you can take on as many clients as you're comfortable with. Plus this will be a job with staying power. A report from Harvard's Joint Center for Housing Studies predicts a prolonged period of recovery and growth for the home-improvement industry as Americans age.

The National Association of Home Builders (NAHB) offers a Certified Aging-in-Place Specialist (CAPS) designation to teach the knowledge and skills required to compete in this fast-growing segment of the residential remodeling industry. The program consists of three individual classes that cover such things as design basics, building standards, how to do a home assessment, and the best methods to market services. Total fees for the combined courses are typically under $1,000. Every three years, continuing education is required to maintain the designation. For details, visit www.nahb.org.

Fitness Trainer

If you've been sitting behind a desk for the past 30 years but prefer a more active lifestyle, working as a fitness trainer could be very rewarding. The greatest need is for skilled trainers who can develop workout routines for people age 65 to 90. Opportunities for senior fitness trainers are projected to grow 13 percent from 2012 to 2022, according to the BLS.

Certification isn't required by law, but most fitness clubs insist on it. The American Council on Exercise (ACE) offers a Senior Fitness Specialty Certification (www.acefitness.org/fitness-certifications/specialty-certifications/senior-fitness.aspx). The International

Sports Sciences Association offers a Senior Fitness Certification (www.issaonline.edu/certification/senior-fitness-certification). The National Strength and Conditioning Association offers a Certified Strength and Conditioning Specialist (CSCS) designation (www.nsca.com/CSCS_Certification_2).

Massage Therapist

Massage therapists are appreciated for their ability to ease muscle soreness and unwind stress for their clients. The employment prospects are swelling, as massage becomes an increasingly mainstream service offered by spas and clinics in recent years. The employment of massage therapists is projected to grow 23 percent by 2022, much faster than the average for all occupations, according to the BLS.

Massage therapists use a smorgasbord of treatments and techniques, and you may choose to specialize in one as a targeted way to build a business as the go-to expert. You may work for a big hotel chain, which offers in-room massages to guests, or a local health club. Or your magic fingers could comfort residents of a retirement or assisted-living community or medical center. After you get a loyal base of followers, you can attract new clients by word of mouth. Then you pack up your own table and linen and head over to their homes or offices for private sessions.

Many states and municipalities regulate the practice, so look into legal requirements for the state and other locality in which you intend to practice. Programs offered at colleges and universities may require 500 hours or more of study and practice to complete. These programs cover more than just hands-on training, covering anatomy, physiology, and business management.

Eco-Landscaper

The green movement is leading more people and organizations to want their own "sustainable" gardens, which use less water and have native plants that are less expensive to maintain. If you have a green thumb, this could be a good business to go into. You'll need to understand horticulture, have wide-ranging knowledge of plants and diseases, and know your way around a graphics program. To get the requisite training, look into the following options:

✔ The Ecological Landscaping Association (www.ecolandscaping.org) holds an annual conference with workshops and educational sessions. The site provides links to seminars and events held around the country.

✔ Many community colleges offer certificates and degrees in sustainable landscape design. George Washington University, for instance, offers a program on a series of weekends, along with an annual landscape design career fair.

✔ The American Horticultural Society offers a Master Gardeners program, typically through universities in the United States and Canada. Visit www.ahs.org/gardening-resources/master-gardeners for additional details.

✔ Check out garden centers in your area for classes and certificate programs. In Pittsburgh, for example, you can earn a certificate in sustainable horticulture at Phipps Conservatory and Botanical Gardens.

✔ The Association of Professional Landscape Designers (www.apld.com) offers certification to members who have at least four years of experience and submit three projects they've completed for review.

Independent Contractor

As an independent contractor, you do what you've been doing (or something else you're good at and that's in demand), but instead of doing it as an employee, you do it on your own, finding and serving your own clientele. Most independent contractors parachute in to problem solve or work on a specific project. You may work for an intense period and then take time out for several weeks or even months. Small and fast-growing companies looking for experienced employees who can tackle a range of duties are great sources of work. Drawback: slow payments at times, and projects that run longer than expected or don't begin on schedule. This line of work is best for those who can hit the ground running and love intensity.

The trick to finding projects is tapping fearlessly into your professional network. Past employers are a good first stop when you're looking for contract gigs. Contact former colleagues and clients for help finding great opportunities. Get involved with a local small business association and network through organizations such as Kiwanis, Rotary, and the Lions Clubs.

Accountant/Financial Manager

If you're skilled at managing personal or business finances, you're well qualified to manage the books for individuals and small businesses in your area. As accountant/financial manager, you take on a variety of roles, including bookkeeper, accountant, cashier, and tax expert. Duties run the gamut from processing payroll checks and expense reports to handling invoicing, accounts receivable, accounts payable, and producing monthly, quarterly, and annual financial reports. Buying office supplies or filing tax returns may even be your bailiwick. Some firms may ask you to monitor checking and savings accounts and track credit card bills.

A degree in accounting or business is generally required. The most common certification is a Certified Public Accountant (CPA). The rigorous exam is administered by the American Institute of Certified Public Accountants (www.aicpa.org). CPAs are licensed to offer a range of accounting services, including tax preparation. Another certification is a Certified Internal Auditor (CIA), which is someone who has passed a four-part test, administered by the Institute of Internal Auditors (na.theiia.org). Relevant experience or formal training in accounting-auditing services is a plus. Other key skills to have in your kit include data entry and being adept with financial and accounting computer software such as QuickBooks.

The American Institute of Professional Bookkeepers (www.aipb.org) lists jobs and offers a national certification for bookkeepers, which may help you land a job if you don't have prior practical experience.

Dietitian/Nutritionist

A dietitian/nutritionist creates special diets for people who struggle with allergies, diabetes, metabolic syndrome, heart disease, and other illnesses. The job involves conducting nutritional screenings, planning meals, and monitoring meal preparation. You may find yourself working for a retirement community, assisted-living facility, a corporation that offers a wellness program for its employees, a health club, or even a sports team. Supermarkets and restaurants may also hire you to whip up a custom menu. An aging population is driving a growing demand for geriatric dietitians at hospitals, nursing care facilities, outpatient care centers, and offices of health practitioners. You may even opt to open your own practice. The number of jobs for dietitians is on the upswing, and BLS expects a jump of 14,200 jobs through 2022, up 21 percent.

The requirements for a state license and certification include a bachelor's degree in food and nutrition or a related area, supervised practice, and passing an exam. One way to become licensed is to earn the Registered Dietitian (RD) credential, which involves passing an exam after completing academic coursework and a supervised internship. You can find more information from the Academy of Nutrition and Dietetics at www.eatright.org.

Chapter 16

Ten Common Interview Questions Answered

In This Chapter

▶ Improving your ability to anticipate interviewer's questions

▶ Checking out sample answers to common questions

▶ Formulating your own responses

*J*ob interviews are tough. Worst-case scenarios may have you feeling as though you're being grilled under hot lights. You're peppered with questions you really shouldn't ever have to answer, like "What are your weaknesses?" and "Why should we hire you?" You may even have to answer loaded questions, such as "What will I dislike about you in three months?" Who asks such questions?! Are these people really human? Perhaps the organization has been taken over by cyborgs.

Unfortunately, to get a job, you must endure the humiliation of the job interview and answer the questions with a certain degree of grace and sophistication. In this chapter, I offer guidance on how to field ten of the most common questions.

What Are Your Weaknesses?

It's imperative not to glaze over your weak spots. We all have them, and most employers are interested in hiring people who have a good bead on who they are and are always looking to improve.

So first, do some soul searching and be honest with yourself about work-related tasks that don't come naturally to you. Maybe you aren't good at delegating tasks or are better at big-picture strategy versus the painstaking details of carrying it out. Pick one or two of these areas and say what you've done and continue to do to sharpen these skills.

Try to find a weakness that won't affect your performance for this particular job. For example, if the job requires a great deal of talking with customers on the telephone, you may want to say that you're not very good at business-management tasks.

Why Should We Hire You?

This is like a slow pitch that you come prepared to knock out of the ballpark. It gives you the opportunity to play your sizzle reel. Recap the chief three or four reasons that *this* employer would want to offer you *this* job. I'm not talking a quick list delivered in a rapid-fire response. Choose job skills that apply to this particular position, as detailed in the job description. Take your time to describe each skill and how you've demonstrated it in context of a work challenge in a previous position. Try to highlight quantifiable accomplishments, as you have on your résumé, such as boosting sales a certain percentage or completing a project so many days ahead of schedule. Describe how a key accomplishment, say, a successful fundraising campaign, reveals your knack for creativity, innovation, and achieving goals. Be choosy. You want to keep your answer to less than two minutes.

In general, employers are looking for evidence of your industry experience and a range of both soft and technical skills.

Why Do You Want to Work Here?

When asked why you want to work for the company, ramp up your passion and enthusiasm as you formulate your answer. Then deliver your answer as follows:

1. **Show that you did your homework.**

   Pick a handful of key factors about the company that you gleaned from your research about the organization and its people. Mention the mission statement or a cause that the organization supports. Sing the praises of its products and services, its commitment to quality, or customer satisfaction. Provide details from your research to support your statements.

2. **Explain how you see yourself fitting in.**

   Describe how your values align with those of the company and how you see yourself fitting into the culture of the organization. Maybe the company is a fun place to work, and you're a fun-loving person. Or perhaps this company is more serious, and that fits best with your strictly business personality.

3. **Lay out how your skills and experience are a perfect match for the company's needs.**

   Pick a few needs out of the job description that align with your skills and experience. You want to show that you've given some thought to how the job makes sense for you now and in the foreseeable future and how you will help the company meet its goals.

What Are Your Goals?

The seed of this question is for a hiring manager to get a feel for the fit factor. Will you be happy in the position and stick around, or are you using it as a stepping stone to what you really want to do? Bringing a new hire up to speed is expensive, and the employer wants to make sure you're going to stick around long enough for the company to get a reasonable return on its investment in you.

Your answer needs to say that the position is perfectly aligned with the goals you've set for yourself at this stage in your career. Your response should be frank and honest. This is the time to express your passion for your work and your excitement at having the opportunity to contribute your time, talent, and expertise to improving the company's success. You may also want to mention that you're looking forward to the learning opportunities that this position offers.

Why Did You Leave, or Do You Want to Leave, Your Current Job?

Hold your tongue, No negative vibes or comments about your present or past employers. This is not a dish session to unload grievances or shortcomings.

Gear your answer along the lines that you're seeking a company with a mission or culture that you feel you're better suited for at this stage in your career. You may say you're looking for new challenges and opportunities to contribute to a company beyond what you've been able to at your current position.

Never say it's because you want more money, were overlooked for a promotion, or are unhappy with a boss or coworkers. The reasons for leaving an employer should always be for positive growth and finding work with purpose or passion and meaning for you.

It's certainly okay to mention that your current or past employer has been undergoing a lot of changes and that the new management, a culture shift, or new strategies have created a situation that's no longer a good fit for you.

When Were You Happiest at Your Job?

Always answer this question with a smile. It's the perfect opportunity to deliver an energetic response that shares something you've succeeded at in a previous position and how that suited your expertise, interests, and personality. If you love to work independently and that's something the position requires, you may describe a time when you were given project X and told to run with it. You loved the autonomy of researching and writing and finding the best solutions. You appreciated that the boss trusted you and your abilities and did not micromanage you and that ultimately you delivered the project ahead of schedule and exceeded your boss's expectations at the same time. What a high!

Conversely, if the position is a team-oriented one or a sales post, you may say, "I'm a people person. I get energy from working with others. In general, I find I'm happiest and most gratified when I am interacting with coworkers and collaborating to solve a problem or when I'm introducing customers to possibilities they had never imagined. Those have always been my brightest moments."

Again, circle back to how you're happiest when you're doing the kind of duties the employer is interviewing you to do.

What Can You Do for Us That Someone Else Can't?

Ahem. This question is designed to demonstrate that you have moxie — confidence with a dash of humility. No long-winded answer, here. Get right to the point. Look the interviewer directly in the eye and be clear that you have the skills to fit their bill and shine but also have a strong desire to continue to learn and improve.

I would throw the question back: "What do I have to offer you that no one else can?" Then say, "I have the passion, the experience at solving problems, the abilities, and the energy to step into this position right now and hit the ground running. Aside from that, my curiosity and desire to keep learning will continue to add to my skillset moving forward."

Keep it short. You want to get across that you aren't arrogant, but you are self-assured, self-directed, and loyal.

What Are Three Positives Things Your Previous Bosses Would Say About You?

With this question, the hiring manager wants to get a feel for your work style and to see whether what you say matches up with how one of your work references may describe you.

Don't toss out too many softballs here, such as the fact that you're a good listener, a hard worker, or are fun to work with. You may say that your boss at company X always said you were dependable or efficient, organized, positive, trustworthy, or had a sense of humor. I like all those descriptions for starters. But then get serious and pull out some business-oriented qualities that previous supervisors attributed to you. For example, you make everyone else around you more productive, or you're always coming up with ways to make everyone else's job easier.

In general, you want this description to be aimed at the attributes essential for this position. Again, study that job description. If the position requires project-management skills, you may point out a time when a supervisor praised your project-management skills on an evaluation. If the position requires problem-solving skills, you may talk about a time when a manager pointed out that you were innovative and seemed to always have a creative solution, such as the time you did _____. This could be a time to toss out an award you received for your work from your previous employer or even a direct quote from a performance review or email your boss or coworker sent you referring to a certain situation.

Prepare for this question by asking one or two previous managers you plan to tap as your references how they would describe your work-related strengths. Focus on your fortes — triumphs, achievements, awards, recognition — that relate to your job.

What Are Your Salary Requirements?

Chapter 14 walks you through researching salaries and how to prepare for this question in an interview. Don't be afraid to aim a little high with your target figure, but be flexible — give yourself some haggle room with the expectation of having to offer some concessions.

As I explain in Chapter 12, preface your answer by saying that your interest in the position doesn't revolve around money, but you would be interested in knowing what the range is. Expect a pause and then a ballpark figure. Try not to show delight or disappointment. This isn't a time to negotiate or even to indicate whether the range is acceptable. Save that for the negotiating table, after you get a formal offer. If the interviewer deflects or struggles to answer, reply smoothly, without missing a beat, that you're looking forward to learning more details when the interviewer is free to share them in your next discussion.

Or, as I explain in Chapter 13, say that although the position is not precisely the same as your last job, you would need to understand your duties and responsibilities in order to establish a fair salary for the job. If pressed to be more specific, ask what the salary range is and factor that in your response. So if the salary range is $50,000 to $60,000 and you want to make at least $55,000, you're probably best off asking for something between, say, $55,000 and $60,000.

For more about negotiating salary and other terms of a job offer, turn to Chapter 14.

Are You a Team Player?

The goal of this question is to gauge your ability to be a team player, to get along with the other kids in the sandbox and collaborate like a pro. Say yes if that's true, and haul out one or two great examples of when you demonstrated that ability.

In general, you want to describe a successful project that involved contributions from several people at varying levels in the company. At this stage in your work life, you should have a slew of examples.

Before you hit the interview hot seat, think of instances when you successfully collaborated on projects with coworkers, and choose a few of the best and most recent to use as examples. More recent examples demonstrate that you're current and up to speed with today's work environment. If an example emphasizes your leadership acumen or your financial smarts, all the better. You may want one example of when you led the group and another showing that you're able to follow someone else's lead.

Chapter 17

Ten Steps for Career Changers

· ·

In This Chapter

▶ Making sure you really want to change careers

▶ Testing the waters

▶ Laying the foundation

▶ Seeking guidance from someone who's been there, done that

▶ Taking small steps toward your goal

· ·

A police officer turned music agent. A Navy captain who became a circus manager. A botanist who traded plants for making chocolate. Those are a few of the major career changes among boomers and retirees I interviewed for my book *What's Next? Finding Your Passion and Your Dream Job in Your Forties, Fifties, and Beyond* (Berkley/AARP). Each person faced a different set of challenges, yet their stories reveal common threads.

Many of these men and women were spurred to discover what really matters to them and transform their work (and, in turn, personal) lives by a crisis or loss that starkly revealed the fleeting nature of life. No one acted impulsively. They paused. They planned. They bypassed helter-skelter approaches and pursued prudent, well-researched moves.

Each person had a flexible time horizon for his or her venture. If necessary, these people added the essential skills and degrees before they made the leap. They often apprenticed or volunteered beforehand. They reached out to their networks of social and professional contacts to ask for help and guidance.

They downsized and planned their financial lives to be able to afford a cut in pay or the cost of a start-up. Several were fortunate to have a spouse's steady income or had some outside investments, retirement savings, and pensions in place to ease the transition to their new line of work.

But what really sticks with me is that they all share confidence in the direction they've taken. They collectively work longer hours, but it doesn't matter. They only wish they had done it sooner.

You might know you want to do something different but don't have the courage to do it yet. Take a breath. Here are my top ten tips for making a career change.

Understand What's Behind Your Desire for a Change

Maybe you're starting to become disillusioned with work. You're in a rut. Perhaps you're no longer on the way up. Maybe your profession changed in a way that has made you less passionate about it. Whatever the reason, your current job or the job you just left or lost isn't or wasn't providing the spark to light your fire, and you need to change careers, or so you think.

Don't base your decision on a negative motivation, such as hating your job. Base it on something positive, such as pursuing a more attractive possibility. Otherwise, you're setting sail with no destination in mind, which is more likely to lead to a shipwreck than a pleasant cruise on placid seas. Besides, maybe you need a vacation or a professional conference or some refresher courses to reignite your passion for your profession, and you really don't need or want to change careers after all. Be warned, career changers often end up mourning their loss. All of a sudden, they realize how much they miss their old career, and they're really not open to replacing it. I don't want that to happen to you.

I encourage you to do some serious soul searching before jumping ship. Think about life more broadly, about what you want to do, workwise, for the next 10, 20, 30, or 40 years. Find an activity or a cause you're passionate about, and if you decide to pursue it as a career, start working in that direction by volunteering, taking a class or two, and so on. In the meantime, keep your day job until you've chosen a destination, mapped your route, prepared your ship, and are ready to set sail.

The longer time frame you have to plan, the better. Start working at age 50 on a career you may not get around to until age 60. If you have lots of time, you can try out some ideas and possibilities; role-play and do a little bit of those things to see if that's the direction you want to go. You might want to check our AARP's Life Reimagined (www.lifereimagined.org) to discover possibilities you never imagined and see where they lead you in your career and life.

Get Your Life in Order

In the time leading up to your career transition, get physically and financially fit. Change is stressful. When you're physically fit, you have more energy and are mentally sharper to face the challenges ahead. Starting a new career later in life takes an incredible amount of strength and energy.

Firm up your finances, too. Debt is a dream killer. It saps your resources and limits your choices. Indeed, the need to be financially responsible tops the list of biggest obstacles to landing one's dream job among those 40 to 59 years old, according to a survey commissioned by Life Reimagined. But financial obligations and pursuing your passions needn't be mutually exclusive. Start by tackling your debt. Without the burden of crushing credit card bills and a big mortgage, you're nimble. Being debt-free gives you the freedom to pursue work that may pay less initially, if you're starting over in a new field. Or if you're starting your own business, it tides you over until you can afford to pay yourself a salary — sometimes a year or more.

A new career is often a spiritual quest, too. So get spiritually fit by finding a space — perhaps through meditation or a yoga class — where you can get away from the stress and fears that go hand in hand with making major changes in your life.

Dream Big, but Be Practical

I don't want to squelch your dreams by advising you to be practical, so instead I advise you to dream big, but be practical. That may sound like contradictory advice, but I believe you can do both. You can change professions, launch your own nonprofit, start your own business, or change course in numerous other ways, but do so in stages as much as possible. The most successful career changers typically spend three years or so laying the groundwork for their switch.

For example, suppose you decide to become a nurse, something you've always dreamed of doing. You don't have to quit your day job and apply to nursing school. Instead, consider taking one class at a time, perhaps a night course, to gauge your interest and see how well you do. You can add more classes as your direction and motivation become clear.

Avoid making costly decisions that further deplete your resources and limit your options. Why shell out the big bucks on an advanced degree when a few courses will suffice? Why invest in a pricey résumé service before you've really thought through your next step? Why quit a current job when it's providing the financial fuel needed to pursue other options? Check out gratis career services from your alma mater. Look into tuition reimbursement options from your current employer (but check for any payback requirements if you leave the company). Take free courses, as explained in Chapter 2.

Volunteer or Moonlight

Before trading in your current career for a newer model, test drive the career(s) you're considering. You may discover that the ride is bumpier than you had anticipated. You may need to test drive several careers before you find the one that's right. If you are aiming for a nonprofit position, check out HandsOn Network (www.handsonnetwork.org), Idealist (www.idealist. org), and VolunteerMatch.org (www.volunteermatch.org). To track down opportunities to practice a profession before deciding to make it a full-time occupation, look around you. Where can you lend a hand? Want to be a landscaper, for instance, see if you can moonlight for a local landscaper on weekends to see if that type of work suits you. Opportunity comes from the unexpected. Be open to it.

Find a Mentor

Seek advice from people who've been successful in the field that interests you. Everyone likes to be asked for counsel. Find a mentor working in your new field. Reach out to your colleagues to see if they can make introductions for you. Two heads may be better than one, and together you can explore possibilities. Sign up with LinkedIn (see Chapter 10) to meet others in a field or profession that interests you. If a particular industry intrigues you, join an association affiliated with it, attend conferences, and recruit a mentor.

Keep Your Hand Out of the Cookie Jar

As you explore career options, don't dip too deep into your core savings. Of all the mistakes older workers make in launching second careers, this is probably the worst. Would-be entrepreneurs aren't necessarily raiding retirement accounts to launch businesses, but they're tapping home equity and other savings, and that has severe repercussions on your future ability to retire in the manner you've become accustomed to.

If you're launching a business, consult an attorney and an accountant to find ways to limit your exposure to financial risk. You shouldn't have to risk your home or retirement savings to launch a business. After all, when you start a business, you're already putting your time and effort at risk.

Be Prepared for Setbacks

Few endeavors in life that are worth pursuing go smoothly, so be prepared for setbacks. The biggest step you can take toward preparing for setbacks is to manage your expectations. Start your journey knowing it'll be difficult. Here are a few additional steps to take to prepare for setbacks:

- ✔ **Draw up a plan.** A good plan doesn't make you immune to setbacks, but it does enable you to avoid some pitfalls and respond more effectively to others.

- ✔ **Anticipate difficulties.** By anticipating difficulties, you won't be blind-sided when they arise, and you may even have plans in place for dealing with them.

- ✔ **Sock away some cash before making a change.** You don't need financial stress on top of the stress of dealing with the setback itself.

- ✔ **Share your burden.** Having your family, your partner, or a dear friend or two at your back or by your side for support helps tremendously. They don't have to own your dream, just be supportive.

It's not all smooth sailing, but if you've laid the proper groundwork, you'll get through the rough patches.

Do Your Homework

Before hopping that train that's heading off in a different direction, find out where it's going. Whether you're looking to make a career change, become a contract worker, buy a franchise, or open your own business, do some research to find out what's involved. The websites mentioned throughout this book provide plenty of resources to help you explore career and business options. Tap into your personal and professional networks for additional input and insight. You don't have to cut your own trail through the jungle; others have trampled the path smooth. Learn from their costly mistakes instead of making your own.

Take a lesson from employers. They carefully vet job candidates to make sure they hire someone with the knowledge, skills, and experience to do the job. They want the candidate to be successful. In the same way, you should try to match opportunities with the skills, knowledge, and experience you've developed through your many years in the workforce. Check out career websites including www.aarp.org/work, Encore.org (www.encore.org), Job-Hunt (www.job-hunt.org), Retiredbrains.com (www.retiredbrains.com), and Workforce50.com (www.workforce50.com) to get a flavor of what others are doing and what jobs are out there. Investigate nonprofits and fields such as healthcare, eldercare, and education that have a growing demand for workers. The Bureau of Labor Statistics' Occupational Outlook Handbook (www.bls.gov/ooh) is a good reference.

Don't Lock Yourself into a Must-Have Salary

Insufficient funds are the biggest roadblock for most career changers. Chances are when you start over in a new field or move to a nonprofit, you'll need to take a salary cut at least initially. If you have an emergency fund to buy you time, you can do a more thoughtful job search. Pare back your discretionary living expenses to reflect a more realistic view of what you'll earn. Consider which expenses are necessary and which may be given up temporarily until you've established yourself in your new career.

Do Something Every Day to Work Toward Your Goal

Changing careers can seem overwhelming. To make the transition more manageable, take small steps toward that vision. Here are a few small steps to consider:

- ✔ Draw a map or create a plan for how you're going to navigate your career change.
- ✔ Create a budget, so you can track the funds you need to finance your transition.
- ✔ Create an extensive to-do list and do one thing on that list every single day.
- ✔ Take a class on a topic that will bring you closer to achieving your career goal.

✔ Design and print a business card for your new venture complete with your name, contact info, website address, and your LinkedIn, Facebook, and Twitter URLs.

✔ Read at least one book per month that's relevant to helping you achieve your career goal.

✔ Identify and master a technology that you'll need to use in your new career.

✔ Find and bookmark at least one website per week that contains valuable information related to your career goal. (Visit the site regularly.)

✔ Contact at least one person every day, preferably by phone, who may be able to bring you closer to your goal.

Do one thing different every day that you're afraid to do. Keep track of them in a journal. This practice starts to build your "risk" muscle, says business and work coach Patricia DiVecchio, author of *Evolutionary Work: Unleashing Your Potential in Extraordinary Time*s (Pearhouse Press) and president of International Purpose (www.internationalpurpose.com), based in Arlington, Virginia, who has been helping people for more than 25 years manage fear and uncover their work potential and purpose.

You may make a phone call, for example, that you have been dreading. Before you call, write what you want to say, list your goals for the call, and visualize the person on the other end as being as human as you are. People are always willing to talk about themselves and their work. Engage them. Make the conversation valuable for them.

Index

● *D* ●

About the Author

Kerry Hannon is a nationally recognized authority on career transitions and retirement, a frequent TV and radio commentator who speaks about and offers advice on career and personal finance trends, and author of numerous books, including *Love Your Job: The New Rules for Career Happiness* (Wiley/AARP), *What's Next? Finding Your Passion and Your Dream Job in Your Forties, Fifties and Beyond* (Berkley Trade/AARP), and *Great Jobs for Everyone 50+: Finding Work That Keeps You Happy and Healthy . . . And Pays the Bills* (Wiley/AARP).

Kerry is a columnist and regular contributor to *The New York Times,* a contributing writer for *Money* magazine, AARP's Jobs Expert and Great Jobs columnist, contributing editor and Second Verse columnist at *Forbes,* and the PBS website NextAvenue.org expert and regular columnist on personal finance and careers for boomer women. Kerry is a fellow of the Columbia Journalism School and the Robert N. Butler Columbia Aging Center's 2015 Age Boom Academy. She is a former Metlife Foundation and New America Media fellow on aging. On June 24, 2015, Kerry testified before the Senate Special Committee on Aging at the invitation of its chairman, Senator Susan M. Collins (R-Maine), and ranking member, Claire McCaskill (D-Mo.) At the hearing, *Work in Retirement: Career Reinventions and the New Retirement Workscape,* Kerry discussed the challenges that Americans who work in retirement or plan to work in retirement may face and the value that older workers can add to the workplace.

Kerry has been covering careers and individual career choices for more than a decade. In 2006, she developed *U.S. News & World Report's* "Second Acts" feature — a regular column that looked at people who successfully navigated a career change in midlife, focusing on their challenges and their motivations. She has spent more than two decades covering all aspects of business and personal finance as a columnist, editor, and writer for the nation's leading media companies, including *Forbes, Money, U.S. News & World Report,* and *USA Today*. Kerry's work has also regularly appeared in *BusinessWeek, Kiplinger's Personal Finance, The Wall St reet Journal,* and *Reader's Digest,* among other national publications. She has appeared as a financial expert on ABC News, CBS, CNBC, NBC Nightly News, NPR, and PBS.

Kerry graduated from Shady Side Academy in Pittsburgh, Pennsylvania, where she serves on the Board of Visitors, and received a bachelor's degree from Duke University, where she is a member of an editorial board.

Kerry lives in Washington, D.C., with her husband, documentary producer and editor Cliff Hackel, and her Labrador retriever, Zena.

Follow Kerry on Twitter @KerryHannon, visit her website at KerryHannon.com, and check out her LinkedIn profile at www.linkedin.com/in/kerryhannon.

Dedication

For my millennial Hannon and Bonney nephews and nieces, who keep me in tune with the beat of today's evolving workplace.

Author's Acknowledgments

Thanks to Stacy Kennedy, acquisitions editor at Wiley, who chose me to write this book and worked tirelessly in the early stages to get it on the right track.

Most importantly, I want to thank the savvy Joe Kraynak, who expertly and smoothly helped me navigate the *For Dummies* book format and style under extremely tight deadline pressure. Joe, we did it! I'm forever grateful for all your calm advice, professional wordsmithing, and top-drawer editing. You have the *magic* touch.

Thanks also to project manager and development editor Linda Brandon for choreographing the production from manuscript to finished product and serving as reader advocate to clarify passages and fill in any bare spots. Another thank you goes to Jennette ElNaggar, copy editor, for her terrific attention to detail.

My deep appreciation also goes out to Debbie Banda for checking the manuscript meticulously for technical errors and offering her sage guidance and insight to make this a top-notch publication. Thanks to Mark Friedlich for his technical review of the financial portions of the text.

Jodi Lipson, director of AARP Books Division, is a woman I admire both professionally and personally. Jodi, once again, I extend my gratitude for your faith in me and your heart-felt commitment to the utmost quality and high standards of your book projects.

Tara Coates, my astute AARP editor, you are an integral member of my editorial team and someone whose judgment and advice I cherish. A tip of the hat to you, my friend.

My respect and deep thanks to my agent, Linda Konner of the Linda Konner Literary Agency, whose encouragement and experience in the publishing industry makes her a delight to work with.

And to my family and friends who bring love and laughter to my life, especially my mother, Marguerite Sullivan Hannon, the Bonney family — Paul, Pat, Christine, Mike, Caitlin, and Shannon — and the Hannon family — Mike, Judy, Brendan, Sean, Conor, and Brian — my brother, Jack, and his wife, Charmaine. Hugs all around.

For taking me far away from my computer to a world earth-people never know, apples, carrots, and peppermints to my beautiful mare, Saintly. And for keeping me on my path walking forward, Zena, my Labrador retriever and road manager.

Finally, my deepest love to my husband, Cliff. Thanks for always having my back, urging me to believe in myself and to never lose my *upbeat* attitude!

Publisher's Acknowledgments

Acquisitions Editor: Stacy Kennedy

Project Manager: Linda Brandon

Development Editor: Linda Brandon

Copy Editor: Jennette ElNaggar

Technical Editor: Debbie Banda, Mark Friedlich

Art Coordinator: Alicia B. South

Production Editor: Kinson Raja

Cover Image: ©GlobalStock/iStock.com

Apple & Mac

iPad For Dummies,
6th Edition
978-1-118-72306-7

iPhone For Dummies,
7th Edition
978-1-118-69083-3

Macs All-in-One
For Dummies, 4th Edition
978-1-118-82210-4

OS X Mavericks
For Dummies
978-1-118-69188-5

Blogging & Social Media

Facebook For Dummies,
5th Edition
978-1-118-63312-0

Social Media Engagement
For Dummies
978-1-118-53019-1

WordPress For Dummies,
6th Edition
978-1-118-79161-5

Business

Stock Investing
For Dummies, 4th Edition
978-1-118-37678-2

Investing For Dummies,
6th Edition
978-0-470-90545-6

Personal Finance
For Dummies, 7th Edition
978-1-118-11785-9

QuickBooks 2014
For Dummies
978-1-118-72005-9

Small Business Marketing
Kit For Dummies,
3rd Edition
978-1-118-31183-7

Careers

Job Interviews
For Dummies, 4th Edition
978-1-118-11290-8

Job Searching with Social
Media For Dummies,
2nd Edition
978-1-118-67856-5

Personal Branding
For Dummies
978-1-118-11792-7

Resumes For Dummies,
6th Edition
978-0-470-87361-8

Starting an Etsy Business
For Dummies, 2nd Edition
978-1-118-59024-9

Diet & Nutrition

Belly Fat Diet For Dummies
978-1-118-34585-6

Mediterranean Diet
For Dummies
978-1-118-71525-3

Nutrition For Dummies,
5th Edition
978-0-470-93231-5

Digital Photography

Digital SLR Photography
All-in-One For Dummies,
2nd Edition
978-1-118-59082-9

Digital SLR Video &
Filmmaking For Dummies
978-1-118-36598-4

Photoshop Elements 12
For Dummies
978-1-118-72714-0

Gardening

Herb Gardening
For Dummies, 2nd Edition
978-0-470-61778-6

Gardening with Free-Range
Chickens For Dummies
978-1-118-54754-0

Health

Boosting Your Immunity
For Dummies
978-1-118-40200-9

Diabetes For Dummies,
4th Edition
978-1-118-29447-5

Living Paleo For Dummies
978-1-118-29405-5

Big Data

Big Data For Dummies
978-1-118-50422-2

Data Visualization
For Dummies
978-1-118-50289-1

Hadoop For Dummies
978-1-118-60755-8

Language &
Foreign Language

500 Spanish Verbs
For Dummies
978-1-118-02382-2

English Grammar
For Dummies, 2nd Edition
978-0-470-54664-2

French All-in-One
For Dummies
978-1-118-22815-9

German Essentials
For Dummies
978-1-118-18422-6

Italian For Dummies,
2nd Edition
978-1-118-00465-4

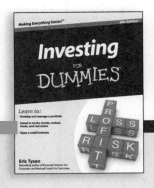 **Available in print and e-book formats.**

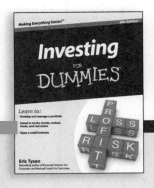
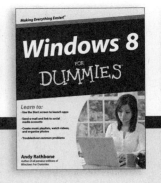

Available wherever books are sold. **For more information or to order direct visit www.dummies.com**

Math & Science

Algebra I For Dummies,
2nd Edition
978-0-470-55964-2

Anatomy and Physiology
For Dummies, 2nd Edition
978-0-470-92326-9

Astronomy For Dummies,
3rd Edition
978-1-118-37697-3

Biology For Dummies,
2nd Edition
978-0-470-59875-7

Chemistry For Dummies,
2nd Edition
978-1-118-00730-3

1001 Algebra II Practice
Problems For Dummies
978-1-118-44662-1

Microsoft Office

Excel 2013 For Dummies
978-1-118-51012-4

Office 2013 All-in-One
For Dummies
978-1-118-51636-2

PowerPoint 2013
For Dummies
978-1-118-50253-2

Word 2013 For Dummies
978-1-118-49123-2

Music

Blues Harmonica
For Dummies
978-1-118-25269-7

Guitar For Dummies,
3rd Edition
978-1-118-11554-1

iPod & iTunes
For Dummies, 10th Edition
978-1-118-50864-0

Programming

Beginning Programming
with C For Dummies
978-1-118-73763-7

Excel VBA Programming
For Dummies, 3rd Edition
978-1-118-49037-2

Java For Dummies,
6th Edition
978-1-118-40780-6

Religion & Inspiration

The Bible For Dummies
978-0-7645-5296-0

Buddhism For Dummies,
2nd Edition
978-1-118-02379-2

Catholicism For Dummies,
2nd Edition
978-1-118-07778-8

Self-Help & Relationships

Beating Sugar Addiction
For Dummies
978-1-118-54645-1

Meditation For Dummies,
3rd Edition
978-1-118-29144-3

Seniors

Laptops For Seniors
For Dummies, 3rd Edition
978-1-118-71105-7

Computers For Seniors
For Dummies, 3rd Edition
978-1-118-11553-4

iPad For Seniors
For Dummies, 6th Edition
978-1-118-72826-0

Social Security
For Dummies
978-1-118-20573-0

Smartphones & Tablets

Android Phones
For Dummies, 2nd Edition
978-1-118-72030-1

Nexus Tablets
For Dummies
978-1-118-77243-0

Samsung Galaxy S 4
For Dummies
978-1-118-64222-1

Samsung Galaxy Tabs
For Dummies
978-1-118-77294-2

Test Prep

ACT For Dummies,
5th Edition
978-1-118-01259-8

ASVAB For Dummies,
3rd Edition
978-0-470-63760-9

GRE For Dummies,
7th Edition
978-0-470-88921-3

Officer Candidate Tests
For Dummies
978-0-470-59876-4

Physician's Assistant Exam
For Dummies
978-1-118-11556-5

Series 7 Exam For Dummies
978-0-470-09932-2

Windows 8

Windows 8.1 All-in-One
For Dummies
978-1-118-82087-2

Windows 8.1 For Dummies
978-1-118-82121-3

Windows 8.1 For Dummies,
Book + DVD Bundle
978-1-118-82107-7

Available in print and e-book formats.

Available wherever books are sold. **For more information or to order direct visit www.dummies.com**

Take Dummies with you everywhere you go!

Whether you are excited about e-books, want more from the web, must have your mobile apps, or are swept up in social media, Dummies makes everything easier.

For Dummies is the global leader in the reference category and one of the most trusted and highly regarded brands in the world. No longer just focused on books, customers now have access to the For Dummies content they need in the format they want. Let us help you develop a solution that will fit your brand and help you connect with your customers.

Advertising & Sponsorships

Connect with an engaged audience on a powerful multimedia site, and position your message alongside expert how-to content.

Targeted ads • Video • Email marketing • Microsites • Sweepstakes sponsorship

21 Million Monthly Page Views & 13 Million Unique Visitors

Custom Publishing

Reach a global audience in any language by creating a solution that will differentiate you from competitors, amplify your message, and encourage customers to make a buying decision.

Apps • Books • eBooks • Video • Audio • Webinars

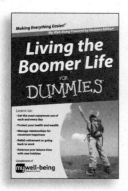

Brand Licensing & Content

Leverage the strength of the world's most popular reference brand to reach new audiences and channels of distribution.

For more information, visit www.Dummies.com/biz

A Wiley Brand

Dummies products make life

- DIY
- Consumer Electronics
- Crafts
- Software
- Cookware
- Hobbies
- Vide...
- Music...
- Games
- and More!

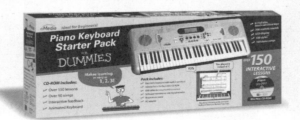

For more information, go to **Dummies.com** and search the store by category.

FOR
DUMMIE...

A Wiley Br...